Faster Smarter

Microsoft® Office

FrontPage® 2003

William R. Stanek
*Award-winning author and
Web technologies expert*

Greg Holden
*Popular author, CNET columnist,
and FrontPage expert*

PUBLISHED BY
Microsoft Press
A Division of Microsoft Corporation
One Microsoft Way
Redmond, Washington 98052-6399

Library of Congress Cataloging-in-Publication Data
Stanek, William R.
    Faster Smarter Microsoft Office FrontPage 2003 / William R. Stanek, Greg Holden.
       p. cm.
    Includes index.
    ISBN 0-7356-1972-7
    1. Microsoft FrontPage. 2. Web Sites--Design. 3. Web publishing. I. Holden, Greg. II. Title

    TK5105.8885.M53S7   2003
    005.7'2--dc21   2003052663

Printed and bound in the United States of America.

1 2 3 4 5 6 7 8 9   QWE   8 7 6 5 4 3

Distributed in Canada by H.B. Fenn and Company Ltd.

A CIP catalogue record for this book is available from the British Library.

Microsoft Press books are available through booksellers and distributors worldwide. For further information about international editions, contact your local Microsoft Corporation office or contact Microsoft Press International directly at fax (425) 936-7329. Visit our Web site at www.microsoft.com/mspress. Send comments to *mspinput@microsoft.com*.

Acquisitions Editor: Alex Blanton
Project Editor: Kristen Weatherby

Body Part No. X09-99968

*To my daughters Zosia and Lucy, who make me move
faster and work smarter every day.*
Greg Holden

Table of Contents

Part 2: Making Your FrontPage Site Content-Rich

Acknowledgments

William R. Stanek

I've used, abused, and written about every version of FrontPage. Nevertheless, writing *Faster Smarter Microsoft Office FrontPage 2003* was quite an experience. *Faster Smarter* is a fairly new series from Microsoft Press that aims to help readers (like you) learn products and technologies quickly. As you'll see, this series is a bit different from other similar ones on the market. You'll find things like Aha! (which provide tips and tricks for efficiency) and Lingo (which define terms) in addition to traditional Notes and Cautions. You'll find 10-Second Summaries that introduce the chapters and Fast Wrap-Ups that conclude chapters. And in between, you'll find a focus on accomplishing tasks with minimal fuss.

No man is an island, and this book couldn't have been written without the help of some very special people. Kristen Weatherby and Carmen Corral-Reid helped me stay on track and get the tools I needed to write this book. Carmen headed up the editorial process for nSight, Inc. As the project manager, she wore many hats, assisted in many ways, and was instrumental in helping me complete the text. I would also like to thank Alex Blanton. Not only did Alex help keep the project on track and resolve issues, but he also helped coordinate communications with the FrontPage team. Being able to work closely with the FrontPage team in the early stages of this project was both very important and helpful. Thank you!

Unfortunately for the writer (but fortunately for readers), writing is only one part of the publishing process. Next came editing and author review. Chris Russo was the technical editor for the book. Thank you Chris for checking the text carefully!

Hopefully, I haven't forgotten anyone but if I have, it was an oversight. *Honest.;-)*

Greg Holden

Preparing this book proved to be a remarkably smooth process due to the participation of a number of dedicated professionals. Neil Salkind, Stacey Barone, Jackie Coder, and David and Sherry Rogelberg of Studio B never fail to brighten my day with an exciting new project or good news on the success of our former collaborations. Laura Sackerman and Kristen Weatherby of Microsoft Press and Carmen Corral-Reid of nSight, Inc. made sure the text was presented clearly, and technical editor Chris Russo made sure it was accurate. Alex Blanton at Microsoft got the project going and was helpful all the way through. Finally, thanks to my coauthor William R. Stanek for his guidance and support.

Introduction

Faster Smarter Microsoft Office FrontPage 2003 is designed to be a concise, readable guide for FrontPage. This concise guide is the one you'll use if you want to learn FrontPage 2003 quickly and you already know the basics. The book covers everything you need to master FrontPage essentials from forms to themes to wizards to Web site administration. Because the focus is on learning FrontPage faster and smarter, you don't have to wade through hundreds of pages of background information to find what you're looking for. Instead, you find exactly what you need to use FrontPage effectively and to get the job done.

This Book Is For You

While *Faster Smarter Microsoft Office FrontPage 2003* discusses FrontPage Server Extensions and SharePoint Team Services, the focus of this book is on Microsoft Office FrontPage 2003. You'll find what you need to learn FrontPage quickly and efficiently. The book is designed for:

- Existing FrontPage users who want to learn the new features
- Web designers who manage medium- to large-scale Web sites
- Webmasters who use or support FrontPage-based Web sites
- Programmers who are writing code for dynamic, data-driven Web sites
- Hobbyists who want to create FrontPage-based pages and sites

To truly allow you to learn FrontPage 2003 faster and smarter, we had to assume that you already know Internet basics and have basic Web skills. With this in mind, the book doesn't discuss the history of the Internet, the evolution of Web design, or markup language fundamentals. The book doesn't discuss scripting, Java, XML, or other Web technologies either, except with regard to how those technologies are used with FrontPage 2003 to create dynamic, interactive Web sites. We do, however, cover themes, style sheets, tables, layers, frames, forms, database-driven sites, collaboration, and much more.

We also assume that you know a bit about HTML and XML. If you want to learn HTML/XML basics, there are many terrific resources, including Laura Lemay's *Teach Yourself Web Publishing with HTML and XHTML*, and William Stanek's *XML Pocket Consultant*.

This Book Is Organized For You

Faster Smarter Microsoft Office FrontPage 2003 is designed to be the guide you turn to to learn FrontPage features. As such, the book can be a tutorial that you read from cover to cover or a daily training resource that you turn to whenever you have questions about a particular feature. If you are reading this book, you should be aware of the relationship between *Faster Smarter* books and *Inside Out* books. Both types of books are designed to be a part of your library. While *Faster Smarter* books are the easy-to-read, get-it-done tutorial guides, *Inside Out* books are the comprehensive tutorials and references that cover every aspect of a particular technology from an end user's perspective.

Speed and efficiency are an important part of this tutorial guide. This book is organized according to FrontPage features and tasks that you will perform in conjunction with these features. The book is broken down into both parts and chapters. Each part contains an opening paragraph or two about the chapters contained in that part.

Part 1, "Getting Starting with Microsoft Office FrontPage 2003," covers the essential details you need to know to start using FrontPage. In Chapter 1, you learn about FrontPage 2003's new features. Chapter 2 discusses FrontPage 2003's redesigned interface. Chapter 3 provides an essential overview of page templates and Web site wizards.

In Part 2, "Making Your FrontPage Site Content-Rich," you'll learn everything you need to know to create effective Web pages. Chapter 4 provides the essentials for creatingWeb pages. The chapter also details how to set page properties, and how to print and preview pages in various browsers. Chapter 5 explores enhancing page design using themes, shared borders, and navigation bars. Chapter 6 discusses how to polish page design with style sheets. You'll learn how to work with in-line, header-defined, and external style sheets.

Chapter 7 covers the specifics of using images in Web pages, providing tips and advice for changing file formats, copying and moving images, adding special effects to images, and much more. Chapter 8 examines techniques for adding background graphics, video, and audio to Web pages. To round out the discussion, Chapter 9 examines HTML tables.

Part 3, "Advanced Web Page Techniques," builds on the previous discussion. Chapter 10 details what you need to know to edit HTML and XML markup. Chapter 11 examines advanced layout with tables and layers. Chapter 12 discusses techniques for using HTML frames with a focus on effectively using frames and designing frames-based interfaces that work.

Part 4, "Making Your Web Site Interactive," is where we dig into FrontPage 2003's extensive goodies bag. In Chapter 13, you'll learn about the many FrontPage components that help you create dynamic, interactive Web sites. The chapter discusses everything from the supported DHTML effects, to included content, to bCentral Web extras. Chapter 14 examines HTML forms, detailing how to effectively use various form elements. Chapter 15 extends this discussion and focuses on additional elements for forms, including labels and keyboard shortcuts. The chapter also discusses validation of form fields, custom scripts, and search forms. Chapter 16 completes the discussion with a look at making a site database-driven.

In Part 5, "Administering and Updating Your Web Site," you'll learn about FrontPage administration, collaboration, and maintenance. Chapter 17 focuses on publishing your site. Chapter 18 discusses collaboration and SharePoint Team Services. Chapter 19 examines site administration. Chapter 20 explains how to customize FrontPage and how to detect and repair problems.

Conventions You'll See

We've used a variety of elements to help keep the text clear and easy to follow. You'll find code terms and listings in monospace type, except when we tell you to actually type a command. In that case, the command appears in **bold** type. When we introduce and define a new term, we put it in *italics*.

Every chapter is introduced with a 10-Second Summary designed to provide a brief introduction to the main topics to be presented and ends with a Fast Wrap-Up to summarize the main ideas. Other conventions include:

- **Aha!** Provide tips, tricks, and additional techniques or insights to help you be more efficient.
- **Caution** Warn you when there are potential problems you should look out for.
- **Note** Provide additional details on a particular point that needs emphasis.
- **Lingo** Define a term that appears italicized in the text.
- **See Also** Contain cross-references to a page, section, or chapter in the book.

Support

Every effort has been made to ensure the accuracy of this book. Microsoft Press provides corrections for books through the World Wide Web at the following address:

http://www.microsoft.com/mspress/support/search.asp

If you have comments, questions, or ideas regarding this book, please send them to Microsoft Press using either of the following methods:

Postal Mail:
    Microsoft Press
    Attn: Faster Smarter Series Editor
    One Microsoft Way
    Redmond, WA 98052-6399

E-mail:
    msinput@microsoft.com

Please note that product support is not offered through the above mail addresses. For support information visit Microsoft's Web site at *http://support.microsoft.com/*.

Part 1
Getting Started with Microsoft Office FrontPage 2003

Whether you're a programmer or a proprietor, you can use Microsoft Office FrontPage 2003 to make the Web work harder for you, and getting started with FrontPage is what this part of the book is all about. In Chapter 1, "Introducing Microsoft Office FrontPage 2003," you'll learn about new features that make it easy to design and publish Web pages using FrontPage 2003. You'll explore the various ways you can work with pages and learn about design tools, coding tools, and other FrontPage extras. Chapter 2, "Touring the Interface," discusses FrontPage 2003's redesigned interface. You'll learn how to create collections of pages called sites, how to work with folders, and how to create pages.

The final chapter in this part, Chapter 3, "Maximizing Template and Wizard Options," provides an essential overview of FrontPage features that can help you quickly create pages and sites. This chapter discusses page templates you should know about, provides tips for creating online discussion sites, and much more. So what are you waiting for? Let's dive in and learn FrontPage 2003 faster and smarter.

Introducing Microsoft Office FrontPage 2003

1

10-Second Summary

- Explore FrontPage 2003
- Learn about page and web site views
- Learn about design and coding tools
- Learn about Web components, page templates and wizards
- Learn about advanced authoring options

FrontPage 2003 is the culmination of a decade of work toward building the best Web site creation and management tool. From previous versions, it inherits a rich foundation of reliable, proven features and support for all standard file formats and protocols. This allows you to design Web pages that take advantage of tables, frames, cascading style sheets, and use many other Internet technologies. For good measure, FrontPage 2003 adds extensive interface enhancements and new capabilities that programmers and designers have been asking for.

When you start working with FrontPage 2003, you'll notice many of the interface enhancements immediately. These changes are hard to miss if you've worked with previous versions of FrontPage – and even if you haven't worked with FrontPage before, it's hard not to see that there is something truly different and unique here.

In this chapter, you'll learn about FrontPage 2003's key features. You'll learn about the various ways you can work with pages and Web sites, and the design and coding tools that are available. The chapter also introduces powerful features that help you do more, and do more quickly, with FrontPage 2003, including page wizards, page templates, Web components and product extensions.

Viewing Your Pages in Different Ways

Figure 1-1 shows a page being edited in FrontPage. Look below the standard menus and toolbars at the top of the figure, and you'll see a row of quick access tabs. These tabs let you quickly access any open resources, including the Web site and pages you are working with. If you have a Web site open, and click the Web Site tab, you have direct access to resources in the site. If you have Web pages open, and click any of the page tabs, you have direct access to the page for editing.

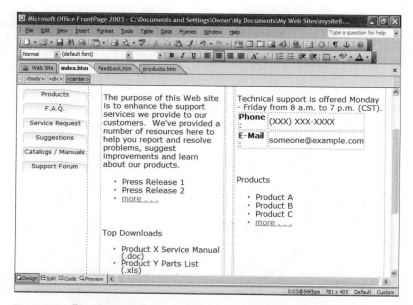

Figure 1-1   FrontPage 2003 provides easy access to menus, toolbars, and open resources, including the active site and any pages you are working with.

> **Lingo**   When working with Web sites in FrontPage, it is important to understand what is meant by the term *Web page*. A Web page, or simply *page*, is any type of Web document that you'll work with in FrontPage.

Speaking of Web pages, FrontPage provides four different ways to view and work with pages. Views you can choose from include:

See Also   For more information on working with Web pages, see the section of Chapter 2 entitled "Getting to Work with Web Pages and Files."

- **Design**   Displays the page much as it will be seen in a Web browser and provides quick access to the HTML tags in the page. Design view is useful when you want to create pages, but don't want to worry about the underlying markup code.

- **Code**   Shows the actual HTML markup and the text of the page. Code view is helpful when you want to edit or insert markup directly. You can also use this view to see what the actual code looks like.

- **Split**   Displays two view panes: one with the code view, the other with the design view of the page. Split view is useful when you want to see what the actual page looks like, yet also be able to work with code quickly and easily. You'll find this view is handy when you're polishing pages just before you publish them.

- **Preview**   Displays a preview of the page as it will appear in Web browsers. Although Design view does provide a view of the page layout, it isn't an exact view of the page as seen through aWeb browser. So if you want to be certain of what the finished page looks like, you'll need to display the page preview.

Look in the lower left corner of Figure 1-1 and you'll see a row of buttons. These buttons correspond to the Views described above and are available whenever you work with Web pages. Switching page views is easy. If you want to use the design view, you click Design. For code view, you click Code, and so on.

Viewing Web Site Files and Folders in Different Ways

FrontPage 2003 also provides different ways to view and work with Web sites. Views you can choose from include:

See Also
For more information on working with Web site files and folders, see the section of Chapter 2 entitled "Getting to Work with Web Sites and Folders."

- **Folders**   Lists all files and folders associated with the current Web site. You can sort file and folder listings by name, title, size, type, modification date, editor and comments. Double-clicking a folder allows you to browse its contents. Double-clicking a file opens it for editing.

- **Remote Web Site**   Lets you publish local files to a remote Web site. You can view the publish status, quickly synchronize files, optimize HTML source as you publish pages, and more.

- **Reports**   Enables you to manage and analyze site content, using reports. Site Summary, the top-level report, provides a summary entry for all available reports. Click a report title to access the report details.

> **Aha!**   Access Individual Reports
>
> Use the Reports selection menu to access individual reports directly. You'll find this selection menu in the upper left corner, just below the row of tabs.

- **Navigation**   Displays the navigation structure of the Web site. Typically, this structure branches out from the site's home page. To view various levels of the site hierarchy, expand the view by clicking the plus nodes (+). Later, you can collapse the view by clicking the minus nodes (-).

- **Hyperlinks**   Allows you to see links to and from selected pages. To take advantage of this view, select a page in any of the other views, then access this view.

- **Tasks**   Enables you to create and manage to-do list tasks for the current Web site. Tasks are listed by status, name, assignment, priority, association, modification date and description. Right-click in the viewing area and select Add Task to create a new task.

Figure 1-2 shows a Web site being edited in FrontPage. Look in the lower left corner of Figure 1-2, and you'll see a row of buttons in the status area. These buttons are available whenever you work with Web sites. You can switch Web site views just as you do with page views—click the button for the view you want to use. If you want to use the Folders view, you click Folders. For the Remote Web Site view, you click Remote Web Site, and so on.

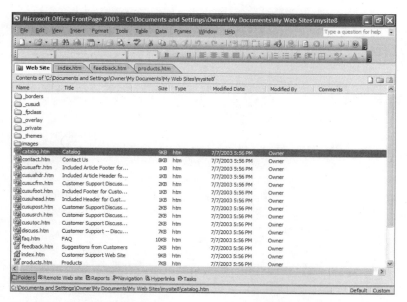

Figure 1-2   FrontPage 2003 also provides many different ways to view and work with Web sites.

Designing Pages with Ease and Precision

As shown previously in Figure 1-1, the Design view allows you to see markup tags, as well as the layout of page content. When working in the Design view, there are many tools that can help you quickly design great-looking pages. The design tools you'll use the most are:

- Reveal Tags for selecting tags and editing tag properties
- Quick Tag Selector for faster editing of tags and their contents
- Rulers and Grids for precise positioning
- Preview In Browser and Page Size for checking the final product

These design tools are discussed in the sections that follow.

Revealing Tags for Quick Selection and Editing

Regardless of which markup language you are using, FrontPage clearly delineates tags. For example, an opening tag, such as <p>, precedes the element you are defining, and a closing tag, such as </p> follows the element—except in the case of empty elements that have only an opening tag. With Reveal Tags enabled, you can:

- Click the opening or closing tag to select the entire element you are defining, including its contents. You can then cut, copy or delete the selected element and its contents.

■ Double-click the opening or closing tag to display a style or properties dialog box for the element. You can then customize the way the element is used.

To see markup tags when you are working in Design view, choose View, and then Reveal Tags. A check mark next to this option on the menu indicates that the feature is enabled. You can quickly turn this feature on or off by pressing Ctrl+/.

Editing Faster with the Quick Tag Selector

Another important design feature is the quick tag selector, which enables you to perform a variety of editing tasks quickly. When you are working with Web pages in Design view, choose View, and then Quick Tag Selector (see Figure 1-3) to enable this feature. A check mark next to this option on the menu indicates that the feature is enabled.

Here's how the Quick Tag Selector works:

1 Click on the opening or closing tag of the element you want to work with.

2 Right-click the related entry for the tag you've selected on the accessory toolbar area (the toolbar area below the quick access tabs).

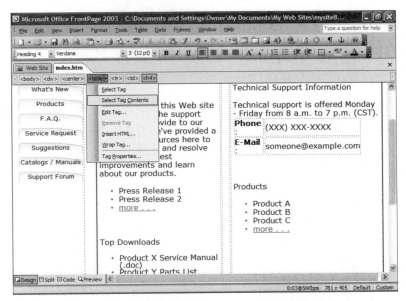

Figure 1-3 You can use the Quick Tag Selector to edit tags and their contents quickly.

3 Use the shortcut menu displayed to perform common editing tasks on the selected element. You can use these options as follows:

● **Select Tag** Selects the tag and its contents—the same as clicking the opening or closing tag in the layout area.

- **Select Tag Contents**   Selects the contents of the tag, and not the tag itself.

- **Edit Tag**   Displays the Quick Tag Editor in Edit Tag mode, which allows you to edit tag attributes directly. For example, with a paragraph tag, you could add the attribute *align="center"* to center the paragraph.

- **Remove Tag**   Deletes the selected tag, but preserves the contents. For example, if you select a paragraph tag, then choose this option, FrontPage removes the opening <p> and closing </p> tags, but preserves the contents within the tags.

- **Insert HTML**   Displays the Quick Tag Editor in Insert HTML mode, which allows you to insert markup directly before the selected tag.

- **Wrap Tag**   Displays the Quick Tag Editor in Wrap Tag mode, which allows you to insert markup that should enclose the selected tag. For example, if you select a paragraph tag and then choose this option, you could type **<div></div>** to define a HTML division element that should contain the paragraph tag and all its contents.

- **Tag Properties**   Displays a style or properties dialog box for the selected tag. This is the same as double-clicking the tag.

Precisely Placing Elements with Rulers and Grids

When you are working with Web pages in Design view, you can also add rulers and grids, making it easier to place elements, such as images or tables, precisely. Select View, then Ruler And Grid, Show Ruler Or View, Ruler And Grid, or then Show Grid to toggle these features on or off.

FrontPage 2003 also supports snap-to-grid. When enabled, this feature aligns elements to grid lines, making it easier to position elements in rows or columns.

> **Aha!**   Get More Control Over Spacing and Grids
>
> If you want a bit more control over how grids and rulers are used, choose View, Ruler And Grid, and then Configure. You can then configure ruler and grid units (pixels, inches, centimeters or points); set grid spacing, line style and line color; and manage snap-to spacing.

Previewing Pages to Ensure Everyone Can Enjoy Them

When you design pages, you should always think about how the page will look to Joe Web-surfer, and design page elements with that average Joe in mind. Back in the good old days of the Web, most pages were designed for 640x480-pixel screen resolution, because, as the thinking went, the average Joe had a system that used this display size. Fortunately, we've come a long way since then, and most computers these days have screens with much higher resolutions. In fact, in many cases, an 800x600 screen is at the low end, and a 1024x768 resolution is more the norm—despite what some of the Web design books might tell you. Keep this in mind when you're designing pages.

If you want to preview a page using a specific display size, FrontPage 2003 makes it easy. Choose File, Preview In Browser, then select the browser and display mode you want to use, such as Microsoft Internet Explorer 6.0 (800x600). Display modes you can choose from include:

- 640x480

- 800x600

- 1024x768

> **Note** 640x480, 800x600 and 1024x768 are standard display sizes for Windows-based computers. These screen sizes don't take into account those used by other operating systems, or the screen sizes available with high-end displays on Windows-based computers. Apple computers use different screen sizes altogether, and other computers may use different screen sizes as well. High-end display resolutions can go up to 2048x1536 and beyond.

One of my favorite Design view interface enhancements is the Page Size feature. With this feature, you can preview Web pages in a specific size without ever having to leave Design view. Best of all, FrontPage 2003 takes into account the screen space used by menus, toolbars and scrollbars when displaying the page at your chosen page size.

To take advantage of the Page Size feature, choose View, Page Size, and then select the page size you want to use. Page sizes you can choose from include:

- 536x196, the default page area available when screen size is 640x480.

- 600x300, the page area available when screen size is 640x480, and the browser is maximized.

- 760x420, the page area available when screen size is 800x600, and the browser is maximized.

- 795x470, the page area available when screen size is 832x624, and the browser is maximized.

- 955x600, the page area available when screen size is 955x600, and the browser is maximized.

> **Note** One important thing to note about these page sizes is that they are set with Internet Explorer in mind. Different browsers might have different page sizes. To accommodate other browsers, you can define additional page sizes. Click View, Page, and then select Page Size, Modify Page Sizes. In the Modify Page Sizes dialog box, click Add to specify the pixel width and height of the new page size.

Getting Page and Web Site Creation Tasks Done Quickly

When you want to—or have to—get it done quickly, the most powerful, timesaving features FrontPage 2003 puts at your fingertips are:

- Web components
- Page templates
- Page and Web Wizards

Let's look at each of these features in turn, and then look at how FrontPage 2003 supports them.

Accelerating the Development Process with Web Components

See Also
Not only can FrontPage components save you time, they can also save you money, as you might not have to hire someone to create the functionality you need. You'll learn all about FrontPage components in Chapter 13, "Using FrontPage Components."

Using Web components, you can add advanced capabilities to your Web site at the touch of a button. Components not only offer drop-in interactive functionality and greatly streamline the development process, they also can, in many cases, eliminate the need to write your own scripts or add complicated HTML commands.

You can think of components as programs that run when needed. Components available in FrontPage 2003 include:

- Dynamic Effects, such as marquees and interactive buttons.
- Web Search, of the current Web Site and the Web, through MSN.
- Microsoft Office System spreadsheets, charts, and PivotTables.
- Web site hit counters in a variety of styles.
- Photo galleries with horizontal, vertical, montage and slideshow layouts.
- Included content, such as page banners and pictures that rotate based on a schedule.
- Links bars to help visitors navigate your Web site more easily.
- Tables of Contents, top 10 lists, and list views.
- Maps, stock quotes, headline news from MSNBC, and weather forecasts.

Before FrontPage introduced Web components, Webmasters and designers had to be master programmers. Now you, as the webmaster, designer—or business owner—can spend more of your time thinking about the look, feel, and content of your pages, and less time worrying about programmatic functions needed to create a professional Web site.

Creating Pages Quickly with Templates

Over the years, thousands and thousands of people have turned to FrontPage to help them create great Web sites. And not all of them have been programmers or webmasters; lots of small business owners and managers have used FrontPage to get their businesses on the Web. That's why, from the beginning, FrontPage has supported a standard set of templates. Whenever you create a page or site in FrontPage, you will usually base the page or site on one of these templates. FrontPage includes dozens of templates designed to make page and site creation easy.

Page templates provide outlines for specific types of pages. You'll find page templates for:

- Bibliography pages
- Frequently asked question (FAQ) pages
- Feedback form pages
- Confirmation form pages
- Guest book pages
- Photo gallery pages
- User registration pages
- Search pages
- Table of Contents pages
- Frames pages in a variety of layout styles

Site templates provide outlines for specific sets of pages. You'll find Web site templates for:

- Customer support Web sites
- Personal Web sites
- Project Web sites
- SharePoint-based Team Web sites

Most templates contain guidelines to help you complete the design; some are basic and very straightforward in use, while others are more complex, requiring a bit of expertise to get the job done. We discuss these templates in Chapter 3, "Maximizing Template and Wizard Options."

Creating Advanced Pages and Sites Fast with Wizards

When you need a bit more than templates offer, you may be able to use a power tool, like a wizard, to get the job done. Wizards help you create complex pages and sites automatically. All you have to do is start the wizard, and work your way through each successive wizard page.

As with templates, FrontPage has both page and Web site wizards. The most commonly used page wizard is the Form Page Wizard, which you can use to create a form page by specifying the types of information you need collect. If you want to learn more about the forms,

See Also
You'll learn more about Web Site Wizards in Chapter 3, "Maximizing Template and Wizard Options."

and the Form Page Wizard, see Chapter 14, "Working with Forms," and Chapter 15, "Crowd Pleasing Forms Extras."

The two most commonly used Web site wizards are the Corporate Presence Wizard and the Discussion Web Wizard. You can use the Corporate Presence Wizard to create a site that helps your business or organization to establish a presence on the Web. You can use the Discussion Web Wizard to create a Web site with multiple discussion groups that company employees and customers can use to discuss topics of interest.

How Does FrontPage 2003 Support Web Components, Page Templates and Wizards?

Most of the crowd-pleasing extras provided by components, templates and wizards cannot be created with HTML alone—this is where FrontPage Server Extensions and Microsoft SharePoint Team Services come into the picture. These add-on technologies for FrontPage make the razzle-dazzle possible.

Not only can you configure FrontPage 2003 to support these technologies, but you can also tell FrontPage "Hey! I don't want to use this technology or a subset of this technology." The following sections take a brief look at FrontPage Server Extensions and SharePoint Team Services, and then examine how you can configure FrontPage to work with these technologies.

What Are FrontPage Server Extensions and What Do They Do For You?

FrontPage Server Extensions are a collection of Web scripts and executable programs. Once installed on a Web server, these extensions allow your Web site to take advantage of FrontPage's most advanced features. They also provide the functionality you need to remotely administer and author FrontPage Web sites.

If FrontPage Server Extensions are not installed on your Web server, there are many tasks you won't be able to perform. You won't be able to use FrontPage to configure authoring permissions. You won't be able to open or manage Web sites that you publish. In addition, you won't be able to use the following FrontPage components:

- Confirmation Field
- Document Library view
- Hit Counter
- List View
- Photo Gallery
- Top 10 List
- Web Search

List views and Document Library views also rely on SharePoint Team Services. Both FrontPage Server Extensions and SharePoint Team Services must be installed on your Web server for these components to function properly.

What Are SharePoint Team Services and What Do They Do For You?

Speaking of SharePoint Team Services, this technology enables team-based Web sites. You know, the stuff you need to collaborate and share documents with other people— everything from the roster for the soccer team you coach to the PTA meeting minutes to the quarterly sales reports of your company. Team-based Web sites are data driven, and rely on an Access or SQL Server database to store information. The information stored in a SharePoint database includes:

- Data for list views, which provide information on tasks, events, actions and whatever else you want to share with members of the team-based web site.

- Data for document libraries, which is used to track document information, such as title, creation date, modification date and size.

- Data for subscriptions and discussions, which includes the actual contents of discussion threads and subscription details.

Security is an important part of SharePoint Team Services. You can configure several types of rights, including:

- **Team Contributor Rights**   To allow users to access team lists and participate in team discussions.

- **Web Design Rights**   To allow users to browse pages, author pages, and apply settings to a site.

- **Web Administration Rights**   To allow users to manage the SharePoint configuration and grant or restrict access to the team-based Web site.

Many FrontPage features rely on SharePoint Team Services, and if this technology is not installed on your Web server, and configured for your Web site, there are many tasks you won't be able to perform. Specifically, you won't be able to implement document discussions, use List or Document Library views, or enable Web subscriptions. By the way, team services are also responsible for important server functions, such as monitoring server health and tracking server usage statistics, so if the services aren't installed, these and other dependent server functions won't be available.

Configuring FrontPage Support for Server Extensions and SharePoint

Don't worry, you don't have to know what features are supported when. All you need to know when designing pages is what's installed on the destination Web server you're going to use. If you know that, you can configure FrontPage so that it doesn't allow you to use unsupported features. And if you're unsure, you can even tell FrontPage not to use any of the advanced features implemented using FrontPage Server Extensions and SharePoint Team Services. As you might imagine, if you decide to design your site without these features, or without a subset of these features, some FrontPage menu and dialog box options won't be available.

How does that work? Well, let's say you want your site to support Web components, but not support SharePoint Team Services. Your reason for this is that you know FrontPage Server Extensions are installed on the server, but you aren't sure if SharePoint is installed or needed. In this case, you configure FrontPage 2003 to support Web components, but not SharePoint. Now when you're working with FrontPage 2003, you won't be able to select menu or dialog box options that require SharePoint. For example, you wouldn't be able to add List views or Document Library views to your pages—these features are implemented as Web components, but require SharePoint to work, so you can't select the related options in FrontPage.

On the FrontPage status bar, you'll see two entries to the right of the page size. These entries specify the current technology and browser support configurations.

- The first entry tells you what FrontPage and SharePoint Team Services technologies FrontPage 2003 is configured to support. An entry of Custom means that the settings are customized based on Web technologies, rather than set to a specific setting.

- The second entry tells you what browser version or versions FrontPage is configured to support. An entry of Custom here means that the settings are customized based on Web technologies, rather than on browser version.

As shown in Figure 1-4, if you double-click either of these entries FrontPage displays the Page Options dialog box with the Authoring tab selected. Another way to display authoring options is to choose Tools, Page Options and then select the Authoring tab.

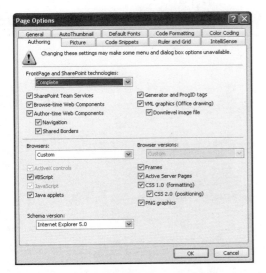

Figure 1-4   FrontPage 2003 gives you precise control over which server and browser technologies you can add to pages—the goal is to ensure any page you develop is compatible with your target server and browser environments.

As shown in Figure 1-4, the Authoring tab has a selection menu labeled FrontPage And SharePoint Team Services Specific Technologies. You can use this selection menu to configure support for various technologies. The options are:

■ **Default**   Select this option to use the default feature set. This means that all FrontPage Server Extensions and SharePoint Team Services technologies are allowed, except shared borders, and Generator/ProgID tags.

■ **None**   Select this option if you are publishing to a server that doesn't support FrontPage Server Extensions and SharePoint Team Services.

■ **Complete**   Select this option to allow all FrontPage Server Extensions and SharePoint Team Services technologies, including shared borders and Generator/ProgID tags.

■ **Custom**   Select this option if you are planning to work with a subset of the available technology options. FrontPage will also change the selection to Custom if you change any of the technology options individually.

Going Further & Doing More with Tables, Layers, Frames and Style Sheets

FrontPage 2003 supports all the latest HTML/XHTML features including:

- Tables
- Layers
- Frames
- Style sheets

Let's look at each of these advanced authoring features in turn, and then look at how FrontPage 2003 supports them.

Control Page Layout with Tables and Layers

See Also For more information on working with tables and layers, see Chapter 11, "Advanced Layout with Tables and Layers."

Tables are used to lay out content in rows and columns. Tables and table cells can have borders and backgrounds, which are different from each other and from the rest of the page, and in addition to text, can include images, form fields and any other type of HTML content. Because tables provide more control over the appearance of the page, you can use tables as a central design element. For example, you could use tables to lay out form fields and their associated text.

If you've worked with previous versions of FrontPage, you know that support for layers is new in FrontPage 2003. When you work with layers, you embed layers of content within a page. Layers are like floating panels that you can size, position and stack one on top of the other.

Browsers position layers using a 3-dimensional axis with X, Y and Z coordinates. The X and Y coordinates allow you to position the layer relative to the top, left corner of the page or other content. The Z coordinate lets you stack layers in front or behind each other or other content on the page. Layers can have unique borders and background shading as well.

Control Formatting Quickly and Easily with Style Sheets

See Also For more information on working with style sheets, see Chapter 6, "Polishing Design with Style Sheets."

Markup languages, such as HTML, define the structure of pages, and for the most part, don't say anything about the way a page should look when you view it in a browser. Therefore, when you include markup that says this element is a level 1 heading, and this element is a paragraph of text, the tags themselves don't say anything about how a browser displays the heading and paragraph. Because of this, your browser might display the page differently from someone else's browser.

To be more specific about how a browser should display a page, you can use style sheets—which allow you to be very specific about formatting and positioning. You can, for example, say that the font face for the heading is bold 24-point Haettenschweiler, the font color is brown, and that the background is highlighted yellow. You could extend this style definition by adding spacing before and after the level 1 heading, a wide right margin, and an inset border.

Two Web technologies specify what features are available for style sheets:

- **Cascading Style Sheets level 1 (CSS1)**   Defines the formatting styles available for use with Web pages.

- **Cascading Style Sheets level 2 (CSS2)**   Defines the positioning styles available for use with Web pages.

FrontPage 2003 makes using style sheets easy, regardless of whether you are using HTML, XHTML, XML or another Web language. You can add style definitions to any single element, groups of elements, or entire pages.

Dividing the Browser Window with Frames

Frames allow you to divide the browser window into sections. Each section, or frame, has its own associated document, and its links can open documents in other frames. For example, you could create a frame-enhanced page with three sections: header, main contents and footer. You create the header, contents and footer as separate documents, specifying that links in the header open new documents in the contents area, and that links in the contents display details or footnote references in the footnotes area.

See Also
You'll find a detailed discussion on designing good framed pages and overcoming the bad reputation of frames in Chapter 12, "Using Frames."

An inline frame is another type of frame. You insert inline frames into a Web page using a fixed or relative size and position. As with a standard frame, the contents of an inline frame come from a separate document. Inline frames offer a unique design opportunity, however, because they have their own scroll bars, and content that flows separately from the main document. You can, for example, click on a link in the inline frame to open a new document in the frame, without the contents of the main page changing.

When used properly, frames can help make your site easier to navigate. Nevertheless, frames also have a bad reputation because they are frequently misused, actually making sites more difficult and confusing to navigate than they would be otherwise.

How Does FrontPage 2003 Support Advanced Features?

You'll find that browser support is the most crucial component for deciding whether to use an advanced feature. The two most popular browsers available today are Internet Explorer and Netscape Navigator. While the latest versions of Internet Explorer and Netscape Navigator support all the advanced features implemented in FrontPage 2003, older versions of these browsers may not.

Just to give you an idea of the complexity involved, Netscape Navigator 3.0 doesn't support formatting or positioning with style sheets. Internet Explorer 3.0 only supports formatting with style sheets. Only Internet Explorer 3.0 and later supported inline frames; that is until

Netscape Navigator 5.0 was released. Support for layers wasn't implemented in either browser until version 4.0, and then both browsers used slightly different implementations. And the list goes on and on.

Don't worry! You needn't know what browser version supports which feature. FrontPage takes care of this for you. All you need to know when designing pages is what browsers and browser versions you want to target—then you simply tell FrontPage to configure itself to support these browsers. As you might imagine, if you decide to design your site for older browsers, some FrontPage features won't be available.

How does that work? Well, let's say you want your site to support both Internet Explorer and Netscape Navigator versions 3.0 or later, so you configure FrontPage 2003 to support these older browsers. Now when you're working with FrontPage 2003, you won't be able to select menu or dialog box options that would make the page incompatible with these browsers. For example, you wouldn't be able to configure CSS1 formatting or CSS2 positioning, and you wouldn't be able to add layers or inline frames. These features aren't supported in Internet Explorer or Netscape Navigator version 3.0, so you can't select the related options in FrontPage.

Not only can you configure FrontPage 2003 to support specific browsers and browser versions, you can also check page compatibility for specific target browsers. We discuss these tasks in the sections that follow.

Choosing Which Browser to Author For

As shown previously in Figure 1-3, the Authoring tab has selection menus labeled Browsers and Brower Versions, as well as fields that allow you to configure support for various Web technologies. Double-click either the FrontPage technology or browser configuration entry to display the Page Options dialog box with the Authoring tab selected. Or choose Tools, Page Options, then select the Authoring tab.

Using the Browsers selection menu, you can specify the browser support as:

- Microsoft Internet Explorer Only
- Netscape Navigator Only
- Both Internet Explorer and Netscape Navigator
- Custom

Using the Browser Versions selection menu, you can specify the browser version support as:

- 5.0/6.0 browsers and later
- 4.0 browsers and later
- 3.0 browsers and later
- Custom

How do you use the browser support feature? Let's say you want your site to support both Internet Explorer and Netscape Navigator versions 3.0 or later. In this case, you would set the browser support to both Internet Explorer and Netscape Navigator, and the browser version support to 3.0 browsers and later.

Then, if you decide that you want to support CSS1, you could select the CSS 1.0 Formatting option. This would change the browser version support to Custom, because the settings you've chosen may not apply to specific browser versions.

> **Aha!**   Careful When You Change Browser Support
>
> If you change the browser support configuration while designing pages or importing pages into FrontPage, FrontPage will not remove incompatible elements. These elements will remain, but you won't be able to edit them, or add new elements of the unsupported type. In most cases, the only actions you'll be able to perform are to delete the unsupported element, or edit its contents. To regain full editing control over the element, you'll need to change the browser support configuration.

Checking Browser Compatibility

FrontPage 2003 lets you check the compatibility of any page against a target browser at any time. The fastest way to check a page for compatibility is to open it for editing and then check it's compatibility as shown in these steps:

1 Open a page for editing, then choose Tools, Browser Compatibility. Then, in the Browser Compatibility dialog box, click Check.

2 FrontPage 2003 checks the current page's compatibility with the browsers and browser versions configured on the Authoring tab of the Page Options dialog box. FrontPage displays any inconsistencies, as shown in Figure 1-5 on the following page.

3 FrontPage highlights the first inconsistency found (if any), allowing you to easily edit or delete its related markup and contents from the page. After you modify or delete the incompatible element as necessary, click Next to highlight the next inconsistency (if any). Repeat this process as necessary until you've reviewed all the inconsistencies found.

4 Click Check to re-check the page after you've made your edits, as necessary. Or click Generate HTML Report to generate a Browser Compatibility Report that you can save or print.

5 Click Close when you're finished working with the page.

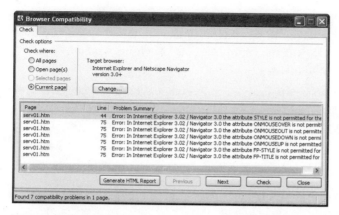

Figure 1-5   Create new code snippets by specifying a keyword, description and code block to use.

You can also check:

- All open pages, meaning all pages open for editing in FrontPage.

- Selected pages, meaning all pages selected in the folder list or Web site view.

- All pages, meaning all pages in the current Web site.

To do this, in Step 1 above, select the appropriate option for Check Where before you click the Check button.

Fine-tuning the Page with Coding Tools

With a click of the Code button, you can change to Code view and easily edit the markup and text that define the look and feel of the Web page you are working with. FrontPage 2003 has many features and tools to help make this job easier.

For starters, FrontPage numbers and indents each line of code by default, as shown in Figure 1-6. You can change these code view options using the General tab of the Page Options dialog box. Choose Tools, Page Options, and then select the General tab. You can now use the fields of the Code View Options panel to manage word wrap, auto indent, line numbers, and the selection margin (the spacing between line numbers and code).

If you are working with a page that has lengthy sections of code, you'll find that line numbering is an invaluable tool you frequently use to zero in on a specific line of code to make a change. Regardless of whether or not they are displayed, FrontPage 2003 tracks line numbers, so that you can jump to a specific line of code using the Go To Line dialog box.

To display and use the Go To Line dialog box, press Ctrl+G, or choose Edit, and then Go To Line. Next, type the line number you want to access, and then press Enter.

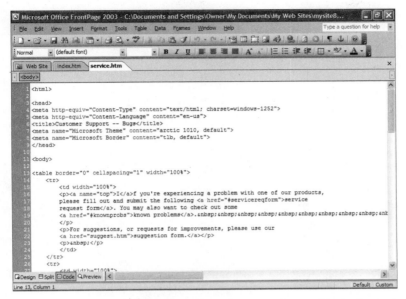

Figure 1-6 Code view makes it easy to edit the markup and text of a page directly.

Other coding features that you'll use frequently include:

- Color coding
- Code formatting rules
- Code snippets

Using Color Coding to Easily Distinguish Elements

In Code view, tags, attribute names, attribute values, and other items are color-coded. You have precise control over the color combinations used. To view or modify the color settings, follow these steps:

1. Choose Tools, Page Options, and then click the Color Coding tab.

2. Use the color selection options shown in Figure 1-7 to specify the colors you want to apply. If you later want to restore the original color settings, click Reset Colors.

3. Click OK when you are finished.

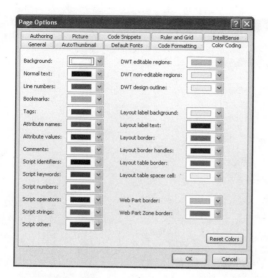

Figure 1-7 Color-code the markup and text of the page to suit your needs.

Using Code Formatting to Get Precise Code

The format of code is important, so FrontPage 2003 applies code formatting according to very specific rules. By default, when FrontPage creates tags, the tag names and their attribute names are lower case. Unlike HTML, where tag and attribute case doesn't matter, you'll find that some other markup languages (including XML and XHTML) require that all tags and attribute names be lowercase. With this default setting, you'll be in good shape if you use these markup languages, or transition to them in the future.

You can view and change the code formatting rules by choosing Tools, Page Options, and then selecting Code Formatting. FrontPage applies these formatting rules only when it generates markup. As Figure 1-8 shows, these rules control:

- Tab size, indentation and right margin
- Line breaks before and after start and end tags
- Whether start or end tags should be omitted when generating tag sets

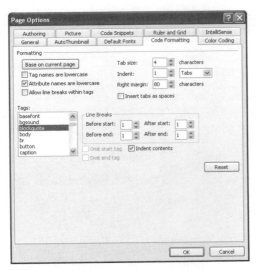

Figure 1-8   FrontPage uses code-formatting rules when generating markup. You can change these rules at any time.

> **Note**   It's important to note that FrontPage will not modify existing code automatically. If you change the formatting rules, FrontPage does not apply these rules to existing code. If you import or open pages that were created outside of FrontPage, the code formatting rules aren't applied, nor is the code of the page changed in any way. The only time FrontPage might change code within pages is if you elect to optimize pages when publishing them. For more information on the Optimize Published HTML feature, see Chapter 17, "Publishing Your Web Site."

Adding Code Quickly with Code Snippets

When you are in Code view, you can add frequently-used code blocks with a few keystrokes, using the Code Snippets feature. All code snippets have a keyword, description and code block.

You use the keyword to specify which code snippet to insert. For example, if you wanted to insert a JavaScript block, you would use the scriptj keyword. This is only one of several code snippets FrontPage defines. Table 1-1 shows a complete list of predefined code snippets.

See Also If you want to learn how to modify existing code snippets or define your own code snippets, see Chapter 10, "Editing HTML and XML Markup."

Table 1-1   Code snippets defined by FrontPage

Keyword	Purpose
dt2	Adds an HTML 2.0 DOC TYPE declaration to the page.
dt3	Adds an HTML 3.2 DOC TYPE declaration to the page.
dt4	Adds an HTML 4.0 DOC TYPE declaration to the page.
Linkrels	Adds a link relationship tag for specifying an external style sheet.

Table 1-1 Code snippets defined by FrontPage

Keyword	Purpose
Metad	Adds a meta tag used to specify the page description for search engines.
Metakey	Adds a meta tag used to specify the keywords for search engines.
Scriptj	Adds a JavaScript block with script and comment tags.
Scriptv	Adds a VBScript block with script and comment tags.

You can easily insert code snippets by following these steps:

1 Press Ctrl+Enter to display a shortcut menu that lists all the available code snippets by keyword and description.

2 Once the shortcut menu is displayed, type the keyword or select the code snippet you want to use.

3 Press Tab or Enter.

> **Aha!**   Use Code Snippets to Learn Faster
>
> The process for inserting code snippets sounds more complex than it actually is—trust me. Once you start using this feature, the process will seem very natural and intuitive. After a while, you'll be able to insert code snippets quickly, without ever looking at the shortcut menu options. For example, if you wanted to add a JavaScript block, you would simply press Ctrl+Enter, type **scriptj**, and then press Tab.

Fast Wrap-Up

- FrontPage 2003 has many new features, including a completely redesigned interface that lets you easily switch between design and code views.

- Design tools and features that you'll use regularly include Reveal Tags, Quick Tag Selector, rulers, grids, Page Size, and Preview In Browser.

- You can add many features to Web pages, including those that require FrontPage components to work properly.

- Some components require FrontPage Server Extensions and others require SharePoint Team Services to work properly.

- Whenever you use advanced features, such as tables, layers, frames or style sheets, keep in mind that some browsers and browser versions might not support these features.

- Whenever you work with code, Code view, or color coding, code formatting options affect how FrontPage displays the code. If you want to quickly add blocks of code to a page, you can use Code Snippets.

Touring the Interface

2

10-Second Summary

- ■ Get to know the FrontPage interface.
- ■ Work with FrontPage pages, sites, folders and files.
- ■ Understand and use hidden folders.
- ■ Save your sites and pages.

Microsoft Office FrontPage 2003 centralizes all the design, coding and publishing functions you'll need as you design, publish and maintain your organization's Web site. Not only does FrontPage make authoring and management easy, it also provides everything you need in a single unified interface. Getting to know the FrontPage 2003 interface is the subject of this chapter, and even if you're a veteran FrontPage user, you're sure to learn a few helpful tricks and techniques, so dive on in.

Using Folder List, Navigation and Task View Panes

Everything you need to get the job done is right at hand with FrontPage 2003, regardless of whether you are working with Web sites and folders, or pages and files. Typically, when you work with Web sites and folders, you'll want to perform high-level tasks, such as viewing Web site reports, checking site structure for navigation, or publishing files. When you work with pages and files, you'll want to perform the nuts-and-bolts authoring tasks of page design and coding.

View panes are a bit different from toolbars. While toolbars have tools for frequently used commands, such as open page or save page, view panes provide quick access for working with various types of page and site resources. You might have worked with the Folder List pane, shown in Figure 2-1 on the following page.

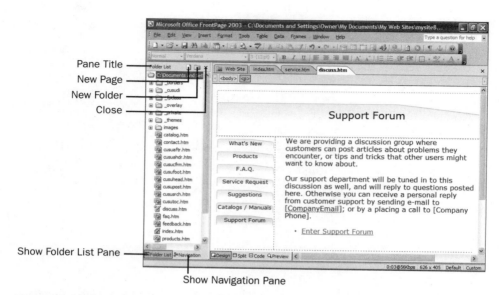

Figure 2-1   Press Alt+F1 to display the Folder List pane; use it as you would the Web Site Folders view.

Managing Folder and File Lists

As with the Web Site Folders view, the Folder List pane helps you work with folders and the files they contain. As the figure callouts show, buttons at the top of the pane allow you to create a new page or folder. Try these techniques to work smarter and faster:

- Right-click a folder or file in the Folder List pane to access a shortcut menu. For example, the shortcut menu for folders allows you to perform quick editing tasks, like cut, copy, rename or delete. You can convert the folder to be a standalone site, view properties, or publish files you've selected in the folder. You can also create a new file, folder, or page, and add it to the selected folder automatically.

- Click the Close button to put the Folder List pane away, and toggle off the Folder List display option. You can display the Folder List again by pressing Alt+F1 or choosing View, Folder List.

Navigating the Site Structure

When you are working with pages, you can also display the Navigation pane. This view pane has the same features as the Web Site Navigation view. It displays the navigation structure of the Web site, which typically branches out from the site's home page.

If you are editing pages, you display the Navigation pane by selecting View, Navigation Pane. To view various levels of the site hierarchy, expand the view by clicking the plus nodes (+). Later, you can collapse the view by clicking the minus nodes (-).

Using the Task Pane

The Task view pane, shown in Figure 2-2, is also important. You can display it by pressing Ctrl+F1, or by choosing View, Task Pane. FrontPage displays the Task Pane automatically when you work with advanced features, or are performing advanced formatting of tables, layers, themes, and more. Standard features of the task pane include a task selection menu, browse forward, browse back, and home tools. The Home task provides quick access to recently opened files and sites.

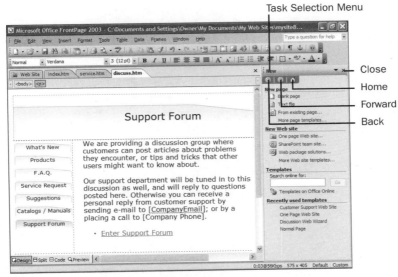

Figure 2-2   Use the Task Pane to help with advanced tasks, such as formatting layers.

Getting to Work with Sites and Folders

In FrontPage 2003, you can work with individual pages, or with collections of pages known as Web sites. The first time you start FrontPage, you'll be in Page view. This view is intended to help you design and code individual pages. While this might be all you require if you design individual home pages, you will most likely need to begin working with FrontPage sites and folders almost immediately.

> **Lingo**   A *FrontPage Web site* is a home page, its associated pages, folders and other files created in FrontPage and stored on a Web server or on a computer's hard drive. A FrontPage Web site also contains files and folders that support FrontPage-specific functionality that allows the site to be opened, copied, edited, and administered in FrontPage. In documentation, and in this book, you may also see a FrontPage Web site referred to as a *FrontPage Web* or simply a *web*.

Typically, your first task will be to create the sites that you will use to store home pages, associated pages and other related files. If you do this, the next time you start it, FrontPage opens the last site you worked with for editing. You also have quick access to recently used sites by choosing File, Recent Sites, then selecting the site you want to open.

Until it is published, a FrontPage Web site is a work in progress. It exists on a computer's hard disk, but generally isn't available for browsing. Use folders to organize the pages and related files in a site, but keep in mind that this folder structure will also be used when the site is published. Don't implement a folder structure that is difficult to maintain. Instead, use a structure that is logical and intuitive to anyone who may work with the site now or in the future.

Aha!   When working with folders and files, you can use the Ctrl key to select multiple files or folders individually. Click the first file or folder you want to select, hold down the Ctrl key, then click individually on other files or folders that you want to select.

Use the Shift key to select a group of contiguous files or folders. Click the first file or folder you want to select, hold down the Shift key, then click the last file or folder.

Creating FrontPage Web Sites

FrontPage makes it easy to create new Web sites. When you create a FrontPage Web site, you can specify the location of the Web site as:

- A folder on your local hard drive, such as C:\MyWebStuff\TestWeb1\.
- A network share specified using a UNC path, such as \\IntranetServer03\WebDev\.
- A directory on a remote web server specified as a URL, such as *http:// www.microsoft.com/support/*.

Usually, you'll want to create the Web site on your local hard drive first, and then publish it later to a network share or remote web server. If you do this, you'll have a local development copy that you can easily author and design, and a separate finished version that can be browsed when you make the site available to others. The default location for local FrontPage sites is My Documents\My Web Sites.

You can create a new site quickly by completing the following steps:

1 Click the down arrow to the right of the New tool (shown in Figure 2-3) on the Standard toolbar, and then select Web Site.

Figure 2-3 The New tool is located in the FrontPage standard task bar.

2 Using the Web Site Templates dialog box shown in Figure 2-4, specify the type of Web site you want to create. Usually, you will want to base your new Web site on one of the following Web templates or wizards:

- **Empty Web Site**   Creates the necessary folders and files for a new Web site, but doesn't create pages or open any pages for editing.

- **One page Web Site**   Creates a new Web site with a single page ready for editing.

- **Corporate Presence Wizard**   Starts a wizard that helps you create a Web site designed for a company that plans to offer products or services.

- **Customer Support Web Site**   Creates a customer support Web site, complete with discussion areas. This site could also be used for general or technical support.

- **Discussion Web Site**   Starts a wizard that helps you create a Web-based discussion group.

- **Personal Web Site**   Creates a personal Web site complete with About Me, Favorites, Feedback, Interests, and Photo Gallery pages.

- **Project Web Site**   Creates a Web site that helps you manage individual or team-based projects, includes knowledge base and requirements discussion areas.

- **SharePoint Team Site**   Creates a team Web site that you can use to manage collaboration and document sharing.

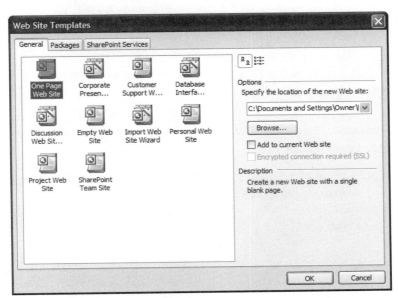

Figure 2-4 Select the Web site template you want to use as the basis of the new site.

3 If you want to specify the location of the site, set the location for the Web site using the field provided in the Options area of the dialog box, or click the Browse button to find a location. The location can be a URL, network path, or local folder.

4 Click OK. If the folder doesn't exist at the given location, FrontPage creates the folder and adds the necessary file and folder structures for a FrontPage Web site. If the folder exists at the given location, FrontPage converts the folder to a FrontPage 2003 Web site.

> **Note**   If you are creating a new site on a server, you may be prompted to provide logon information. Be sure to use the user name and password for an account that is authorized to access the server you are working with.

Opening, Closing, and Saving Web Sites

FrontPage sites that you've worked with recently are accessible by clicking File, Recent Sites, and then selecting the site you want to work with. You can also open a site by completing these steps:

1 Click the down arrow to the right of the Open tool (shown in Figure 2-5) on he Standard toolbar, then select Open Site. Or choose File, Open Site. This displays the Open Site dialog box.

Figure 2-5 The Open tool appears on the standard FrontPage toolbar, but may appear as a folder with the Earth inside it. This indicates that this tool was last used to open a site.

2 If you know the location of the web you want to open, type this location in the Site Name field. Otherwise, use the Look In list box or other options to browse for available webs.

3 When you find the site you want to use, click Open. Each open site is managed in a separate instance of FrontPage. Use the Windows taskbar to switch between the FrontPage instances that are running.

When you are finished working with a site, you can close it and save your work by choosing File, Close Site. If you've made changes to any files in the site, you are prompted to save the changes. You can avoid individual prompts for each file by choosing File, Save All, and then choosing File, Close Site.

Bringing Existing Web Pages and Sites Into FrontPage

Web sites that you've created in other authoring environments, as stand-alone folders, or on a remote server, can be retrieved, stored locally and converted to a FrontPage Web site. To do this, you'll use the Import Web Site Wizard. This wizard can import Web sites using:

- **Extensions** If FrontPage Server Extensions or Microsoft SharePoint Team Services are installed on the remote server, you can use the extensions to transfer the Web site from the remote location. Using extensions should help ensure that all the files FrontPage needs are transferred with their source code intact.

- **DAV** Web distributed authoring and versioning (WebDAV) is a protocol for authoring and publishing files using a standard set of permissions. If the remote server is WebDAV-compliant, you can use this technology to retrieve Web sites that you want to import. Again, this technique should ensure the files are transferred with their source code intact.

- **FTP** File Transfer Protocol (FTP) is a standard Internet protocol for transferring files. To import files using this protocol, the remote server must be running FTP server software. Typically, you'll use this protocol if the remote server isn't compatible with FrontPage, FrontPage Server Extensions, SharePoint Team Services, or WebDAV.

- **File System** File system allows you to transfer a Web site's files using the operating system. If the files are stored on a local disk drive, or are accessible on a network share to which you have access, you can use this option to directly transfer files.

- **HTTP** Hypertext Transfer Protocol (HTTP) is a standard Internet protocol for transferring files over the World Wide Web. If you can't access files any other way, you can use this technique to retrieve files from a remote server. The files may not be transferred with their complete source code, however. Instead, you may get the source as viewed in an end-user's browser.

To import an existing Web site into FrontPage, follow these steps:

1 Choose File, Import. Then, in the Import dialog box, choose From Site to start the Import Web Site Wizard.

2 Choose the import technique. As Figure 2-6 on the following page shows, the options are:

- FrontPage Server Extensions or SharePoint Team Services
- DAV
- FTP
- File System
- HTTP

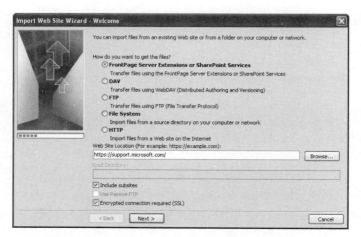

Figure 2-6 Determine the transfer technology, then specify the location of the import files.

3 Type the path to the Web site or folder you want to import, or click Browse to use the New Publish Location dialog box to find the Web site or folder you want to import. Note the following:

- When importing from files on a local drive or network share, you can type the path to a local file system, such as C:\docs\supportsite, or the UNC file path to a network server, such as \\InternetServer03\docs\testsite.

- When importing from a Web site, click Browse, then in the New Publish Location dialog box, click the Search The Web tool on the dialog box's toolbar. This starts Internet Explorer. Browse to the source Web site, then close Internet Explorer. The URL is entered in the Site Name field. Click Open.

4 If you are using extensions, or the file system, you can transfer the root folder and any associated subsites in that folder by selecting Include Subsites.

5 Click Next. The Web site is given a default save location. You can change this by:

- **Typing a new location**   Set the location for the Web site using the field provided, or click the Browse button to find a save location.

- **Selecting Add To Current Web Site**   Add the Web site's files and folders to the current site. If any files or folders being imported have the same name as files or folders in the current Web site, FrontPage will warn you. You'll be able to replace the existing file by clicking Yes, or keep the existing file by clicking No.

6 With extensions, DAV, and HTTP, you can make a secure SSL connection to the remote server by selecting Secure Connection Required (SSL). Click Next.

7 If you are importing from a Web server using HTTP, you can set import limits. You can choose to limit according to levels of folders and subfolders, or total kilobytes. You can also limit the transfer to text and images. Click Next.

8 Click Finish to begin the import process.

Deleting Web Sites

If you no longer need a FrontPage Web site, you can delete it. Instead of deleting the site using Windows Explorer or another tool, you should use FrontPage. If you delete the site using FrontPage, you have more control over how the site's files are deleted and can be sure references to the site are removed from FrontPage.

To delete a site in FrontPage, follow these steps:

1 Open the site for editing in FrontPage, then change to the Folders view, or access the Folder List panel.

2 Right-click the top-level folder for the web, then select Delete.

3 In the Confirm Delete dialog box, select one of the following deletion options:

- **Remove FrontPage Information From This Web Site Only**   Removes folders and files used by FrontPage Server Extensions and SharePoint Team Services, but doesn't remove standard pages or files from the site. You may want to use this option if you discover you are publishing to a server that doesn't support FrontPage Server Extensions or SharePoint Team Services.

- **Delete This Web Site Entirely**   Deletes the entire contents of the site. The contents of the site are not placed in the recycle bin and cannot be recovered from the recycle bin once they are deleted.

4 Click OK.

Creating Folders

Sometimes you may want to create subfolders for files and pages within a site. To do this, follow these steps:

1 Change to the Folders view, or access the Folder List panel.

2 Right-click any open space, point to New, then select Folder.

3 FrontPage creates a new folder with the folder name highlighted for editing. Enter a name for the folder.

> **Note**   You can move pages, images, and other files into the new folder. When you do this, you don't have to worry about breaking links within pages. FrontPage automatically updates all references to the files.

Hiding Folders

All folders and files are accessible to users that access your site in FrontPage and browse your published site unless you specify otherwise. One way to block user access is to hide folders so that they aren't listed in FrontPage and then ensure that directory browsing is disabled on the Web server when the Web site is published.

> **Note**   In FrontPage 2003, hidden folders are visible by default in FrontPage 2003. This is a change from previous versions.

Creating Hidden Folders

To create a hidden folder, use the underscore as the first character of the name. The underscore tells FrontPage the folder is private and shouldn't be listed when browsing folders in FrontPage. You still need to tell the Web server that the folder shouldn't be browsed and may also need to change the folder permissions so that it cannot be accessed.

Displaying Hidden Folders

If you want to show or hide the hidden folders in FrontPage, you'll need to follow these steps:

1 Choose Tools, Site Settings. This displays the Site Settings dialog box.

2 On the Advanced tab, select Show Hidden Files and Folders.

3 Click OK. When FrontPage prompts you to refresh the site, click Yes. When you refresh a site, FrontPage updates the views of the site using the new settings.

> **Aha!**   When you create a new site, a hidden folder called _private is created automatically. This folder is typically used to store form results that you do not want people browsing the web site to see. Visitors to the site aren't allowed to view the contents of this or any other hidden folder as long as directory browsing is disabled. _private is the only hidden folder displayed in FrontPage regardless of the hidden folder settings.

Renaming Folders

When you work with Web site folders, you should perform all of your editing tasks in FrontPage, especially when renaming folders. The main reason is that you don't have to worry about breaking links within pages. FrontPage automatically updates all references to the files in the folders—as long as those files are in the current Web site.

To rename a folder, follow these steps:

1 Right-click the folder in the Folder view or Folder List pane, then select Rename.

2 The folder name is highlighted for editing. Edit the filename. When you are finished, press Enter.

Deleting Folders

When you delete a folder in FrontPage, the folder and all its contents are removed. The contents of the folder are not placed in the recycle bin and cannot be recovered from the recycle bin afterward. To delete a folder, follow these steps:

1 Change to the Folders view, or access the Folder List panel.

2 Right-click the folder you want to delete, then select Delete. You can use Shift+Click and Ctrl+Click to select multiple folders.

3 In the Confirm Delete dialog box, select Yes or Yes To All to delete the selected folder or folders.

Getting to Work with Web Pages and Files

In FrontPage 2003, you can work with many different types of pages. FrontPage is configured as the default editor for most types of text and markup files.

Creating Web Pages

Before you can edit or work with a page, you must first create it. You can create a blank page in any view by pressing Ctrl+N, or by clicking the New Page tool on the Standard toolbar.

You can create new pages based on templates as well. To do this, follow these steps:

1 Click the down arrow to the right of the New button, then select Page. This displays the Page Templates dialog box.

2 Select the template you want to use, then click OK. You'll find more information on working with templates in Chapter 3, "Maximizing Template and Wizard Options."

Another useful technique for creating pages is to use the New task pane. Follow these steps:

1 Choose File, New. This displays the New task pane.

2 Choose a page creation option:

- **Blank Page**   Creates a new page with an HTML header and body, but no contents, and names the file with the .htm extension.

- **Text File**   Creates a new text file with no contents, and names the files with the .txt extension.

- **From Existing Page**   Creates a new page that is a copy of the page you selected in the New From Existing Page dialog box, and names the file with the .htm extension.

Opening Existing Pages and Files

When you open a site for editing, all the pages and files in the site are easily accessible in the Folder Web Site view and in the Folder List pane. Simply double-click a file to open it. You can open multiple files for editing, using Shift+Click and Ctrl+Click. Once you've selected multiple files, right-click, then choose Open.

You can also open existing pages or files by clicking the Open tool on the Standard toolbar. This displays the Open File dialog box, which lets you open files based on their location. You can open files from the current site, on your hard drive, or on the Web.

Editing Pages

You can enter text in FrontPage just as you do in Microsoft Office Word 2003. FrontPage generates the necessary markup for you behind the scenes. If you want to modify the markup yourself, click the Code or Split tab, and then edit the markup directly.

When you open a page for editing in FrontPage, the document title is displayed with a quick access tab. If you make changes to the page, an asterisk is added to the tab title to indicate that there are unsaved changes. The asterisk is displayed until the next time you save the page.

Saving Pages

To save a page in FrontPage, select File, Save, or click the Save tool on the toolbar. Pages are saved to the location from which you opened them, which is usually the current site.

If you are saving a new page, the Save As dialog box is displayed when you choose File, Save, or click the Save tool. This lets you set the page title, file name, save as type and save location. Usually, you'll want to set a new title and filename. To do that, follow these steps:

1 Click the Change Title button, enter the title in the Set Page Title dialog box, and then click OK. This title is displayed in Web browsers, and should accurately describe the contents of the page.

2 Enter the filename in the File Name field. The filename should end with the appropriate extension, such as .htm or .html for an HTML document.

3 Click Save.

Maintaining Pages and Files

You should perform all of your page editing tasks in FrontPage, especially when you are renaming, moving or deleting files. If you do this, FrontPage will automatically update references to the pages and files you've changed in the current site, ensuring those pages and files are still accessible from within other pages—as long as those pages and files are in the current site.

Renaming Pages and Files

To rename a page or file, right-click the filename in the Folder view or Folder List pane, then select Rename. The filename is highlighted for editing. When you are finished editing, press Enter.

> **Aha!**   Another way of renaming files is to use two single clicks to enter filename edit mode. Click the filename, pause, then click the filename again. The filename will be highlighted for editing, as with the Rename option.

Moving Pages and Files

Using the Web site Folders view or the Folder List pane, you can move pages and files just as you would in Windows Explorer. You can:

- **Drag and Drop**   Left-click the file, hold the mouse button, and then drag the file to the new location. The file is moved to the new location.

- **Copy and Paste**   Right-click the file, choose Copy. Navigate to the new location, right-click and then choose Paste. A copy of the file is created at the desired location.

- **Cut and Paste**   Right-click the file, choose Cut. Navigate to the new location, right-click, then choose Paste. The file is moved to the new location.

Unlike previous versions of FrontPage, you can also use these techniques when moving files between sites. To drag and drop between sites, follow these steps:

1 Open the Web sites you want to work with in FrontPage. Note that each Web site has its own instance of FrontPage, which is accessible from the taskbar.

2 In the destination Web site, display the Web Site Folders view, or the Folder List pane.

3   In the source site, left-click the file, hold the mouse button down, and drag the file to the taskbar area. Multiple files can be selected using Shift+Click or Ctrl+Click.

4   Move the pointer over the FrontPage instance containing the destination web.

5   Continue to drag the file into the Folder view or Folder List pane, then drop the file in the desired location.

To copy and paste or cut and paste between sites, follow these steps:

1   Open the Web sites you want to work with in FrontPage.

2   In the destination site, display the Web site Folders view, or the Folder List pane.

3   In the source site, right-click the file, then select Copy or Cut. Multiple files can be selected prior to right-clicking using Shift+Click or Ctrl+Click.

4   On the taskbar, select the FrontPage instance containing the destination site.

5   In the Folder view or Folder List pane, paste the file in the desired location by right-clicking and choosing Paste.

Deleting Pages and Files from the Current Site

To delete a file, follow these steps:

1   Select the file in the Web site Folders view, or the Folder List pane. Multiple files can be selected using Shift+Click or Ctrl+Click.

2   Press the Delete key, or choose Edit, Delete.

3   FrontPage asks you to confirm that you want to delete the file. Click Yes.

Fast Wrap-Up

- The FrontPage 2003 interface makes it easy to switch between design and code views.

- When working with Web sites, you can quickly switch between folder, navigation, link, report and remote Web site views using the buttons provided on the lower portion of the window.

- When you work with sites and folders, you can toggle the view of the Folder List using the View, Folder List option.

- Hidden folders can't be accessed directly by Web site visitors. They can be created by naming a folder with an underscore (_) as the first character of the folder name.

- When you are finished working with FrontPage, you can save your sites and pages to the local file system, a local web, or a remote Web site.

Maximizing Template and Wizard Options

3

10-Second Summary
- Learn about page templates.
- Create discussion Web sites.
- Learn guidelines for Customer Support Web sites.
- Explore the possibilities of Project Web sites.
- Get strategies for Corporate Presence Web sites.

Whether you're building a Web site to support customers, internal teams, or just creating Web pages for fun, you'll want to learn how to get the most out of the templates and wizards available in Microsoft Office FrontPage 2003. Templates contain guidelines to help you complete the design of individual pages, and even entire Web sites. While some templates are basic and straightforward in use, others are a bit more complex and require a bit of expertise to accomplish the task at hand—and these are the ones that we'll focus on in this chapter.

The chapter also looks at wizards. Wizards provide a step-by-step approach to creating Web pages and sites, and two wizards in particular can come in very handy when you're creating sites to support customers and internal teams. These wizards are the Discussion Web Site Wizard, used to create discussion Web sites, and the Corporate Presence Wizard, used to create a professional-looking Web site for an organization.

Creating and Working with Page Templates

When you are working with pages in FrontPage, you can create a new page based on a template by completing the following steps:

1 Click the down arrow to the right of the New tool, then select Page.

2 In the Page Templates dialog box, select the template you want to use, then click OK.

That's it. It's that simple. What isn't so simple, however, is the way to get the maximum benefit from templates. So now let's look at the templates that are available, and identify ways they can be used to save time and effort. In this section, we'll look at:

- Bibliography templates
- Frequently Asked Questions (FAQ) templates
- Table of Contents templates
- Creating your own page templates

> **Note**   While FrontPage 2003 does provide other page templates, these templates are discussed in more appropriate chapters later in the book. For example, Search Page, Feedback Form, Confirmation Form and Guest Book templates use forms, and are discussed in Chapter 14, "Working with Forms," and Chapter 15, "Crowd Pleasing Form Extras." These chapters focus on forms, and because forms are fairly complicated, it is better to discuss the form-related templates later.

Quick Tips for Bibliography Pages

Figure 3-1 shows the bibliography page template. You can use the bibliography template to create a bibliography for your site, which is useful if you reproduce material from another source. You could also use this page to list company contacts, or members of a project team. Bibliography entries are created as bookmarks. Bookmarks use anchor tags, and allow you to add internal page links to individual entries.

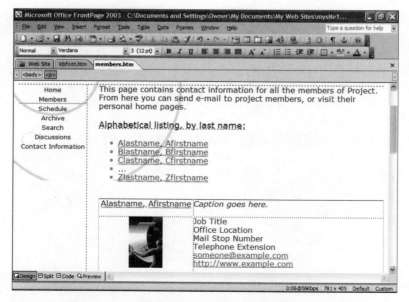

Figure 3-1   You can use bibliography pages whenever you want to create a list of references, team members or contacts.

The fastest way to create and link bibliography entries is to follow these steps:

1 Open a bibliography page for editing in FrontPage 2003 or create one using the bibliography template.

2 Triple-click an existing entry. This will select the entire entry for editing.

3 Press Ctrl+C to copy the entry. Move the insertion point to where you want to add the new entry, then press Ctrl+V.

4 After you modify the text of the entry as necessary, double-click the author's last name, then press Ctrl+G to display the Bookmark dialog box.

5 Enter the author's last name in the Bookmark Name field and click OK.

6 Press Ctrl+S to save the updated page.

7 Open the page containing the referenced resource, then triple-click the text that you want to link to the bookmark.

8 Press Ctrl+K to display the Insert Hyperlink dialog box.

9 Select the bibliography page in the list of pages available, or browse to the page as necessary.

10 Click Bookmark, then select the appropriate bookmark in the Bookmark list.

11 Click OK twice, then press Ctrl+S to save the page.

Quick Tips for FAQ Pages

Figure 3-2 on the following page shows the Frequently Asked Questions or FAQ page template. As the figure shows, the FAQ template begins with a table of contents showing a list of questions, which is followed by individual sections containing answers to the questions. You can use FAQ pages to help your organization in many ways. You could create a FAQ to answer common customer questions, to examine the benefits of a team project, or to respond to common questions about your organization's products or services—and that's only the beginning.

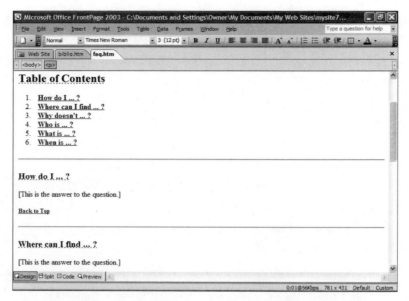

Figure 3-2 You can create FAQ pages whenever you want a list of questions and answers, such as a Q&A list for commonly asked customer questions.

Caution   As you work with the FAQ template, keep in mind that it contains many links and bookmarks, which you don't want to accidentally erase. Links are shown with solid underlining; bookmarks are shown with dashed underlining. You'll learn all about creating links and bookmarks in Chapter 4, "Crafting Pages."

Here are some tips to keep in mind when working with the FAQ page:

■ When you replace text, be careful not to accidentally delete links or bookmarks.

■ When you add new questions, place them at the end of the TOC section, and then add new answer sections in the document body.

■ Don't forget to create bookmarks linking the questions to the answers.

Aha!   Create Answers First – It's Easier That Way

The fastest way to create a new question and answer section is to create the answer section first, and then create the question section. That way, you can link the question to a bookmark in the answer section.

The fastest way to add and link a new question in the table of contents is to follow these steps:

1 Double-click an existing question to select it, then press Ctrl+C.

2 Move the insertion point to the end of the question that precedes the question you want to add, then press Enter to add a blank line. For example, if you want to add question 5, you would move the insertion point to the end of question 4, then press Enter.

3 Press Ctrl+V to paste the previously selected question.

4 Press Ctrl+K to display the Edit Hyperlink dialog box.

5 In the Text To Display field, type the question, then select the bookmark to this question, using the Select A Place In This Document list.

You can create an answer section by following these steps:

1 Position the cursor before the horizontal line that precedes the answer section you want to copy. Left-click and drag down until all the text to the end of the Back To Top link is selected.

2 Press Ctrl+C to copy the selected section.

3 Move the cursor to where you want to paste the new section, then press Ctrl+V.

4 Double-click the bookmarked question to select it, then type the new question.

5 Press Ctrl+G to display the Bookmark dialog box, then type the name of the bookmark for the question.

6 Replace the existing answer text with the answer text for the current question.

Quick Tips for Table of Contents Pages

A table of contents (TOC) section, like the one in the FAQ page, is useful. But sometimes you want a table of contents for an entire Web site, or a section of a Web site, rather than for an individual page. This is where the table of contents template comes in handy. Rather than creating a table of contents page by hand, you can have FrontPage 2003 create one for you.

FrontPage 2003 builds a table of contents page for a Web site by examining all of the links contained in a starting point page that you specify, then examining the pages that are linked from that page. For example, if your organization had a main products page that listed all your beverage products, and provided links to associated pages describing different flavors, you could easily create a table of contents for this section of your Web site. Here, you would specify the main products page as the starting point for the TOC, and let FrontPage build the linked table of contents to each of your products.

The best way to create a table of contents page is to follow these steps:

1 Click the down arrow to the right of the New tool, then select Page.

2 In the Page Templates dialog box, select Table Of Contents, then click OK.

3 On the TOC page, double-click Table Of Contents Heading Page. This opens the dialog box shown in Figure 3-3.

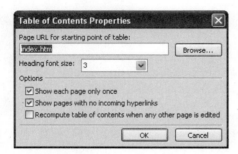

Figure 3-3 Using the starting point, you can configure the table of contents for an entire site, or a section of a site.

4 Enter the starting point page in the field provided. Click Browse to find the page you want to use.

5 If you want the TOC to be updated when pages are changed, select Recompute Table Of Contents.

6 Click OK. Press Ctrl+S to save the page.

7 To see what the TOC looks like, press F12.

> **Aha!**   Save Time By Turning Off Automatic TOC Updates
>
> Recomputing the TOC when other pages are edited will ensure the Table of Contents is always up to date. However, whenever you save changes to pages that are listed in the TOC, FrontPage will update the TOC page, and this can make it seem like FrontPage is very slow when saving pages. In reality, however, FrontPage is spending time updating the TOC. To avoid this, don't select Recompute Table Of Contents. Instead, manually update the page as necessary by opening the TOC page and saving it. Saving the TOC page forces FrontPage to generate a new TOC.

Creating Your Own Page Templates

With FrontPage 2003, you can create new templates for your own use, or for the use of others in your organization, whenever you want. Once you create a page template, it is added to the page template list, and you or others can select it in the Page Templates dialog box.

Page templates you create are either available globally, meaning for all Web sites you work with on a computer, or locally, meaning for a specific Web site you work with on the computer. Thus, if you create global page templates, you can access them from any existing Web site, or any Web site you create. However, if you create a local page template, it is only available when you work with a specific Web site.

You can create page templates, by following these steps:

1   Create or open the page you want to use as a template in FrontPage 2003. Select File, and then Save As.

2   In the Save As dialog box, select FrontPage Template (*.tem) as the Save As Type, then click Save. This displays the Save As Template dialog box shown in Figure 3-4.

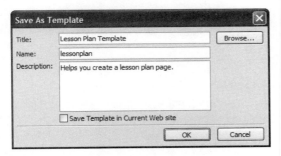

Figure 3-4 You can create your own global and local templates using the Save As Template option.

3   Enter a title, name, and description for the page template.

> **Note**   Don't use the same template name and title as an existing page template. The template title, name and description should clearly and uniquely identify the page template, so that it can be used effectively.

4   Select Save Template In Current Web Site to create a template that is only available for use with the current Web site. Otherwise, the template will be available for all Web sites. Click OK.

> **Note**   Page templates you create are only available on your computer. If you want other people to have access to the templates, you'd need to send them the template page and have them save it as a template, or copy the template file to the appropriate folder on their computer.

Tips for Discussion Web Sites

Want to give your customers or team a place to discuss topics of interest? Well, why not create a discussion Web site? With a discussion Web site, you create a forum where your organization's customers, project team members or others can express their opinions and discuss important issues. Customers may want to learn about upcoming products or learn more about product features. Team members may want a place to discuss project planning, vendor options, or upcoming presentations (such as the nationwide rollout of your new Guava Fizz drink).

Not only does a discussion forum allow users to post articles, it also allows them to search for existing articles on topics of interest. Existing articles can be a gold mine for solving customer problems, answering team member questions, and more. Does this sound like fun? Well, what are you waiting for? Let's create a discussion Web site, and take it for a test drive.

Creating Discussion Web Sites

You can create a discussion Web site as a stand-alone FrontPage Web site, or as part of an existing FrontPage Web site. If you want to have tighter control over access to the discussion, you can also specify that only registered users are allowed, which ensures that all users must register to gain access to the discussion, and that all posted articles have the registered name of the user who submitted them.

A key thing to know up front about discussion Web sites is that they require FrontPage Server Extensions. To create a discussion Web site, follow these steps:

1 Click the down arrow to the right of the New tool, then select Web Site.

2 In the Web Site Templates dialog box, select the Add To Current Web Site check box if you want to add a discussion area to the current FrontPage web.

3 Double-click Discussion Web Site Wizard. Click Next.

4 As shown in Figure 3-5, Discussion Web sites have a submission form, table of contents, search form, threaded replies, and a confirmation page by default. Click Next.

> **Note** If you want all articles posted to the discussion to be in a single list, clear Threaded Replies before clicking Next. Clearing this option specifies that replies to articles should not appear as subtopics.

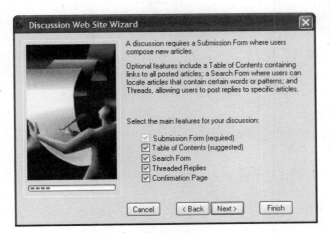

Figure 3-5 You can configure the discussion Web site in several ways, but most of the time you'll want to have a submission form, table of contents, search form, threaded replies and a confirmation page.

5 Enter a descriptive title for the discussion, such as Network Project Discussion or New Product Discussion Forum, in the field provided. Note the name of the discussion folder. This is where articles posted to the discussion will be stored. Click Next.

6 You'll post articles to the discussion using a submission form. As you can see from Figure 3-6 on the following page, you can now set the input fields for this form. The Category and Product fields provide drop-down lists that can be used to sort discussion topics by category name or by product type. Click Next.

> **Note**   If you use the Category or Product field, you'll need to define the categories or products for the discussion later. For more information on working with drop down lists, see Chapter 14, "Working with Forms."

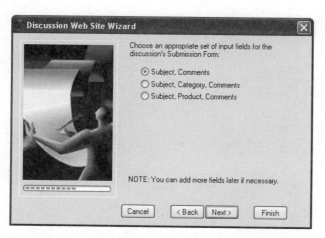

Figure 3-6 You can select several different field combinations for the submission form. Choose the one that makes the most sense, based on how you think the discussion will be used.

7 Click Next to accept the default access setting, and make the discussion group *open*, meaning anyone with access to the discussion can post articles. Or click Yes, Only Registered Users Are Allowed, to make the discussion *closed*, meaning only registered users can post articles to the discussion. Then click Next.

> **Note**   If you chose to restrict access to the discussion, you'll also need to create a registration page, or create the accounts users will need to access the discussion manually.

8 If you choose to add a table of contents to the discussion:

- You'll be able to specify the sort order for articles posted to the discussion. Choose Oldest To Newest or Newest To Oldest, and then click Next.

- You'll then be able to specify whether you want the table of contents to be the home page for the Web site. Choose Yes or No, and then click Next.

9 If you choose to add a search form, select the search options you want to include in the form, including: subject, size, date, and score. The score is a measure of the relevancy of the query term to a particular article. Click Next.

10 Now, you can specify the layout of the discussion. Choose No Frames if you want each discussion area to have its own page, or choose Dual Interface (the default) if you want to allow the use of frames (if the user's browser supports them). With dual interface frames, a table of contents is displayed in the top frame, and articles and other pages are displayed in the bottom frame.

11 Click Finish so that the DiscussionWeb Site Wizard can create the new discussion Web site.

12 Edit the discussion pages as necessary. When you're finished, publish the discussion Web site to a server with FrontPage Server Extensions.

How to Use and Manage Discussion Web Sites

The discussion Web site gets going when a customer, team member or other user posts an article to it. Users can then reply to posts, or create new articles with new subjects to start new discussions. Articles are stored in a discussion folder—a hidden folder that only administrators can access.

Once the discussion gets going, you may need to monitor what is being posted. Sometimes an inappropriate article or reply may be posted to the discussion, and if so, you may want to modify or remove the message. You may also want to periodically modify or remove old articles from the discussion, so that it is easier to keep track of the current discussion.

Articles posted to the discussion Web site are saved as individual Web pages. To modify articles, follow these steps:

1 Open the discussion Web site in FrontPage 2003. If necessary, press Alt+F1 to display the Folder List.

2 Double-click the Hidden Discussion Folder to access its contents.

3 Articles posted to the discussions are named sequentially. To find the article you want to remove, increase the width of the Title column so that you can read the article subjects.

4 Double-click the article you want to modify.

5 Edit the article and then press Ctrl+S to save the changes.

To remove articles, follow these steps:

1 Open the discussion Web site in FrontPage 2003, then select Tools, and then Options to open the Options dialog box.

2 In the General tab, select Warn When Text Index Is Out of Date, and click OK.

3 If the index is out of date, you should get a warning telling you that FrontPage needs to re-index the Web site. Click Yes—you want the index to be up to date before you delete any messages. By updating the index, you ensure the article you are removing isn't listed in search results.

4 If necessary press Alt+F1 to display the Folder List.

  5 Double-click the hidden discussion folder to access its contents.

  6 Articles posted to the discussion are named sequentially. To find the article you want to remove, increase the width of the Title column so that you can read the article subjects.

  7 Right-click the article you want to delete and then select Delete.

Guidelines for Customer Support Web Sites

Most organizations that sell products or services have online customer support Web sites, and you can too. The great thing about a customer support Web site is that it can serve your customers 24 hours a day, every day. Customers are able to get answers to most of their questions (such as store locations, business hours, or nutrition facts) whether it's a weekday, weekend or a holiday.

Creating a Customer Support Web Site

FrontPage 2003 provides a ready-to-use customer support Web site that comes with a standard set of pages designed to make it easy to support your customers' needs.

You can create a customer support Web site by completing the following steps:

  1 Click the down arrow to the right of the New tool, then select Web Site.

  2 In the Web Site Templates dialog box, select the Add To Current Web Site check box if you want to add a customer support area to the current FrontPage web.

  3 When you double-click Customer Support Web Site, FrontPage 2003 will create the Web site for you, complete with all the pages you need to get started.

Understanding and Customizing the Customer Support Web Site

Figure 3-7 shows the main page of the customer support Web site. After you create this Web site, you'll want to tailor the Web site to the needs of your organization, giving it your own customized look and feel. Before you get started, take an inventory of the pages provided and open pages in your browser (open the page for editing then press F12).

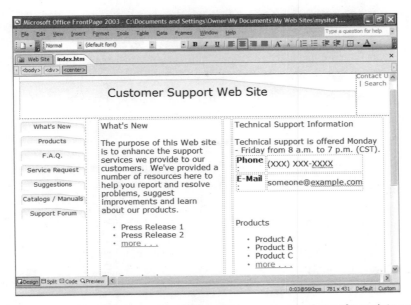

Figure 3-7 The customer support Web site has a standard set of templates and most pages are accessible from the home page shown here.

When you browse the customer support Web site, you'll find the following pages:

- **Catalog** An area for links to product catalogs and manuals.

- **Contact Us** Provides contact information, so that customers can get in touch with the support team.

- **Customer Support Discussion** A discussion area where customers can submit questions and get answers.

- **FAQ** A page for listing answers to frequently-asked customer questions.

- **Products** A page for listing your organization's products.

- **Search** Allows users to search the customer support Web site.

- **Service Request** Allows customers to submit a service request related to a product.

- **Suggestions** Allows customers to submit suggestions for enhancing products or improving customer service.

- **What's New** A page for listing what's new in the customer support Web site, and providing other important announcements.

Tailoring the Customer Support Web Site

The customer support web site is meant to provide a starting point, and, as such, it is far from being a finished site that you'd want customers to browse. So before you publish this site and make it available for browsing, you'll want to tailor it for your organization.

Some of the things you may want to do to prepare the customer support Web site for use are as follows:

- Change the look and feel of the Web site using themes.

   1) Select Format, and then Theme. In the Theme task pane, right-click the theme you want to use, then select Apply As The Default Theme.

   2) Click Yes when prompted to confirm the action.

See Also
For more about themes, see Chapter 5, "Enhancing Design with Themes."

- Update the page banner and navigation bar settings for each page in the Web site.

   1) Open a page for editing, then double-click the page banner or navigation bar you want to change.

   2) Use the Link Bar Properties dialog box to set a new look and style.

- Tailor the text of pages within the Web site to meet the needs of your organization.

   1) Open a page for editing.

   2) Change the page text to replace placeholder text for contact information, and add descriptions appropriate for your organization.

   3) Press Ctrl+S to save the changes you've made.

- Check feedback, service request and suggestion form configurations.

   1) Feedback, service requests or suggestions submitted by users are saved to text files in the Web site's private folder (_private).

   2) Using the techniques discussed in Chapter 14, "Working with Forms," customize the form properties to meet your organization's requirements.

Rules for Project Web Sites

Projects and project teams are the lifeblood of any organization. To help team members stay in touch with each other, and provide forums for discussion, you may want to create a project Web site.

Creating a Project Web Site

FrontPage 2003 provides a ready-to-use project Web site that comes with a standard set of pages designed to make it easy for teams to collaborate. You can create a project Web site by completing the following steps:

1 Click the down arrow to the right of the New tool, then select Web Site.

2 In the Web Site Templates dialog box, select the Add To Current Web Site check box, if you want to add a project area to the current FrontPage web.

3 When you double-click Project Web Site, FrontPage 2003 will create the Web site for you, complete with all the pages you need to get started.

Understanding the Project Web Site

Figure 3-8 shows the main page of the project Web site. After you create a project Web site, you'll want to update the site to meet the requirements of your team. Start by examining the pages that are available, including:

- **Archive**   A page you can use to provide links to important documents, files and reports.

- **Contact Us**   A page for listing contact information, so that others in the organization can contact the project team.

- **Knowledge Base**   A discussion area for common questions and answers about the project.

- **Members**   A bibliography page for listing team members and their contact information.

- **Requirements Discussion**   A discussion area, where team members can discuss project requirements.

- **Schedule**   A page for listing the project timeline and milestones.

- **Search**   Allows team members or others to search the project Web site.

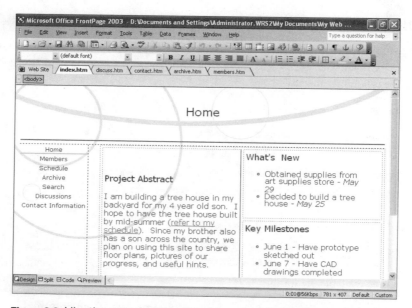

Figure 3-8 Like the support Web site, the project Web site's main page provides the key links to other pages, and introduces the purpose of the site.

Customizing the Project Web Site

The project Web site is an excellent starter site, but it isn't meant to be a finished product. So, before you publish this site and make it available for browsing, you'll want to tailor it for your project.

The things you may want to do to prepare the project Web site for use are the same as for the customer support Web site. You may want to:

- Change the look and feel of the Web site, using themes.

- Update the page banner and navigation bar settings for each page, so it is specific to your project.

- Tailor the text of pages within the Web site for your project.

Don't forget to tailor both the knowledge base discussion and the project requirements discussion. Start with the main discussion page (discuss.htm), and work your way to the individual pages for each discussion (reqtoc.htm and kbtoc.htm).

Strategies for Corporate Presence Web Sites

Every organization should have a presence on the Web, and a great way to get a fast start is to use the Corporate Presence Web site. If you're interested in establishing a corporate presence for your organization, read on!

Introducing Corporate Presence Web Sites

You can build a corporate presence Web site using a FrontPage wizard that customizes the site for the way your organization does business. As a starter site, the Corporate Presence Web site is quite good. It's professional, polished, and has all the features most organizations are looking for in a starter site:

- A corporate home page to establish your presence on the Web.

- A feedback page for getting input from customers.

- Pages for your company's products and services.

- Table of Contents, What's New, and Search pages to make the site more accessible.

- Pages for press releases that provide additional information.

As you can see, the kinds of pages included with the corporate presence Web site are similar to pages in other Web templates discussed in this chapter. What is unique about the corporate presence Web site, however, is that you use a wizard to customize dozens of aspects of the site, so that it's just right for your organization. You decide what features are included, and how those features are presented.

Creating a Corporate Presence Web Site

So, are you ready to give this corporate presence thing a try? Well maybe so, but before you begin, take a moment to consider who your target audience is, what information will be most valuable to them, and how you can effectively present this information to the site's visitors. Once you have clear answers for those questions, you're ready to get started.

You can create a corporate presence Web site by following these steps:

1 Click the down arrow to the right of the New tool, then select Web Site.

2 Double-click Corporate Presence Wizard. When the Corporate Presence Web wizard starts, click Next.

3 With the audience and the site's visitors in mind, select the kinds of pages that you want to include in the Web site (as shown in Figure 3-9).

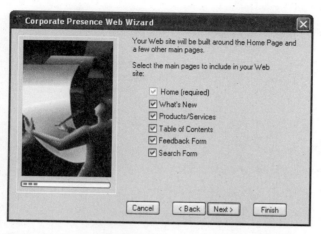

Figure 3-9 Start by selecting the kinds of pages that will be included in your corporate presence Web site.

4   Click Next, then select the topics you want to appear on the site's home page. Because the home page is the first page most visitors see, you'll want to let them know right up front what your organization does. For that reason, you may want the home page to include at least an introduction, mission statement, and profile.

5   Continue through the wizard pages by clicking Next.

- If you decided to include a What's New page, you can choose its topics. Ideally, you'll use the page as a tool to introduce new developments within the organization, such as the introduction of new products or services, and also feature articles, reviews, press releases and other bits of information that will help keep visitors informed about the organization.

- If you decided to include products and services pages in the web site, you can now determine how many links are provided on the main products and services directory page, and how many individual product and service pages FrontPage will create. If your organization only sells products or only offers services, you can enter zero (0) in the product or service field, which tells FrontPage not to include this section, or the related subpages. Next, you'll be able to tailor the topics for the individual product and service pages. All product and service pages have title, description, and benefits areas.

- If you decided to get feedback from customers, which usually is a good idea, you can specify which fields to include on the feedback form. Most of the time, you'll want to get the visitor's full name (so you know who you are speaking with), e-mail address or phone number (so you can e-mail or call them back if necessary), and comments (so you know what the visitor wants or needs help with). Next, you can choose whether feedback is posted to a text file (choose tab-delimited format), or to a Web page (choose Web-page format). You'll find that the Web-page format is easy to read, but not easy to manipulate if you'd like to store submissions in a database or spreadsheet.

- If you decided to have a table of contents page, you'll be able to specify how the TOC is used, much as discussed previously in this chapter in the section "Quick Tips for Table of Contents Pages."

6 When you finish tailoring individual pages, you'll be able to specify the standard elements used in most pages (as shown in Figure 3-10). You'll find two types of elements: Top of page elements are your company's logo, page title, and links to your main web pages. Bottom of page elements are links to your main web pages, the e-mail address of your Webmaster, your copyright notice, and the date the page was last modified.

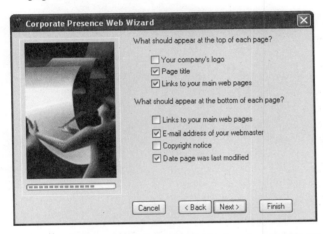

Figure 3-10 After you customize individual pages, specify the standard elements for the top and bottom of the site's pages.

7 Click Next. Select No—you don't want to include an "under construction" icon on your pages, as most search engines won't list pages that are under construction— and then click Next again.

8 Next, enter the company name and address information. Don't leave any of these fields blank. Your organization's name and proper contact information is important in building a Web presence, so be sure to think about how you want this presented on appropriate pages throughout the site.

9 Click Next, then enter contact phone and fax numbers, and e-mail addresses for getting additional information. Again, don't leave these blank (unless of course, you really don't want customers to contact you).

10 Click Finish. When FrontPage finishes creating the Web site, review the tasks provided. You'll need to complete these tasks to get the Web site ready to publish.

Fast Wrap-Up

- FrontPage 2003 has many page templates that can be used as the basis of your Web pages.

- Web templates and wizards can be used as the basis of entire sites, but you'll need to update the page text and design to suit your own needs.

- Use the Customer Support Web when you want to create an area to support customers and receive feedback.

- Use the Project Web when project team members need to collaborate on a project.

- Use the Corporate Presence Web to help you build a basic Web site for your company.

Part 2
Making Your FrontPage Site Content-Rich

Now that you know more about Microsoft Office FrontPage 2003, let's look at how you can use FrontPage to create polished, professional Web sites that are content-rich. To start with, Chapter 4 looks at the key features you can use when crafting pages, including horizontal lines, bulleted lists, and hypertext links. Once you get the hang of these core features, we'll help you take your Web design skills to the next level. Chapter 5, "Enhancing Design with Themes," and Chapter 6, "Polishing Design with Style Sheets," explore more advanced features, including themes and style sheets. With themes, you can use custom designs built in to FrontPage to polish the look and feel of your Web site. With style sheets, you get precise control over the placement of elements and their style.

To add pizzazz to your Web pages, Chapter 7, "Using Pictures in Web Pages," and Chapter 8, "Going Beyond the Ordinary: Photo Galleries, Soundtracks, Video and Picture Maps," show you how to use multimedia in Web pages. Multimedia is a catchphrase for the various types of media that are available, including still images, video and audio. FrontPage includes many helpful tools for working with these types of media. So whether you want to add clip art, a background image, or a soundtrack to a Web page, you'll find the answers in Chapter 7 and Chapter 8.

The final chapter of this part discusses tables. Not only will you learn how to create tables, you'll also learn how to customize the appearance of tables, using background colors, images, custom borders and spacing techniques. The chapter doesn't discuss using tables for layout, however. You'll find a separate design discussion covering layout tables in Chapter 11, "Advanced Layout with Tables and Layers."

Crafting Pages

4

10-Second Summary

- Start crafting the text elements of your Web pages.
- Use line breaks and horizontal lines.
- Create bulleted and numbered lists.
- Link to and within other pages.
- Optimize page properties for the audience and search engines.

When I hear the term "crafting pages" I think of an artist sitting down in front of a blank canvas, preparing to use oil paints to bring the images in her mind's eye to life—and I hope you do too, because there's so much involved in creating Web pages, especially if you want to create *great* Web pages. Great Web pages are designed. Great Web pages are crafted.

Wondering what kinds of pages you can create? Well, there are many. Here are just a few of the ones you might use:

- Product brochures, documentation and announcements
- Project meeting minutes, task lists and milestone timelines
- Classroom lesson plans and bulletins for students or faculty
- Daily, weekly or monthly newsletters
- Service announcements or service plan details

In this chapter, you'll learn how to add the essential features you'll use in these, and any other kinds of pages. We discuss everything from text to line breaks to horizontal lines to lists and links. 99% of all Web pages have these basic elements, and before you use these features, you should read the tips and advice in this chapter.

Getting Started with the Basics

In some books, they tell you to forget everything you learned previously, because everything is different. Well, I'm not going to do that. Instead, I'm going to let you in on a little secret—a big secret, actually. Here goes: When it comes to the basics of entering and editing text, working with a document in FrontPage 2003 is very similar to working with a document in Microsoft Office Word 2003.

You'll find similar or identically-named menus, menu options, toolbars, and tools, and these basic features work much like they do in Word 2003. So, rather than spending several chapters discussing things you already know, let's take a quick look at the basics of working with text, and then go on to more challenging tasks.

Entering and Manipulating Text

FrontPage makes it easy to enter and manipulate text. You enter text by typing it. When you type, the characters appear at the cursor position. Unlike Word, FrontPage doesn't allow you to switch between insert and overwrite mode. FrontPage is always in insert mode, meaning that, when you type, characters are inserted at the cursor position, and any existing characters are pushed to the right.

You can correct typos and manipulate text using the Word techniques you know. For line-editing:

- **Backspace**　Press Backspace to erase characters to the left of the cursor.
- **Delete**　Press Delete to erase the character to the right of the cursor.
- **Enter**　Press Enter to complete a paragraph and move the cursor to the next line in the document.

If you want to select text so that you can manipulate or delete it, you have several options. You can:

- **Select single word**　Double-click the word to select it.
- **Select paragraph**　Triple-click anywhere in the paragraph to select it.
- **Select section of text**　Click at the beginning of the text section, drag the mouse to the end of the selection, and then release the mouse button.
- **Select all text from cursor to beginning of document**　Press Ctrl+Shift+Home
- **Select all text from cursor to end of document**　Press Ctrl+Shift+End
- **Select entire document**　Press Ctrl+A

Getting Text Just the Way You Like It

You can format text using headings, paragraphs and alignment. Headings help you organize your ideas. For example, the chapters of most nonfiction books use many levels of headings. You will usually find chapter headings and section headings that pertain to each major topic, and subheadings pertaining to subtopics.

FrontPage provides six levels of headings. You set the heading level using the Style drop-down list on the Format toolbar. Select Heading 1 for a 24-point font size, Heading 2 for an 18-point font size, Heading 3 for a 14-point font size, and so on. When you enter a heading and press enter, FrontPage returns to the Normal style, which is the style for regular paragraphs.

Paragraphs help to visually break up the page, and are normally styled using a 12-point font. Don't overlook the importance of the way text is used on the page. To better organize and control text more precisely, use:

- **Alignment**   To align a paragraph, heading, or other text element, just move the insertion point to the text element you want to align, then select the alignment you want to use from the Format toolbar. The alignment options are Align Left, Center, Align Right, and Justify.

- **Font Size**   To the right of the alignment options, you'll find the Increase Font Size and Decrease Font Size tools. Click Increase Font Size to step up the font size incrementally. Click Decrease Font Size to step down the font size incrementally.

- **Indentation**   You can indent text using the Format toolbar's Increase Indent tool. Each time you click this tool, FrontPage indents the text element about an inch. To decrease the indentation, use the Decrease Indent button.

Entering Line Breaks and Horizontal Lines

If you've browsed the Web, you've probably seen pages with line breaks and horizontal lines. Line breaks enable you to break a line without adding a space between the lines. Horizontal lines are graphical lines drawn across the width of the page. When used effectively, line breaks and horizontal lines create necessary spacing in a page—which helps make it easier to understand the text, and gives the reader's eyes a break.

Adding Spacing with Line Breaks

You can use a line break to format text in many ways. Line breaks can highlight text by creating a column or a simple list, which not only adds to the visual impact of the page, but also gets the reader's attention. Sometimes you don't want a space between lines of text, or you want to highlight an example by breaking the line and starting a new line showing the example.

To add a line break, press Shift+Enter. If you want to clear the left, right, or both margins after placing a picture or other element on the page, select Break from the Insert menu, choose the appropriate setting in the Break dialog box, and then click OK.

If you make a mistake and want to remove a line break, or change its properties, you can do this by following these steps:

1 Click Show All on the Standard toolbar (hint: it looks like a paragraph mark). You should now see line breaks and paragraph marks.

2 Double-click the line break you want to remove or change.

3 Press Delete to remove the line break or press Alt+Enter to set the Break properties, using the dialog box shown in Figure 4-1 on the following page.

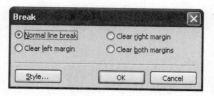

Figure 4-1 Line break properties control whether the left, right or both margins are cleared after the line break.

Adding Spacing with Horizontal Lines

Horizontal lines also provide an easy way to organize, or visually break up the text of a page. Horizontal lines are entered as either shaded (default) or solid lines, and can be as wide as the browser window, a percentage of the browser window, or a specific size in pixels. The thickness of a horizontal rule is determined by its height, which is set in pixels.

To add a horizontal line to a page, choose Insert, Horizontal Line. Double-click the line to set its properties as shown in Figure 4-2. The properties of horizontal lines are as follows:

- **Width**   Sets the length of the horizontal line in pixels, or as a percentage of the browser window.

- **Height**   Sets the height (thickness) of the horizontal line in pixels.

- **Alignment**   Aligns the horizontal line. Choose Left, Center or Right.

- **Color**   Sets the color of the horizontal line. Choose Automatic to use the default color, or base the color on the current theme.

- **Solid Line**   Specifies that the line is solid without shading.

Figure 4-2 Horizontal lines can be optimized for your pages using different width, height, alignment and color settings.

Organizing Your Ideas with Lists

Lists give order to your ideas, and can add to the visual impact of the page. With a list, you can get the reader's attention, give their eyes a break, and help clarify your main points. You probably are familiar with the two most commonly used types of lists: bulleted and numbered. FrontPage also adds another type of list: definition lists. You use definition lists to define a term, and then provide its definitions. We'll examine all three types of lists in this section.

Using Bulleted and Numbered Lists

Bulleted and numbered lists are the types of lists you'll use most often:

- Bulleted lists are best when you want to outline goals, objectives, or tasks with no specific order.
- Numbered lists are best when tasks must be performed in a particular order, or when you want to be very specific.

The easiest way to create a bulleted or numbered list is to use the Numbering or Bullets tool on the Format toolbar. Follow these steps:

1 Position the cursor at the point you want to begin the list, and click either Numbering or Bullets tools on the Standard toolbar, as appropriate. If you click Numbering, a number 1 is inserted in the page. If you click Bullets, a bullet character is inserted.

2 Create the list by typing an item and pressing Enter. FrontPage moves to the next line, and adds another bullet, or the next number, depending on the type of list you are working with.

3 End the list by pressing Enter twice.

To change the way bullets or numbering are used, choose Format, Bullets And Numbering. This displays the List Properties dialog box shown in Figure 4-3 on the following page. You can then choose a different bullet or number style by clicking the tab you want and then clicking the style you like in the preview window. When you click OK, the new style is applied automatically.

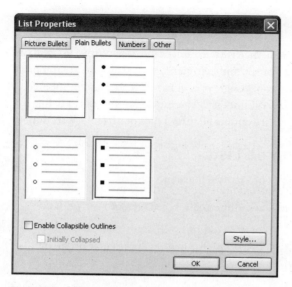

Figure 4-3   You can change the style of bullets and numbers using the List Properties dialog box.

> **Note**   Use the Picture Bullets tab to define pictures to use as bullets. If the current web has a theme, you'll probably want to use pictures from the current theme. Otherwise, you can specify your own pictures to use.

Using Definition Lists

You use definition lists to define a term, and then provide its definitions. Well, that's the official reason anyway. It doesn't mean that you *must* use definition lists that way. In fact, you can use definition lists anytime you want, to associate keywords, phrases, or sentences with concepts.

Items in definition lists contain two elements:

- Keyword, phrases or sentences you are defining, called the defined terms.
- Associated concepts, called definitions.

To create a definition list, follow these steps:

1 Position the cursor at the point you want to begin the list, and choose Definition Term from the Formatting toolbar's Style pull-down list.

2 Type the keyword or phrase you want to define. After you press Enter, you can enter a definition for the keyword or phrase. You can continue to add keywords and definitions to the list in this way, and FrontPage will alternate between the two styles for you automatically.

3 End the list by pressing Enter twice.

Connecting Pages with Links and Bookmarks

Links and bookmarks help readers navigate your Web site, and find pages on other Web sites. Clicking a link takes you to a new page. Clicking a bookmark takes you to a precise location within the current page or another page.

Linking Pages

Links connect pages in Web sites and can be created using text, pictures or other page elements. To create a link in a Web page, follow these steps:

1 Select the item that you want to link by highlighting the text, or clicking the picture, or other page element that you want to use.

2 Press Ctrl+K. This opens the Insert Hyperlink dialog box, shown in Figure 4-4.

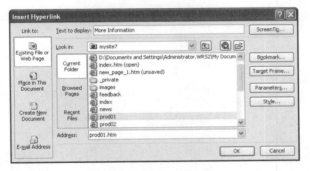

Figure 4-4 You can add links to existing pages, a new document, and email addresses.

3 Specify whether you want to link to an existing Web page, a new document, or an email address by clicking the appropriate Link To option. The options of the dialog box change based on your selection.

4 Choose the file to which you want to link if it is displayed in the Look In list, or enter the Web address in the Address field. With e-mail addresses, you'll be able to enter an e-mail address and a subject. Here, clicking the link starts the reader's e-mail program and creates a new e-mail message, using the information you provided.

5 When you click OK, FrontPage will create the link.

Linking within Pages Using Bookmarks

Bookmarks point to precise locations within Web pages. Creating a bookmark is a two-part process that involves labeling the bookmark, and creating a link to the bookmark. The label is the name of the bookmark so that it can be referenced in the bookmark link.

To label a bookmark, follow these steps:

1 Select the item that you want to use as the label by highlighting the text, or clicking the picture, or other page element that you want to use.

2 Press Ctrl+G. This opens the Bookmark dialog box, shown in Figure 4-5.

3 In the Bookmark Name field, enter the name of the bookmark. Bookmark names must be unique within a page, and can include spaces.

4 Click OK to create the label.

Figure 4-5 Set a unique name for each bookmark.

To create a link to the bookmark, follow these steps:

1 Select the item that you want to link by highlighting the text, or clicking the picture, or other page element that you want to use.

2 Press Ctrl+K. This opens the Insert Hyperlink dialog box, shown previously in Figure 4-4.

3 To link to a bookmark in the current Web page, choose Place In This Document, then select the bookmark you want to use in the Bookmarks list.

4 To link to a bookmark in another Web page, choose Existing File Or Web Page, then choose the file to which you want to link, if it is displayed in the Look In list, or enter the Web address in the Address field. Afterward, click Bookmark, then select the bookmark you want to use in the Bookmarks list.

5 When you click OK, FrontPage will create the link.

Editing Links and Bookmarks

Editing links and bookmarks is easy. Place the pointer anywhere in the text containing the link, or select any part of the link, then press Ctrl+K. This opens the Edit Hyperlink dialog box, where you can now change the link's attributes.

To change a bookmark, select the bookmark, then press Ctrl+G. This opens the Bookmark dialog box. You can change the name of the bookmark's label by entering a new name.

Removing Links and Bookmarks

Removing links and bookmarks is easy, too. Place the pointer anywhere in the text containing the link, or select any part of the link, and then press Ctrl+K. Click the Remove Link button in the lower right corner of the Edit Hyperlink dialog box.

To remove a bookmark, select the bookmark, then press Ctrl+G. This opens the Bookmark dialog box. Click the Clear button in the Bookmark dialog box, then click OK.

Behind the Scenes... Setting Page Properties

Every Web page you create or edit in FrontPage has page properties. Page properties specify the general attributes of the page, covering everything from the page title, to the descriptions and keywords that search engines should use, to the colors of text, links and backgrounds.

In this section, we'll take a look at the page properties you'll want to work with right now, including page titles, descriptions, keywords, and colors.

Creating Useful Page Titles

Every page you create in FrontPage should have a title. The title is displayed at the top of the browser window. If you don't specify a title, FrontPage will create one for you using the page's file name. Trust me—you don't want that. Instead, you should optimize the page title for the people who visit your site or for search engines.

- If you decide to optimize a page title for your site's visitors, use a short, but descriptive title. Style the title like a heading. Don't add extra formatting or markup. For example, use "Welcome to Adatum.com's Web Site" instead of "Adatum web".

- If you decide to optimize a page title for search engines, enter two or three keywords that are in the text of the page as the title. Use lower case, and separate keyword groupings with commas. For example, use "tourist information, tourism" instead of "Information and Tourism Bureau."

To specify the page title, follow these steps:

1 Right-click an open area within the page, then select Page Properties. This displays the Page Properties dialog box.

2 Enter the page title in the Title field, then click OK.

Customizing Text and Link Colors

Most browsers display Web pages using default colors for text, links and backgrounds. Typically, this means black text, blue links and white backgrounds. However, this isn't always the case. Sometimes, the default colors for text, links, and backgrounds may be completely different.

To ensure consistency or add a bit more pizzazz to your pages, you can specify the colors you want to use. To do this, follow these steps:

1 Right-click an open area within the page, then select Page Properties.

2 Select the Formatting tab as shown in Figure 4-6. On the Colors panel, you'll find the following options:

- **Background**   Sets the color for the open area of the page.
- **Text**   Sets the color for text.
- **Hyperlink**   Sets the color for unvisited links.
- **Visited Hyperlink**   Sets the color for links readers have clicked on before.
- **Active Hyperlink**   Sets the color for selected links.

See Also If you use themes in your pages, colors and backgrounds are already determined for you. Therefore, to change colors and backgrounds, you must either change your theme or not use themes. For more information, see Chapter 5 "Enhancing Design with Themes."

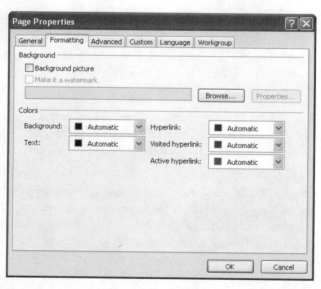

Figure 4-6 You can customize the colors used for backgrounds, text and links.

3 The standard color palette has 16 basic colors, such as yellow, blue or green. To use one of these colors, click the pull-down list , then choose the color you want to use.

4 The extended color palette has 216 colors. To use one of these colors, click the pull-down list, select More Colors, then, in the More Colors dialog box, choose the color you want to use. If you want to use a color that's displayed on the screen, click Select, move the color selection cursor over the color that you want to use, and then click. Click OK.

5 Click OK to close the Page Properties dialog box.

> **Note**   Are you wondering why the extended palette has only 216 colors, when most computers display at least 256 colors? It's because the extended colors provided by FrontPage are based on the browser-safe color palette used by professional designers. The idea here is to ensure that colors are consistent from browser to browser, and from computer to computer, whether you are using Windows, Macintosh or Unix.

Helping Readers Find Your Pages in Search Engines

Even though Internet search engines are becoming more and more sophisticated, it is becoming harder and harder to find the information you are looking for on the Web. One of the reasons for this is that the Web is growing at a phenomenal rate—by some accounts, by millions of pages each week. To help readers find your pages in the ever-growing Web, you should add descriptions and keywords to every page you publish.

To specify descriptions and keywords, follow these steps:

1 Open a page for editing, and study its contents. Think of how you could best describe this page to others, and then make a list of important words and phrases that highlight the purpose of the page.

2 Right-click an open area within the page, then select Page Properties. This displays the Page Properties dialog box shown in Figure 4-7 on the following page.

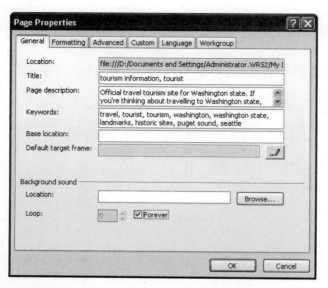

Figure 4-7 To help search engines index your pages, and help people find your site, enter an accurate description and keyword list.

3   Enter a description in the Page Description field, making sure to use complete sentences, and that the description relates directly to the purpose of the page. The description should be no more than 4 or 5 average-length sentences, or about 250 characters. The most important information should be in the first 100 characters.

4   Type your list of important words or phrases in the Keywords field. Enter a comma after each word or phrase. Don't use more than 25 or 30 keywords, and be careful not to repeat keywords.

5   Click OK, then press Ctrl+S to save the page.

Fast Wrap-Up

■   While it's easy to add text to Web pages, there are a few tips and tricks to getting things just right.

■   You can add line breaks and horizontal lines to Web pages to break up the page visually.

■   If you want to organize text, one technique to use is a bulleted or numbered list.

■   To access other resources and pages, define hypertext links.

■   You can also define links to places within pages using bookmarks.

■   Before you finish a page, don't forget to optimize page properties for your audience and for search engines.

Enhancing Design with Themes

5

10-Second Summary

- Use and customize themes to suit your needs.
- Use shared borders, link bars and page banners.
- Remove themes from pages and Web sites when no longer desired.

Now that you know the basics of crafting pages, you're ready to polish the page design. One way to do this is to add items such as:

- Themes that customize the way graphics and text elements are used on pages.
- Shared borders that add common headers and footers to pages in a site.
- Link bars that make it easy to navigate the pages of your sites.
- Page banners that add introductory graphics or text to pages.

Not only can these features turn ordinary sites into extraordinary sites, they also can save you time and effort. By the time you finish this chapter, you'll have a polished site with professional-quality design and graphics. Along the way, you'll also learn how to customize themes; use shared borders; add page banners or link bars to pages; and remove these features if they are no longer needed.

Spicing Up Your Sites with Themes

Designing a professional-looking Web site takes a lot of time. You have to plan the overall look and the navigation structure of the site down to the most minute detail. To be thorough, your planning should include everything from color schemes, font types and font styles to background graphics, banners, headers, footers, and links. Wouldn't it be great if you didn't have to waste hours and hours trying to come up with a design that works, and could instead simply experiment with existing designs to see which ones you prefer? Well, you can—this is where themes come into the picture.

With themes, you get ready-to-use designs, complete with all the essential elements you need, and you can apply these elements to individual pages, groups of pages, or entire Web sites at any time. If you later decide to use a different theme, or no theme at all, you can make the necessary changes with a few simple mouse clicks. You can even customize themes to meet your needs more precisely.

Working with Themes

In Microsoft Office FrontPage 2003, themes can use vivid colors, active graphics and background graphics. With the vivid colors option, pages have bright colors in text and graphics. With the active graphics option, pages have graphic buttons that change when the mouse is passed over them (these are called "hover buttons") and more contemporary graphics. With the background graphics option, pages have background graphics, rather than a plain background color, such as white or black.

To work with themes, you'll use the Themes task pane, shown in Figure 5-1. Display the Themes task pane by selecting Format, Theme. Under Select A Theme, you'll find the following options:

- **Current Theme**   Denotes the theme that is currently selected and displayed in preview mode. The theme information isn't written to the site, unless you also set it as the default theme. Click the plus sign (+) to see sub-entries that specify the settings for vivid colors, active graphics and background graphics.

- **Web Site Default Theme**   Denotes the default theme for the current site. The default theme can be different from the theme for the page you are currently previewing.

- **Recently Used Themes**   Denotes themes that you've worked with recently. This is handy if you are looking for a particular theme that you may have used before, and don't know the name.

- **All Available Themes**   Lists all the themes that are available for you to use. Themes are listed alphabetically by name.

Figure 5-1   The Themes task pane makes it easy to preview and select the themes you want to use.

You can preview themes by clicking them in the Select A Theme list. Clicking a theme makes it the current theme, and sets the theme display mode to read-only. To get different views of the same theme, select or clear Vivid Colors, Active Graphics or Background Graphics at the bottom of the pane, then click the theme again to see how the theme changes.

Applying Themes

Once you've decided on a theme that you want to use, you can apply it to the Web site by right-clicking the theme in the Themes task pane, and selecting Apply As Default Theme. Then click Yes when prompted to confirm the action.

Another way to apply themes is to do so only for selected pages. To apply a theme to a group of pages, but not to all pages within a site, follow these steps:

1   Press Alt+F1 to display the Folder List.

2   Click the first file you want to select, hold down the Ctrl key, then click individually on other files that you want to select.

3   Choose Format, Theme. In the Themes task pane, right-click the theme you want to use, then select Apply To Selected Pages.

Customizing Themes

Sometimes you won't care for a particular aspect of a theme, such as the color of text, or the style of bullets. Well, you don't have to accept the default settings. You can change any aspect of a theme by right-clicking the theme, then choosing Customize. This displays the Customize Theme dialog box.

Using the Customize Theme dialog box, you can modify the theme's colors, graphics, and text settings. Follow the techniques discussed in the sections that follow.

Modifying Theme Colors

Is there something about the colors in a theme that you just don't like? Wouldn't you love to fine-tune the colors just a bit? You can. In the Themes task pane, right-click the theme you want to modify, select Customize, then click Colors. You can now modify the theme's colors, using the options of the Customize Theme dialog box, as shown in Figure 5-2.

In the bottom section of Figure 5-2, you'll see an entry for Theme Color Set. Each theme has two color sets associated with it: normal colors and vivid colors. The normal color set is used when you select Normal Colors; it uses traditional, less bright colors. The vivid color set is the one used when you select Vivid Colors; it has brighter colors than the normal colors set.

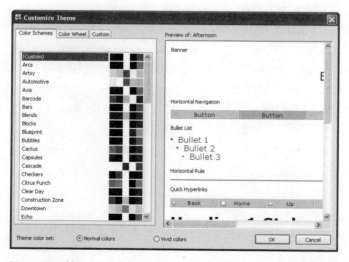

Figure 5-2   You can customize a theme's colors by using predefined color schemes, the color wheel, and settings for individual page elements.

Choose the color set you want to modify, then follow these steps to customize the color set:

1 Options of the Color Schemes tab are used to coordinate every aspect of colors used in the theme. To preview what the current theme would look like with a different color scheme, click any of the color schemes provided.

2 Options of the Color Wheel tab allow you to change the colors used in the themes. You can, for example, make them more red, more green, or more blue. You adjust the colors, and the contrast between colors, by clicking on a new area of the color wheel, as shown in Figure 5-3, or by dragging the pointer to a new location. You adjust brightness using the Brightness slider.

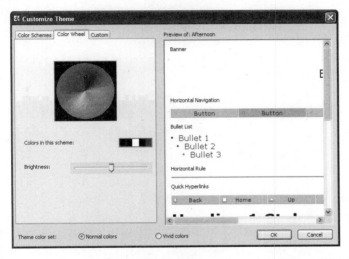

Figure 5-3 The color wheel helps you set the colors you want to use in the color scheme.

3 Options of the Custom tab allow you to change color settings for individual page elements, such as backgrounds, headings, and hyperlinks. To change color settings, select the element you want to work with in the Item list, then select a color in the Color list.

4 When you are finished making changes, click OK, then click Save As to save the theme. When prompted, enter the name of the new theme, then click OK.

> **Note** Keep in mind that each theme has two colors sets. If you make changes to one color set, you may want to apply similar changes to the theme's other color set as well.

Changing Theme Graphics

Sometimes you might love a theme, but dislike the graphics it uses, or you may want to replace a graphic in the theme with one you've created. You can do this, and this section shows you how. Start by right-clicking the theme that you want to work with in the Themes task pane, then selecting Customize. In the Customize Theme dialog box, click Graphics to display the options shown in Figure 5-4.

As with colors, each theme can have two different sets of graphics. One set of graphics is used when you select Normal Graphics. Another set of graphics is used when you select Active Graphics. Use the Theme Graphics Set options to choose the graphics set you want to modify. If the buttons are dimmed, it means that the same graphics are used in both sets.

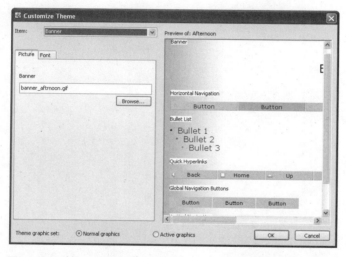

Figure 5-4   You can also customize the graphics used in themes—everything from background pictures to bullets and buttons can be changed.

Once you choose the graphics set you want to modify, follow these steps to customize the graphics set:

1   Use the Item list to select the type of graphic you want to work with, such as background picture or banner.

2   Options of the Picture tab let you change the graphic files used. You'll find the file name for the currently-selected graphic on this tab. Click Browse to find another graphic, using the Open File dialog box.

3   Options of the Font tab let you specify the font face, style, size, and alignment of any text that might be associated with the graphic. Use the selection lists provided to change the text style. The default entry for the font face typically is a series of fonts, such as *Verdana, Arial, Helvetica, sans serif.* Here, the first font is the primary font that should be used, and the rest of the fonts are alternates. If the options of this tab are dimmed, no text can be associated with the type of graphic you've chosen.

> **Note** Specifying alternate fonts to use is important, because some fonts may not be installed or supported on a user's computer. If you want to provide a list of alternate fonts, click the primary font you want to use in the Font list, enter a comma, and then type the name of the next font to use. Separate any additional fonts to use with commas as well. Keep in mind that the last entry should not have a comma. You'll learn more about font faces and styles in Chapter 6, "Polishing Design with Style Sheets."

4 Repeat steps 1 through 3 to change the graphic files and fonts used with other graphics in the currently selected graphics set.

5 When you are finished making changes, click OK, then click Save As to save the theme. When prompted, enter the name of the new theme and click OK.

Optimizing Theme Text Styles

Many of the FrontPage themes use *Verdana*, *Arial*, and *Helvetica* as the primary fonts for body text and headings. While these fonts display well on most computers and operating systems, they may not be the ones you want to use with your site. In this case, you can change the text styles used with the theme. Right-click the theme that you want to work with in the Themes task pane, then select Customize. In the Customize Theme dialog box, click Text to display the options, as shown in Figure 5-5.

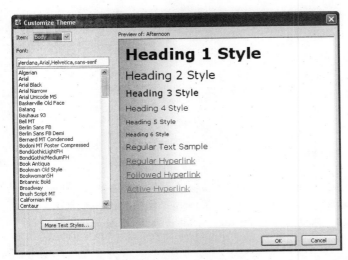

Figure 5-5 The body text and headings used with themes normally have a standard font, such as Verdana, but you can change this if you'd like.

You can now modify the text style used with the theme by completing the following steps:

1 Use the Item list to select the type of text you want to work with, such as Body (for standard paragraph text) or Heading 1 (for level 1 heading).

2 The Font field shows the current default fonts. Select a different font, or type the fonts to use in a comma-separated list, such as *Verdana, Arial, Helvetica, sans serif.*

3 Repeat steps 1 and 2 to change the fonts used with other text styles.

4 When you're finished making changes, click OK, then click Save As to save the theme. When prompted, enter the name of the new theme and click OK.

Removing Themes

If you no longer want a site, or a group of pages within a site to use themes, you can remove the theme. Although this won't restore the site's original settings for backgrounds, fonts, colors and other features, it will let you stop using the theme.

You can remove a theme from an entire site by following these steps:

1 Open the site for editing in FrontPage, then select Format, Theme.

2 In the Themes task pane, right-click No Theme in the Select A Theme list, then select Apply As Default Theme.

3 Click Yes to confirm your selection.

You can remove a theme from a group of pages within a site by following these steps:

1 Open the site for editing in FrontPage, then press Alt+F1 to display the Folder List.

2 Click the first file you want to select, hold down the Ctrl key, then click individually on other files that you want to select.

3 Choose Format, Theme. In the Themes task pane, right-click No Theme in the Select A Theme list, then choose Apply To Selected Pages.

4 Click Yes to confirm your selection.

Using Shared Borders

Most sites have common page banners, navigation structures and contact information. But individually editing page banners, link bars or contact information in pages isn't the best use of your time. Instead, you should define common areas, called *shared borders*, that pages within the site share, and then add the common elements to these shared border areas.

Understanding Shared Borders

Sites you create using advanced templates and wizards have shared borders. Your sites should have shared borders, too. Not only does it make sites easier to manage, it also gives sites a consistent look and feel.

You can add shared borders to four areas of the page:

- **Left**   When you share the left sides of pages, the pages have a common left border. Most of the time, the left border area is used to provide navigation links and buttons, called link bars. Link bars are also used with other shared borders.

- **Right**   When you share the right sides of pages, the pages have a common right border. Right borders are used less frequently than other types of shared borders, but are another alternative.

- **Top**   When you share the tops of pages, the pages have a common header. Typically, page headers will have a banner or other graphic that introduces the purpose of the page, as well as a link bar.

- **Bottom**   When you share the bottom of pages, the pages have a common footer. Typically, page footers will have contact information, copyright notifications, and the date the page was last modified.

Figure 5-6 shows a page with top, left and bottom borders. As you can see, the top and left borders use a link bar, and the bottom border includes contact, copyright and update information.

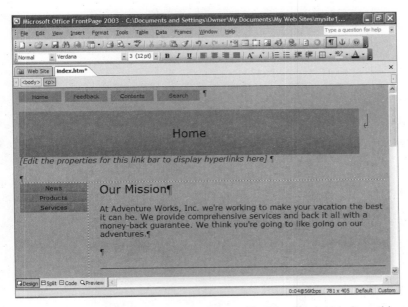

Figure 5-6   Pages can have top, left, right and bottom shared borders; this page uses all but a right shared border.

Top and bottom borders stretch across the entire width of the page. The height or size of a top or bottom border is determined by the amount of information within it.

> **Note**   Because you don't want these border areas to fill the browser window, you should limit the amount of text and graphics you add to these areas. Use only what is necessary and you'll have happier visitors.

Between the top and bottom border you'll find the main text of the page, as well as the left or right borders, if they've been defined. Left and right borders stretch down the length of the page, and are as wide as their widest element. Don't create wide left or right borders. If you do, users may have to scroll left and right to see the contents of the page.

Adding Shared Borders to Sites and Pages

You'll use shared borders in one of two ways. Either set default borders for an entire site, or add borders to individual pages.

1 To assign shared borders to a site, open the site for editing in FrontPage, then select Format, Shared Borders.

> **Note**   If the Shared Borders option is dimmed, you won't be able to select it. To fix this, enable shared borders as a page option. Click Format, Page Options. Afterward, on the Authoring tab of the Page Options dialog box, select Shared Borders and then click OK.

2 To assign shared borders to individual pages within a site, select the pages in the Folder List, then choose Format, Shared Borders.

3 Choose the shared borders that you want to display. If you use the top or left border, you can add link bars as well.

Once shared borders are added to a site, editing the contents of a border area in any page and saving the page updates the contents of the border area for all pages. The reason for this is that the borders are actually saved as separate Web pages, so when you edit the contents of a border area, you're actually editing the individual page that defines the shared border. Thus, you can make a change once, and be sure it is applied throughout the site.

Editing Shared Border Properties

Shared border properties determine the background color or picture that is used in the shared border area. By default, the background color is set to automatic, and the background picture is undefined. If the site uses themes, these default settings tell FrontPage to get the property values from the theme. Otherwise, the default color and background of a particular browser is used.

If you want to set the background color or picture for shared borders, follow these steps:

1 Right-click an open area of the shared border, then select Shared Border Properties. This displays the Border properties dialog box, as shown in Figure 5-7.

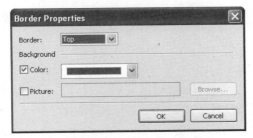

Figure 5-7 Shared borders can get their background colors and pictures from the current theme, or you can specify your own background colors and pictures as shown here.

2 Use the Border list to select the shared border area you want to work with first.

3 If you want to set the background color, click Color, then use the Color selection list to choose the color you want to use.

4 If you want to set a background picture, click Picture, then click Browse. Afterward, use the Open File dialog box to find the background picture you want to use.

> **Note**   You can select both a background color and a picture. In this case, the user's browser will display the border area using the color while the picture is loading. If the user has elected not to display pictures, or their browser doesn't support pictures, only the background color is displayed.

5 Repeat steps 2 through 4 if you want to set the background color or picture for other shared borders.

6 Click OK when you are finished.

Using Link Bars to Help Users Navigate Your Site

Link bars are common elements used in shared borders. A link bar is a textual or graphical menu that links to pages in the site, or to pages in other sites. Two types of link bars can be added to pages:

- **Navigation link bars**   Link bars that are based on the navigation structure of the site.

- **Custom link bars**   Links bars whose links must be specified explicitly.

> **Note**   We realize there is a third type of link bar listed as an option for the Link Bars component. However, the Bar With Back And Next Links option doesn't work the way you think it will. It is, in fact, a bar with custom links, and you can configure it just like you do a custom link bar.

The sections that follow discuss how you can use navigation and custom link bars in your pages.

Working with Navigation Structures and Link Bars

Before you add navigation link bars to your pages, you should plan the site's navigation structure, using the Navigation site view. Then, you should add the appropriate shared borders to the site, so that the link bars can be a common element of the site's pages.

When working with site hierarchies, such as the one shown in Figure 5-8, it is important to understand what is meant by the terms *global, parent,* and *child.* Your site should have a home page, which is the top-level page for the entire site. Any pages that are at the same level of the site's navigation structure are referred to as global pages. In Figure 5-8, *Feedback, Contents,* and *Search* are global pages.

Pages that have links to and from other pages are referred to as *parents* or *children.* In FrontPage's navigation hierarchy, parent-child relationships are limited to a single level of pages. A child is a page immediately below the page containing the link bar. The pages above it are the parents of that level. Pages can be referred to as both parents and children, depending on whether they have pages above and/or below them in the navigation structure. In Figure 5-8, *Home* is the parent of *News, Products,* and *Services.* You could also say that *News, Products,* and *Services* are child pages of *Home.*

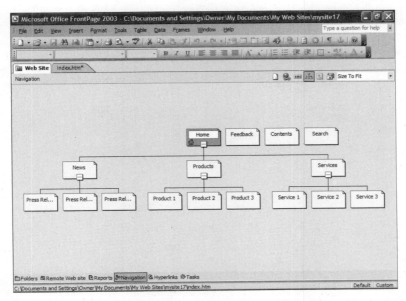

Figure 5-8   Study the navigation structure shown in this example to better understand how parent, child, and global structures are defined.

Each subsequent level in the navigation hierarchy contains its own child pages. *News* is the parent of *Press Release 1*, *Press Release 2*, and *Press Release 3*. *Products* is the parent of *Product 1*, *Product 2*, and *Product 3*. *Services* is the parent of *Services 1*, *Services 2*, and *Services 3*.

Now that you know a bit about navigation structures, you are ready to add navigation link bars to your pages. You can add a link bar to your site by completing the following steps:

1   Position the pointer on the page where you want to insert the link bar, then select Insert, Navigation.

2   The Insert Web Component dialog box is displayed with the Link Bars component type selected in the left pane. In the right pane, choose Bar Based On Navigation Structure, then click Next.

3   Choose a style for the link bar, then click Next. Link bars with graphic styles are shown first in the list. Link bars with text-only styles are shown last.

4   Choose the orientation of the link bar, either horizontal or vertical, and then click Finish. Horizontal link bars work best with the headers and footers used with top and bottom shared borders respectively. Vertical link bars work best as side menus with left or right shared borders.

5   The Link Bar Properties dialog box is displayed as shown in Figure 5-9 on the following page. Use the options provided to choose the navigation level for links, and to add links for the home or parent pages as necessary.

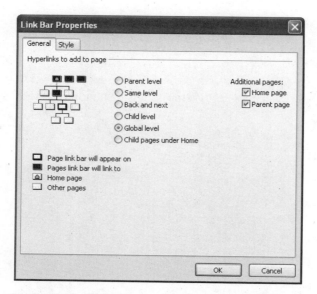

Figure 5-9 You define the navigation levels using the Link Bar Properties dialog box.

6   Click OK to insert the link bar, using these settings. If you want to change the settings later, just double-click the link bar.

Adding Custom Link Bars to Pages

You can create a custom link bar if you don't want to use the navigation structure of your site for determining which links to use. With a custom link bar, you define the links that are used, and in which order they appear. You can add a custom link bar to your site by completing the following steps:

1   Position the pointer on the page where you want to insert the link bar, then select Insert, Navigation.

2   The Insert Web Component dialog box is displayed, with the Link Bars component type selected in the left pane. In the right pane, choose Bar With Custom Links, then click Next.

3   Choose a style for the link bar, then click Next. Link bars with graphic styles are shown first in the list. Link bars with text-only styles are shown last.

4   Choose the orientation of the link bar, either horizontal or vertical, and then click Finish. Horizontal link bars work best with the headers and footers used with top and bottom shared borders, respectively. Vertical link bars work best as side menus with left or right shared borders.

5   If this is the first custom link bar you're creating for the site, the Create New Link Bar and Link Bar Properties dialog boxes are both displayed. Type a name for the new link bar and then click OK.

6   If an existing custom link bar is available, only the Link Bar properties dialog box is displayed, as shown in Figure 5-10.You have the option of choosing an existing link bar, or creating a new one. Use the Choose Existing selection list to choose an existing link bar, or click Create New to set the name of a new link bar.

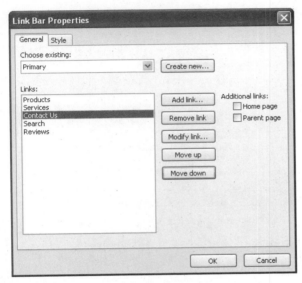

Figure 5-10 When you work with custom link bars, you define the links that are displayed on the link bar.

7   Links that you've added to a custom link bar are displayed in the Links list box. You manage custom links using the following options:

-   **Add Link**   Click Add Link, then use the Add To Link Bar dialog box to set the text to display and the link address.

-   **Remove Link**   Click a link, then click Remove Link to delete it from the Links list.

-   **Modify Link**   Click a link in the Links list, then click Modify link to edit the text to display or link address.

-   **Move Up/Move Down**   Click a link, then click Move Up or Move Down to change the position of the link on the link bar.

-   **Additional Links**   Select Home Page or Parent Page to add the appropriate links to the link bar.

8   When you click OK, FrontPage will add the link bar to the page.

Creating Page Banners

Page banners introduce pages with a banner that specifies the title or purpose of the page. Banners can be text-only, or they can be text on a graphical backdrop. When you add a top border to a page, or create a site using a template or wizard, FrontPage may create page banners for you.

You can add a banner to a page manually by following these steps:

1 Position the pointer on the page where you want to insert the banner, then select Insert, Page Banner.

2 The Page Banner Properties dialog box is displayed, as shown in Figure 5-11. If the site uses themes, and you want the banner to have graphics and text, select Picture under Properties. Otherwise, select Text to have a text-only banner.

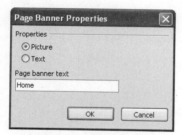

Figure 5-11 Page banners can be text-only or with graphics.

3 Use the Page Banner Text field to set the banner text. By default, page banners have text that corresponds to the page title.

4 Click OK to insert the page banner.

You can change the settings of an existing page banner at any time. Just double-click the banner, make the necessary changes in the Page Banner Properties dialog box, and then click OK.

> **Note**   The way FrontPage uses page banners is simple, yet powerful. The background graphic is the same throughout the site, and only the text label for the banner changes. This means when a user goes from page to page within the site, FrontPage changes the text label as necessary, but doesn't need to load a new banner graphic each time. The banner graphic is loaded only once, which reduces the amount of information the browser has to download, and speeds up the display of your pages.

Fast Wrap-Up

- Use themes to get ready-to-use designs, complete with all the essential elements you need. Themes can be added to individual pages or to all pages within a site.

- Use shared borders to define common areas that pages within the site share, and then add the common elements to these shared border areas.

- Use link bars to add textual or graphical menus that link to pages in the site, or to pages in other sites.

- Use page banners to add a banner that specifies the title or purpose of the page. Banners can be text-only, or they can be text on a graphical backdrop.

- When you use themes, shared borders, link bars, and page banners, you are using a FrontPage component that requires you to publish the page to aWeb server that supports the FrontPage Server Extensions.

- You can easily customize themes, shared borders, link bars and page banners to suit your needs, and when you no longer want to use them, these features can be removed.

Polishing Design with Style Sheets

6

10-Second Summary
- Learn how to use style sheets
- Add style definitions to your Web pages
- Create style classes to apply to multiple page elements
- Create linked style sheets for use with multiple pages
- Remove style links and definitions when they are no longer needed

Your Web pages should be looking pretty good by now. You've learned how to craft pages, and how to enhance design with themes. You're probably thinking about ways to make your pages more interactive, or maybe you're thinking about publishing your pages. Before you do that, you should consider refining your site's design, using style sheets or at the very least, learn about what style sheets have to offer.

Style sheets allow you to separate page content from page formatting. They provide additional options to you as the designer, and, in some cases, also provide better control over how page elements are used. Several techniques can be used to work with style sheets. Each kind of style sheet has its own benefits. We could fill several chapters discussing the various kinds of style sheets and their uses. However, the goal of this book is to teach you how to use Microsoft Office FrontPage 2003 faster and smarter.

So, with this in mind, we'll focus on working with the kinds of style sheets you'll most likely want to use, and those that you can use most effectively. The tasks covered include using style sheet definitions, style classes and linked style sheets.

Getting Stylish: The Essentials

You already know about one way to style elements on the page—the Format menu. Using the options of the Format menu, you can add style to individual headings, paragraphs and other page elements. Defining the style of elements in this way is easy, but you have to define the way each element looks individually.

Not only does it take a lot of time to define the look of each individual element, it's also difficult to maintain that way. Wouldn't you rather be able to define how you want a particular page element to look, and have FrontPage apply that definition throughout the page automatically? Probably so. And this is where style sheets come in handy.

Working with Style Sheets

When you work with style sheets, you refer to each element by its unique identifier, called a selector. The selector for a level 1 heading is H1, which is simply the markup tag for the element without the first and last characters (<>). Table 6-1 shows a list of the most commonly used elements and their selectors.

Table 6-1   Commonly Used Selectors for Page Elements

Element Name	Selector
Active Hypertext Link	A:active
Unvisited Hypertext Link	A:link
Visited Hypertext Link	A:visited
Data cell within a table	TD
Definition in a glossary	DD
Embedded objects	EMBED
Header cell within a table	TH
Hypertext link	A
Image	IMG
Input field	INPUT
Item in a list	LI
Level 1 heading	H1
Level 2 heading	H2
Level 3 heading	H3
Level 4 heading	H4
Level 5 heading	H5
Level 6 heading	H6
Numbered list	NL
Ordered list	OL
Paragraph text	P
Row within a table	TR
Table	TABLE
Unordered list	UL

You can define the formatting and positioning of any of these page elements, as well as other page elements that are available. This definition is then used throughout the page—and you need do nothing more to have similar elements use the style already assigned.

For example, you could specify that all paragraphs use blue, 12-point Times New Roman on a gray background and have a solid inset border around them. Or, that all level 1 headings have a yellow background and brown text. If you later decide that you'd rather have paragraphs use black, 11-point Helvetica on a white background with no border, or that all level 1 headings have a brown background and yellow text, simply make the changes to the style definition in one location. The style of all paragraphs or headings on the page is updated automatically. It's that simple, fast and effective.

To take the discussion a step further, you can also create definitions that are applied to multiple elements. You do this by defining a style class, and then applying the class to page elements that should use it. For example, you could create a style class that defines the basic formatting of all text on the page. This would ensure that all headings and paragraphs have the same basic formatting.

Adding Style Based on Element Type

Think about the kind of style improvements you'd like to make in your Web pages. Go ahead, take a moment. What would you change if you had complete control over the appearance and positioning of elements on the page? Maybe you'd like to set a background color for headings and paragraphs that's different from the page default background color. Maybe you'd like to add decorative borders to headings or paragraphs. Or maybe you'd like to position pictures in a very specific way.

Now that you're thinking about the style improvements you'd like to make, you can add style based on element type by following these steps:

1 Select Format, Style to open the Style dialog box shown in Figure 6-1 on the following page. The Styles list should show a list of HTML tag selectors. If it doesn't, click the List selection list and then chose HTML Tags.

2 Select the identifier for the element you're defining, then click Modify. You should now see the Modify Style dialog box.

3 Click Format, and then use the following options on the shortcut menu to configure the style:

   ● **Font**   Displays the Font dialog box, which you can use to set font characteristics. You'll find options for setting the font face, style, size, color, effects, and character spacing within the text of the element.

   ● **Paragraph**   Displays the Paragraph dialog box, which you can use to set the alignment, indentation, and spacing before and after the element. You can also set the line spacing of text within the element.

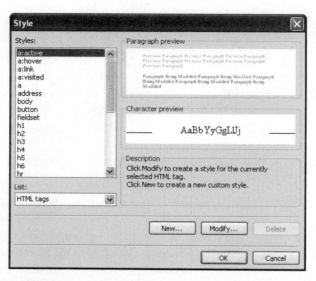

Figure 6-1 Use the Style dialog box to create, modify and delete style definitions.

- **Borders**   Displays the Borders And Shading dialog box, which you can use to add borders and padding around the element, and to fill the element's background with color, a picture, or a pattern.

- **Numbering**   Displays the Bullets And Numbering dialog box, which you can use to specify the bullets and numbering to use with any ordered and unordered lists the element may contain.

- **Position**   Displays the Position dialog box, which you can use to precisely position the element. The element position can be fixed within the page itself, or relative to other elements on the page.

4   Repeat Steps 2 and 3 for other elements you want to work with. When you are finished, click OK.

5   When you're finished with all style assignments, click OK to close the Style dialog box. You can update these style assignments at any time by repeating this procedure.

Using Style Classes

When you want to apply a style definition to multiple elements, you can use a style class. For example, if you want all table cells and table headers as well as all text paragraphs to have the same basic formatting, you can use a style class to do this.

Start by creating the style class:

1   Select Format, Style to display the Style dialog box, and then select New.

2   In the New Style dialog box, enter a name for the class, such as the one shown in Figure 6-2.

> **Note**   The class name should be unique and easy to type. You'll use this name to refer to the class in your pages—and in some cases, you'll have to type the class name by hand.

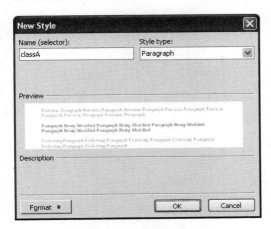

Figure 6-2 Define the style class; be sure to use a unique name that is easy to remember and type.

3   Next, specify whether the style type is Paragraph or Character.

- Paragraph style types are for block-level elements, which can be aligned relative to other elements, and can also have borders and padding. Pictures, paragraphs, and headings are examples of paragraph styles.

- Character style types are styles that apply to individual characters within block-level elements. Bold, italics, and underline are examples of character styles.

4   Click Format, then use the Font, Paragraph, Border, Numbering and Position options to configure the style.

After you create the style class, you can apply the class to any element in your Web page. For all elements except paragraphs and headings, apply the style class as discussed in the steps that follow:

1   Right-click the element, and then select the element's Properties dialog box from the shortcut menu. For example, with a picture, you'd select Picture Properties.

2   In the Properties dialog box, click Style to open the Modify Style dialog box, shown in Figure 6-3.

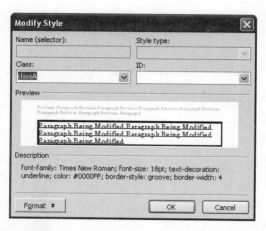

Figure 6-3 Choose the class you want to use.

3 Using the Class selection list, choose the style class that you want to use.

4 Click OK twice.

For paragraphs and headings, apply the style class by highlighting the text that you want to style and then selecting the appropriate style on the Style selection list. For example, if you created a style class called classA, you could select several paragraphs by clicking and dragging the mouse until the paragraph text is selected. Then you could click the down arrow on the Style selection list and then click classA.

Once you get used to working with style classes, you may also want to add style classes to paragraphs and headings by completing these steps:

1 Click Code to switch to code view. Locate the tag that defines the start of a paragraph or heading that you want to work with, such as <p> or <h1>.

2 Within the tag, after the tag selector, type **class="className"**, where *className* is the actual name of the class you created after the selector name within the HTML tag. For example, if you created a class called classA, and you wanted a paragraph tag to use this class, you would type **class="classA"** and the paragraph tag would look like this: <p class="classA">.

3 Click Design to switch back to design view. Now use the Format Painter to apply the format to other headings and paragraphs on the page. To do this, position the insertion point within the paragraph or heading to which you applied the style class, then click Format Painter on the Format toolbar. Afterward, click within the paragraph or heading to which you want to apply the style class. Repeat this step as necessary.

Removing Style Classes

If you later decide that you don't want to use a style class, you can remove the style class by completing the following steps:

1 Select the element or elements you want to change. You'll select most elements by clicking on them. For paragraphs and headings, however, you must position the insertion point within the paragraph or heading, and then triple click.

2 Press Ctrl+Shift+Z to remove the style class definition.

> **Aha!**   Remove Style Class Definitions
>
> In most cases, selecting the element and then using Ctrl+Shift+Z to remove the element's formatting is the fastest way to remove style class definitions. If you have a lot of definitions to remove, you could also change to code view, and then remove the class definition from the elements themselves.

Applying Style Sheets to Multiple Pages

So far you've learned how to create a style sheet for a single page. But what if you want multiple pages, or even all the pages in your Web site to use the same style definitions? Can you do this without having to define the style sheet separately in each page? Yes, you can.

The best way to apply style definitions to multiple pages is to use a linked style sheet. With linked style sheets, you store the style definitions in separate files and reference the style sheet file in the pages that should use them. Not only does a linked style sheet make it easy to apply style definitions to multiple pages, but it also provides a single location for managing the style definitions. To make changes, you simply edit the contents of the linked style sheet—you don't have to edit each affected Web page.

When you work with linked style sheets, you'll need to create a style sheet, then link the style sheet to pages that should use it. FrontPage makes the process of creating and linking style sheets fairly easy. You can use any of the available style sheet templates as starting points. You can also copy previously created style definitions into your style sheets.

Creating Style Sheets from Templates

To create a style sheet from a template, follow these steps:

1 Click the down arrow to the right of the New tool on the Standard toolbar, then select Page.

2 In the Page Templates dialog box, click the Style Sheets tab.

- To start with an empty style sheet, select the Normal Style Sheet template, then click OK.

- To start with a predefined style sheet, select any of the other templates available, then click OK.

3 Any existing style definitions are listed in the page, as shown in Figure 6-4. The Style toolbar is also displayed. If you want to create new style definitions, or modify or delete existing style definitions, click the Style button in the Style toolbar.

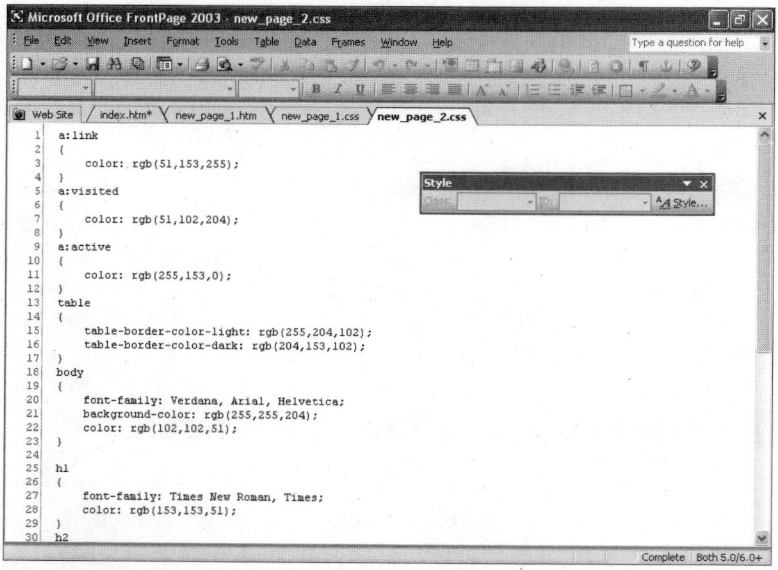

Figure 6-4 Any existing style definitions for the template are listed as the text of the style sheet.

4 To list User-defined styles, select this option for List. You can then modify an existing style by selecting it in the Styles list and clicking Modify.

5 To define additional styles for other HTML tags, select the HTMLTags option for List, click the selector that you want to use in the Styles list, then click Modify.

6 To define a new style class, click New, then define the class, as discussed in the section of this chapter entitled "Using Style Classes."

7 When you are finished creating style definitions and classes, click OK to close the Style dialog box.

8 Press Ctrl+S to save the style sheet. When prompted, select a save location and file name for the style sheet.

> **Note**   All style sheets are saved as CSS (Cascading Style Sheet) files with the .css extension. If you later want to open the style sheet you just saved, press Ctrl+O; then, in the Open File dialog box, select CSS Files (*.css) as the file type, or look for files with the .css file extension in the file list.

Creating Style Sheets Using Previous Definitions and Classes

Any style definitions and classes you've created previously using the techniques discussed in the section of this chapter entitled "Getting Stylish: The Essentials" can be copied into a linked style sheet and used with multiple pages. If you plan to copy existing style definitions into a linked style sheet, follow these steps:

1 Click the down arrow to the right of the New tool on the Standard toolbar, then select Page.

2 In the Page Templates dialog box, click the Style Sheets tab, select the Normal Style Sheet template, then click OK.

3 Open the page in which you previously made style definitions for editing.

4 Click Code. Near the top of the page, you'll see a begin style tag <style>, followed by markup for your style definitions, and completed with the end style </style>.

5 Select and then copy the style definitions without the begin and end style tags.

> **Aha!** Cut and Paste In-Page Style Definitions into Linked Style Sheets
>
> If you're confident that you want to use linked style sheets, rather than the in-page style definitions, cut the style definitions using Ctrl+X, then paste them into the style sheet with Ctrl+V. Afterward, be sure to save the page so that the in-page style definitions aren't used the next time you publish the page.

6 Click Window, then select the new style sheet template you just created.

7 Press Ctrl+V to paste the style definitions you previously copied into the template.

8 Press Ctrl+S to save the style sheet. When prompted, select a save location and file name for the style sheet. All style sheets are saved with the .css extension.

Linking Style Sheets

The best way to manage links to linked style sheets is to use the Folder List view. If Folder List view isn't shown, press Alt+F1. In Folder List view, you can link style sheets to all the pages in your site at once or you can create links to any pages you select. To create links to style sheets, follow these steps:

1 Select the pages that you want to use linked style sheets. You can select multiple pages using Ctrl or Shift. You don't need to do this if you want all pages in the Web site to use the style sheet.

2 Select Format, Style Sheet Links. In the Link Style Sheet dialog box, the All Pages or Selected Page(s) button is selected automatically, based on whether you previously selected pages in the Folders List view.

3   The URL field shows any current style sheet links. Select any style sheets that you don't want linked, then click Remove.

4   Click Add, then use the Select Style Sheet dialog box to select the style sheet you want to use.

5   If you want to use additional style sheets, you can add those as well. The first linked style sheet always has the highest precedence, meaning its settings override the settings of other linked style sheets.

6   Click OK. FrontPage will then add style sheet links to the appropriate pages in the Web site.

Removing Style Sheet Links

If you no longer want to use style sheets, you can remove the links to the style sheet by completing these steps:

1   In the Folder List view, select the pages that you want to stop using linked style sheets. You can select multiple pages using Ctrl or Shift. You don't need to do this if you want all pages in the Web site to stop using style sheets.

2   Select Format, Style Sheet Links. In the Link Style Sheet dialog box, select the style sheet to remove in the URL list, then click Remove. Repeat this step as necessary to remove other style sheet links.

3   Click OK.

Fast Wrap-Up

- Style sheets give your Web pages a unified look and feel.

- When you work with style sheets, you refer to each element by its unique identifier, called a selector. The selector is simply the markup tag for the element without the first and last characters (<>).

- When you want to apply a style definition to multiple elements, you can use a style class. After you create the style class, you can apply the class to any element in your Web page.

- The best way to apply style definitions to multiple pages is to use a linked style sheet. With linked style sheets, you store the style definitions in separate files and reference the style sheet file in the pages that should use them.

- When they are no longer required, you can remove style sheet definitions from Web pages quickly and easily.

Using Pictures in Web Pages

10-Second Summary

- Add pictures to Web pages
- Size and align pictures
- Obtain pictures from clip art and more
- Use background pictures
- Cut, copy, paste and save pictures

In this chapter, you'll learn how to obtain pictures from various sources, and how to use background pictures. Web pages without pictures are dull. If you really want to promote your organization, sell your goods or services, or attract attention to your cause, you'll want to use pictures to help make a lasting impression on your site's visitors. Pictures highlight the text, showcase products or services, and catch the reader's eye. They help you create visually stunning pages that are a joy to browse, and make readers want to come back to your Web site time after time.

Inserting Pictures

The sections that follow discuss how to add pictures to pages, and how to size, align and space them. You'll also find discussions on cutting, copying and pasting pictures; linking pictures to other files; and specifying low-resolution pictures that are displayed before high resolution ones. You'll use these techniques whenever you add pictures to Web pages.

> **Lingo** FrontPage uses the term *picture* to mean any graphic image that you insert into a Web page. A picture can be a page graphic, a digital photo, a banner graphic, clip art, or any other image. Most pictures you use on the Web are either in GIF or JPEG format.

Adding Pictures to Web Pages

Microsoft Office FrontPage 2003 makes it easy to insert and precisely place pictures. Your pictures can come from a variety of sources, including local files, the current Web site, the network and the World Wide Web. When you insert a picture that is not in the GIF or JPEG format, FrontPage needs to convert the picture to either GIF or JPEG format before saving it. You'll find complete details on the conversion process in the section of this chapter entitled "Saving Pictures to the Current Web."

To insert a picture into a Web page open for editing in FrontPage, follow these steps:

1 Move the insertion point to where you want to insert the picture, and then choose Insert, Picture, From File.

2 Using the Picture dialog box, locate and double-click the file name of the picture you want to use.

3 After you add a picture, right-click it, and then select Picture Properties. This displays the Picture Properties dialog box.

4 Click the General tab, as shown in Figure 7-1, and then type a description or title of the picture in the Text field under the Alternative Representations section. The text you enter is displayed whenever the cursor is over the picture. Click OK when you're finished.

Figure 7-1 Add a text description to your pictures to help visitors to your site understand what they're seeing.

> **Note** Wondering why you'd want to add text descriptions to pictures? Well, the text you enter is displayed whenever the cursor is over the picture. The text is also displayed if, for some reason, the user's browser cannot display pictures—if the user turns off picture display, for example. If you link the picture to another file, the text can also tell users what page or file is accessed when they click the picture.

Setting Picture Layout

Adding a picture to a page is one thing, but getting the picture so it is just right in size, alignment, and spacing is something else entirely. Pictures can be sized, aligned and spaced in many different ways. The default alignment and spacing for pictures is very simple. FrontPage 2003 aligns the bottom of the picture with the bottom of any text element that might be associated with the picture, and doesn't add a border or any spacing to the picture.

The default layout may work in some cases, but it probably isn't optimal. In most cases, you'll want to use a different layout. For example, you may want to center the picture on the page, and add a 5-pixel border. Or, you may want to align the picture to the left or right of existing text on the page, and use vertical spacing to ensure that the picture is set clearly apart from the text.

You can change the layout for pictures by completing the following steps:

1 Right-click the picture, and then select Picture Properties. This displays the Picture Properties dialog box shown in Figure 7-2.

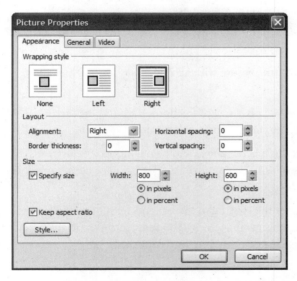

Figure 7-2 Use the Picture Properties dialog box to specify the layout and sizing of pictures.

2 Use Wrapping Style to specify how text wraps around the picture:

- **None**   Ensures the text doesn't wrap around the picture.
- **Left**   Wraps text around the left side of the picture.
- **Right**   Wraps text around the right side of the picture.

3 Use the Alignment drop-down list to set the picture's alignment. The available options are:

- **Absbottom**   Aligns the bottom of the picture with the bottom of the line of text associated with the picture.

- **Absmiddle**   Aligns the middle of the picture with the middle of the line of text associated with the picture.

- **Baseline**   Aligns the picture and text along the baseline of the text. Text elements like s, k and l are aligned along the baseline, and text elements like j, g and p extend below the baseline.

- **Bottom**   Same as baseline.

- **Center**   Centers the picture on the page.

- **Left**   Aligns the picture in the left margin.

- **Middle**   Aligns the middle of the picture with the bottom of the text.

- **Right**   Aligns the picture in the right margin.

- **Texttop**   Aligns the top of the picture with the top of the tallest element in the line of text associated with the picture.

- **Top**   Aligns the top of the picture with an imaginary line slightly above the text.

4 Use Border Thickness to set the pixel size of the border around the picture. Set the value to zero to display the picture without a border.

5 Use Vertical Spacing to set the spacing above and below the picture in pixels. If you set the vertical spacing to zero, you remove any extra spacing above or below the image.

6 Use Horizontal Spacing to set the spacing to the left and right of the picture in pixels. If you set the horizontal spacing to zero, you remove any extra spacing to the left or right of the image. Click OK when you're finished.

Sizing Pictures

Most pictures are sized using pixels, to ensure that they are displayed at a specific fixed size, such as 150 pixels wide and 120 pixels high. Pictures can also be sized as a percentage of the window size, which allows the picture size to change, based on the width and height of the browser window. For example, if you created a page banner using a picture, you might want the banner to fill the width of the browser window. To do this, you would set the picture width to 100 percent of the browser window.

You can size pictures by completing the following steps:

1 Right-click the picture, and then select Picture Properties.

2 On the Appearance tab of the Picture Properties dialog box, select Specify Size, then type the desired width and height for the picture.

3 Use the In Pixels or In Percent options to specify whether the width and height values are expressed in pixels, or as a percentage of the browser's window. Click OK.

> **Aha!**   Preserve the Original Proportions to Correct Picture Distortion
>
> Some pictures won't display properly if the original proportions are changed. As a result, the picture may look blurred or distorted. You may be able to correct this problem by selecting Keep Aspect Ratio. With this option selected, the width and height are sized relative to their original proportions. For example, if a picture is 600x400 pixels, and you change the width to 300, the height would automatically be set to 200, to maintain the original aspect ratio.

Cutting, Copying, and Pasting Pictures

FrontPage lets you manipulate pictures in much the same way as you manipulate text, using the familiar Cut, Copy, and Paste commands. You can also cut a picture from your favorite paint program, and paste it directly into a Web page. Here's how you would do this:

1 In your favorite paint program, create, or open for editing, the picture you want to use.

2 Select the picture, and copy it to the Windows Clipboard.

3 In FrontPage, open a Web page for editing, then move the insertion point to where you want to add the picture. Press Ctrl+X to paste the picture into the page.

> **Note**   FrontPage 2003 automatically converts the picture to either GIF or JPEG format, if necessary. Pictures with 256 or fewer colors are converted to GIF. Pictures with more than 256 colors are converted to JPEG.

Using Pictures as Hyperlinks

Pictures can be clickable entryways to other pages and files. You could, for example, show a small picture of your new digital music player on your home page and link it to a product page that provides more detailed information. When a customer clicks on the picture, they quickly and easily access the product page.

If you want to link a picture to a Web page or file, complete the following steps:

1   Right-click the picture, and then select Picture Properties.

2   On the General tab of the Picture Properties dialog box, click Browse (to the right of the Location field).

3   Specify whether you want to link to an existing Web page, a new document, or an email address, by clicking the appropriate Link To option. The options of the dialog box change, based on your selection.

4   Choose the file to which you want to link, if it is displayed in the Look In list, or enter the Web address in the Address field. Click OK to close the Picture dialog box.

> **Aha!**   Test the Link
>
> Want to check the link you just added to the picture? Move the mouse pointer over the picture, press and hold Ctrl, and then click. The page or file to which you've linked should open in FrontPage. If it doesn't, you may have entered an invalid location or there may be some other problem accessing the resource.

Using Low-Resolution Pictures

It really is true that a picture is worth a thousand words, and sometimes the best way to showcase your organization's products or services is to do so with high-resolution pictures. You don't, however, want visitors to get bored waiting for large pictures to download. Remember, not everyone has a fast connection to the Internet—even some businesses have slow speed dial-up connections.

One way to make it seem as if your pages load faster is to specify low-resolution pictures that browsers can download before they download your high-resolution pictures. In this way, compliant browsers, such as Internet Explorer 6.0, load the low-resolution pictures first—and then, when all other page elements are loaded, they go back and get the high-resolution pictures you've specified. These high-resolution pictures are faded in over the low-resolution pictures.

To specify a low-resolution picture as an alternate picture for an existing picture, follow these steps:

1   Right-click the picture, and select Picture Properties.

2   On the General tab of the Picture Properties dialog box, click Browse (to the right of the Low-Res field).

3   Use the Select Alternate Picture dialog box to locate the low-resolution picture, then double-click its file name. You can use pictures from the current web, your hard drive, the network, or the Web. Click OK when you're finished.

> **Note** Your low-resolution pictures should act as placeholders, and should be the same size on the page as the high-resolution picture. This will ensure the text on the page doesn't shift when the high-resolution picture is displayed.

Obtaining and Importing Pictures

So far, we've talked about inserting pictures from existing files, but we haven't talked about other ways that you can obtain and import pictures. One way to obtain pictures is to create them, using WordArt or AutoShapes. You can also obtain pictures from Clip Art, scanners or digital cameras.

Adding WordArt to Pages

FrontPage allows you to use the WordArt feature of the Microsoft Office System in Web pages. This feature works just as it does in Word and other programs in the Microsoft Office System. You can insert WordArt by completing the following steps:

1 Position the cursor where you want to insert the WordArt, and then choose Insert, Picture, WordArt.

2 Select a WordArt style, and then click OK.

3 In the Edit WordArt Text dialog box, use Font and Size to set the font type and size for your text.

4 Type the text you want to be formatted as WordArt, and then click OK to insert the WordArt into the page.

5 Select the WordArt by clicking it. The WordArt toolbar is displayed. Use these tools on the toolbar to optimize the WordArt settings:

- **WordArt Same Letter Heights** Sets each text character in the WordArt to use the same height.

- **WordArt Vertical Text** Toggles the text display. Click this if you want the text to be displayed as a vertical text banner. Click again to use horizontal text.

- **WordArt Alignment** Sets the alignment of text within the WordArt area.

- **WordArt Character Spacing** Sets the spacing between characters, allowing text characters to be tight (closer together) or loose (farther apart).

> **Note** If you later want to edit the text of the WordArt, simply click Edit Text on the WordArt toolbar. To change the WordArt format, right-click it, and then select Format WordArt.

Adding AutoShapes to Pages

You can also use FrontPage to draw AutoShapes, including lines, block arrows, flowcharts, stars, banners, and callouts. To insert AutoShapes, complete these steps:

1 Choose Insert, Picture, AutoShapes, and then use the AutoShapes toolbar to select the AutoShape you want to use.

2 Position the insertion point where you want to insert the picture.

3 Click and hold down the mouse button, sizing the AutoShape by dragging the pointer.

4 Release the mouse button to create the AutoShape.

> **Note**   If you later want to edit the AutoShape, click it, and then use the size or rotation points to modify the shape. To change the formatting of the AutoShape, right-click it, and then select Format AutoShape.

Getting Pictures from Clip Art, Scanners, and Digital Cameras

In addition to being able to create pictures using WordArt and AutoShapes, you can get pictures from Clip Art, scanners and digital cameras. FrontPage supports the previewing of clip art, scanned pictures, and digital pictures in a wide variety of formats, allowing you to see what the picture looks like before you add it to the page. When you insert a picture that isn't in GIF or JPEG format, FrontPage will convert the picture to either GIF or JPEG format before saving it.

To use clip art in a page, choose Insert, Picture, Clip Art, and then use the Clip Art task pane to find the clip art you want to use. If you want to get a picture from a scanner or digital camera picture, ensure the scanner or digital camera is connected to your computer and turned on, and then choose Insert, Picture, From Scanner Or Camera. FrontPage 2003 will attempt to connect to the scanner or digital camera, and then you will be able to scan in pictures or transfer pictures from your digital camera.

Saving Pictures to the Current Web

Anytime you insert, import or scan in new pictures, FrontPage adds the picture to the page, but doesn't necessarily save the picture file to the current web. To save pictures to the current Web, press Ctrl+S to save the page, and then use the Save Embedded Files dialog box to specify how you want FrontPage to handle the pictures you've inserted, imported and scanned in.

You will then have the option of setting the picture file name, save folder, and picture file type—or simply clicking OK to accept the default options. If you accept the default options, the pictures are saved to the base folder of the web using the original file name, and FrontPage will automatically convert the picture to either GIF or JPEG format as necessary. Pictures with 256 or fewer colors are converted to GIF. Pictures with more than 256 colors are converted to JPEG.

As Figure 7-3 shows, the Save Embedded Files dialog box displays files to save to the current web by name, folder location, and associated action. You can change the default options, using the options provided, including:

- **Rename**   Click the picture file name to select it, and then use Rename to change the file name of a selected picture.

- **Change Folder**   Use Shift and Ctrl to select pictures, and then use Change Folder to select a new folder location for the selected pictures within the current web.

- **Set Action**   Click the picture file name to select it, and then use Set Action to determine whether to save the picture to the web, or use the current file on disk.

- **Picture File Type**   Click the picture file name to select it, and use Picture File Type to override the default conversion settings for pictures. You'll be able to specify whether the picture should use GIF, JPEG, PNG-8 or PNG-24 formatting, and each time you make a change, the Picture File Type dialog box is updated, so that you can see the new file name and approximate file size.

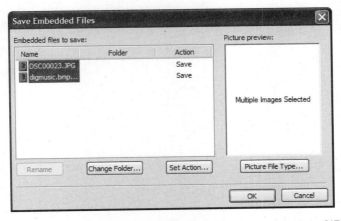

Figure 7-3 When you save pages with pictures that aren't in GIF or JPEG format, you'll see the Save Embedded Files dialog box, where you can accept or change the conversion settings.

Using Background Pictures

FrontPage not only allows you to insert pictures into pages, but also lets you make pictures the backgrounds for pages. The best background pictures help pages stand out, yet aren't distracting. Generally, you'll want all the pages in your site to use the same background picture. This will ensure your site has a consistent look from page to page.

One way to apply a background is to use a FrontPage theme. With themes, the theme settings control which background is used, and you can only modify the background by changing the theme settings, as discussed in Chapter 5, "Enhancing Design with Themes." If you don't want to use themes, you can assign background pictures to pages individually, which is the technique we discuss in this section.

To set a background picture for pages individually, complete the following steps:

1   Open a page for editing in FrontPage, and then display the Page Properties dialog box by selecting File, Properties.

2   On the Formatting tab, select the Background Picture check box, as shown in Figure 7-4, and then click Browse.

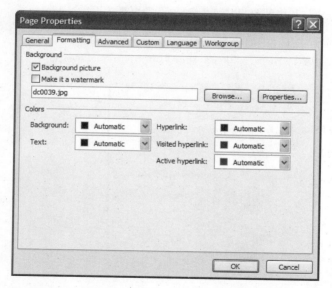

Figure 7-4 Specify the location of the background picture, using the options of the Formatting tab.

3   Use the Select Background Picture dialog box to select the background picture. You can select a picture from the current web, your hard drive, the network, or the Web.

Lingo A *watermark* is a background picture that does not scroll with the text on the page. If you want the background picture to remain fixed in the background, select Make It A Watermark as a formatting option.

4 Click OK to close the Page Properties dialog box, and then press Ctrl+S to save the page.

5 If the background picture isn't in GIF or JPEG format, it will need to be converted to an appropriate format, and the Save Embedded Files dialog box will be displayed. Click Picture File Type to confirm or change the conversion settings.

> **Note** If the Background Picture option is not available, it means that the current web is using a theme. You will need to modify the background picture setting, using the Modify Theme dialog box, as discussed in Chapter 5.

Fast Wrap-Up

- Many types of pictures can be added to Web pages, including pictures in GIF and JPEG format.

- Pictures that aren't in GIF or JPEG format are converted automatically to GIF or JPEG format by FrontPage. You can change formats manually as well.

- Pictures can be obtained from many sources. You can add WordArt, AutoShapes, and Clip Art pictures to pages. You can also get pictures from scanners and digital cameras.

- Pictures can also be used as page backgrounds. A background picture that doesn't scroll with the text of the page is called a watermark.

Going Beyond the Ordinary: Photo Galleries, Soundtracks, Video, and Picture Maps

---

8

10-Second Summary

- ■ Create photo montages, photo albums, and slide shows
- ■ Add soundtracks to Web Pages
- ■ Add video clips to Web pages
- ■ Create graphical menus with clickable hotspots

As you learned in the previous chapter, pictures provide a wonderful entry point into the world of multimedia. Now it's time go beyond ordinary pictures, and explore the many multimedia possibilities available in FrontPage. You'll learn how to use photo galleries, soundtracks, Web video, and picture maps. With photo galleries, you can create photo-montages, photo albums, and slide shows. With soundtracks and video, you can create pages that play music or videos. With picture maps, you can create pictures with clickable hotspots that act as graphical menus.

Doing More with Pictures: Photo Montages, Albums, and Slide Shows

FrontPage makes creating photo galleries easy. In fact, most photo galleries can be created in a just few minutes. That's because all you need to do is provide the photos, the captions, and the descriptions, and FrontPage does the rest of the work—including creating the necessary thumbnail images, links, and markup. Although designed for high-resolution photos, we've found this feature is also useful for showcasing products and services. With this approach, each photo could be a picture of a product, a page from a product brochure, or even a full-color ad.

Inserting a Photo Gallery into a Web Page

Using the photo gallery feature in FrontPage 2003, you can create:

- **Photo montages**   With a photo montage, your photo gallery has thumbnail images of your pictures that are displayed in a pattern like a collage. Clicking on a thumbnail image displays the full-size picture in a new window. Picture captions are displayed when the mouse pointer is over a thumbnail image.

- **Photo albums**   With photo albums, you can choose a horizontal or vertical layout for the thumbnail images in your photo gallery. Captions and descriptions of each thumbnail are displayed below or to the right of the picture, depending on layout. Clicking on a thumbnail image displays the full-size picture in a new window.

- **Slide shows**   With slide shows, thumbnail images of your pictures are arranged in a row that scrolls across the top of the page, and the selected picture is displayed full-size in the center of the page, along with its caption and descriptive text. Clicking on a thumbnail image in the top row displays the full-size picture in the center of the page.

You can insert a photo gallery into any existing page, or create a new page in the web in which the gallery will reside. Once you have a page open for editing, you can create a photo gallery by completing the following steps:

1 Choose Insert, Picture, New Photo Gallery. This displays the Photo Gallery Properties dialog box, shown in Figure 8-1.

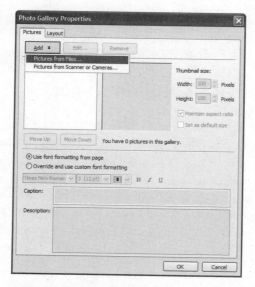

Figure 8-1 Use the Photo Gallery Properties dialog box to add and organize the pictures for your photo montage, album or slide show.

2 Click Add, and then choose Pictures From Files. Next, use the File Open dialog box to choose the photos you want to add to the gallery. Select multiple files, using the Shift and Ctrl keys.

3 Pictures you've added to the gallery are displayed in alphanumeric order in the Add list box, as shown in Figure 8-2. You can adjust the order of photos by selecting a picture, and then clicking Move Up or Move Down, until the picture is in the desired location in the list. Repeat this step to change the order of other pictures.

Figure 8-2 Once you add pictures to the gallery, you can size thumbnails, order the pictures, and add captions and descriptions.

4 Thumbnails for pictures are generated automatically. To set the size of a thumbnail, select the filename in the Add list box, and then use Width and Height options to set the desired size.

> **Note** It's a good idea to maintain the original aspect ratio, which will reduce the possibility that the thumbnail graphic will be blurred or distorted. If you want all thumbnail images to be the same size, select Set As Default, and then use the Width and Height options to set the default size for all thumbnails in the photo gallery.

5 Each thumbnail can have a separate caption and description associated with it. In the Add list box, select the filename of the photo you want to work with, and then type the text for the caption and description in the fields provided.

> **Caution**   Don't enter a description if you plan to create a photo montage. Descriptive text is not displayed with photo montages.

6 On the Layout tab, select the layout for the photo gallery: Horizontal Layout, Montage Layout, Slide Show, or Vertical Layout, as shown in Figure 8-3. If you use a horizontal or vertical layout, set the number of pictures per row. You can have from 1 to 10 pictures per row.

7 Click OK to add the photo gallery to the page.

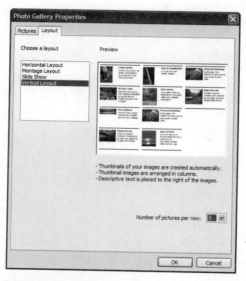

Figure 8-3 Select the layout you want to use; with vertical or horizontal layout, don't forget to set the number of pictures per row.

Customizing the Formatting of Captions and Descriptions

By default, the text used in captions and descriptions is formatted using the font settings from the Web page in which the photo gallery resides. In most cases, this is a good setting to use, if your Web site uses themes. Still, you may find that you want a particular picture to have a different font face and formatting for captions and descriptions, and you can do this by completing the following steps:

1 Open the page containing the photo gallery, and then double-click on any of the photo gallery components.

2 In the Photo Gallery Properties dialog box, select the filename for the picture that you want to use the custom settings, and then choose Override And Use Custom Font Formatting.

3 Select the caption, or a portion of the caption text, and then use the font options to set the font type, size, color, and highlighting for the selected text. You can use different settings for different sections of the caption.

4 Select the Description, or a portion of the description text, and then use the font options to set the font type, size, color, and highlighting for the description. You can use different settings for different sections of the description.

5 Repeat Steps 2-4 to customize the font formatting of other pictures, and click OK to save the changes.

Managing Existing Photo Galleries

You can change photo gallery settings, rotate or crop photos, and add or remove pictures, at anytime. To manage a photo gallery, follow these steps:

1 Open the page containing the photo gallery, then double-click on any of the photo gallery components.

2 To add pictures, click Add in the Photo Gallery Properties dialog box, and then select Pictures From Files. Next, use the File Open dialog box to choose the pictures you want to add to the gallery.

> **Note**   Select multiple files using the Shift and Ctrl keys. New pictures are added to the end of the current list, and you can use the Move Up and Move Down buttons to change picture order, as necessary.

3 To rotate, resize, or crop the full-size pictures in the gallery, select a picture you want to edit in the Add list box, and then click Edit. This opens the Edit Picture dialog box, shown in Figure 8-4 on the following page. You can now choose from the following options:

- **Set Picture Size**   Set the desired size of the picture, using the Width and Height options. If you want all full-size pictures to be the same size, select Set As Default, after you enter the desired width and height.

- **Rotate Picture**   Use the Rotate Right, Rotate Left, Flip Horizontal and Flip Vertical buttons to rotate the picture to the desired position.

- **Crop Picture**   Click Crop and then position the pointer in the upper left corner of the area you want to crop. Afterward, click and hold the mouse button, and drag down and right until the desired crop area is highlighted.

Figure 8-4 Use the Edit Picture dialog box to resize, rotate and crop the pictures in the photo gallery.

4 To remove pictures from a gallery, select the filename of a picture you want to delete, and then click Remove.

> **Caution** When you remove a picture, any associated caption and description are deleted, as well. If you later decide to add the picture back into the gallery, you will need to enter the caption and description again.

5 Click OK to close the Photo Gallery Properties dialog box when you are finished.

Adding Soundtracks to Web Pages

Soundtracks are another feature that can help your pages go beyond the ordinary. When you use soundtracks, you specify an audio file that begins playing when a browser finishes loading a Web page. Most browsers that support soundtracks, including Microsoft Internet Explorer, can play audio files in AIFF, AIFF-C, AU, SND, MIDI, RA and WAV formats.

While soundtracks can contain music, they don't have to be a soundtrack in the traditional sense. They can also be a greeting from executives, a brief introduction to a product or service by a product manager, or the highlights of an important announcement from a company spokesperson.

> **Caution** One thing you should know about soundtracks is that some users don't like to hear any soundtracks on Web pages. These users might close the browser window or click away to a different site. With this in mind, plan carefully before you use a soundtrack, and consider the possible reactions of users.

To add a soundtrack to a Web page, follow these steps:

1 Right-click anywhere in a page open for editing, and choose Page Properties.

2 On the General tab, you'll find the Background Sound panel, as shown in Figure 8-5. Click Browse, then use the Background Sound dialog box to find the sound clip you want to use.

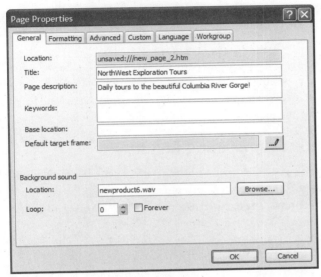

Figure 8-5 Specify the location for the soundtrack file, and configure how it plays.

3 By default, sound files play as long as the reader is on the page. As this can become annoying, clear Forever, and enter a specific number of times that the audio should play in the Loop field, such as 0, 1 or 2. Click OK when you're finished.

> **Note**   If you set Loop to zero, the sound file will play only once, which I recommend in most cases. If you are testing a sound file that you don't loop and want to play the sound clip again, choose Refresh from your browser's View menu.

Creating Video Showcases

Ever wanted to create your own infomercial, or showcase your company's products or services on the Web, using video? Well, you can, and it's easier than you might think. All you need to do is record a video, save it to your computer as a video clip, in the Windows Video, or a Windows Media file format, and then add the video clip to a page in your Web site.

While books like *Faster Smarter Digital Video* (Microsoft Press, 2002) will help you with the process of creating your video clip, and recording it to your computer, this section focuses on adding the finished video clip to a Web page.

When you add a video clip to a Web page, you have two options. You can use a picture as a placeholder for the video, or you can add the video directly to the page. We recommend using a picture as a placeholder, because the picture is displayed, even if, for some reason, the user's browser doesn't support the video format. In this way, compliant browsers, such as Internet Explorer, display the video, and non-compliant browsers, such as Netscape Navigator, display the picture.

Usually, you'll want the picture and the video clip to be displayed at about the same size. This ensures the page flow is similar, whether the picture or the video clip is displayed. If you add a video clip to an existing picture, FrontPage will take care of resizing the picture for you. In most cases, this means setting the picture size to 321x321 pixels (width x height).

Adding a Video Clip to an Existing Picture

One way to add a video clip to a page is to use an existing picture as a placeholder. With this approach, browsers that support the video clip format will show the video and other browsers will show the picture you've designated as a placeholder. If you want to add a video clip to an existing picture, follow these steps:

1 Right-click the picture, and then select Picture Properties.

2 On the Video tab of the Picture Properties dialog box, click Browse, and then use the Video dialog box to find the video clip you want to use. Remember that the video clip should be in a Windows Video or a Windows Media file format, such as the Microsoft AVI format.

3 As shown in Figure 8-6, use Loop to set the number of times the video plays. In most cases, you don't want the video to loop constantly as this can become annoying, so don't select Forever.

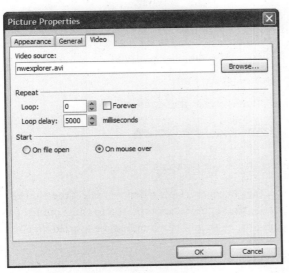

Figure 8-6 Specify the location of the video clip, as well as its looping and play values.

4   Use Loop Delay to specify how long the video waits after playing before playing again (this is called looping). The loop delay is set in milliseconds: for example, if you wanted to wait 10 seconds before looping, you would enter a value of 10000.

5   Specify when the video starts. Choose On File Open to play the video automatically when the browser finishes loading the page and opens the video file. Or choose On Mouse Over to play the video only if the user moves the mouse over the video. Click OK when you're finished.

Adding a Video Clip Directly to a Page

If you want to add a video clip directly to a Web page, without using a placeholder picture, choose Insert, Picture, Video, and then use the Video dialog box to find the video clip you want to use. Afterward, follow Steps 3-5 in the previous section.

Creating Visual Menus with Pictures

Do you have a product diagram, an aerial photo of your college campus, or some other type of picture to which you want to add multiple clickable areas? If so, you might want to create a visual menu using an image map. In an image map, one or more areas of a picture are keyed to a hidden menu of links. When someone clicks on one of these keyed areas, called a hotspot, their browser opens the Web page, or file resource, specified in the associated link.

Hotspots are added to pictures using the Pictures toolbar, shown in Figure 8-7. Three buttons in particular are the most useful:

- **Rectangular Hotspot**   Used to create rectangular hotspots.
- **Circular Hotspot**   Used to create circular hotspots.
- **Polygonal Hotspot**   Used to create polygonal hotspots.

Figure 8-7   You'll use the Pictures toolbar to add hotspots to pictures.

After you add hotspots to a picture, they become visible when you select the picture in which they are defined. You can use the Highlight Hotspots button to white out the picture, and highlight all the hotspots it contains. Highlight Hotspots can be toggled on and off with a mouse click.

The sections that follow discuss the techniques you'll use to create and work with visual menus, including adding hotspots to pictures, modifying existing hotspots, and deleting hotspots.

Adding Clickable Hotspots to Pictures

You can add hotspots to a picture by completing the following steps:

1 Right-click the picture that you want to turn into an image map, and then choose Show Pictures Toolbar.

2 Use the hotspot shape buttons to highlight an area of the picture where you will be placing a hotspot. Hotspots shouldn't overlap, and can be in any of the following shapes:

- **Rectangle**   For a rectangular hotspot, click Rectangular Hotspot. Position the pointer where you want to place the upper left edge, and click and hold the left mouse button while dragging the mouse down and to the right to size the hotspot. Release the mouse button when the hotspot is sized appropriately.

- **Circle**   For a circular hotspot, click Circular Hotspot. Position the pointer where you want to place the center of the circle, and click and hold the left mouse button while dragging the mouse to the right to size the hotspot. Release the mouse button when the hotspot is sized appropriately.

- **Polygon**   For a polygonal hotspot, choose Polygonal Hotspot. Then, click at any point on the perimeter of the shape, move the pointer to a point where the shape outline should change direction, and click again. A line appears that connects the two points. As you add more points, more lines will appear until you return to your starting point to complete the polygon.

3 When the hotspot outline is completed, the Insert Hyperlink dialog box is displayed, as shown in Figure 8-8. This is the same dialog box you use to create other hyperlinks, and the techniques to define the hyperlink are the same as discussed in Chapter 4. After you specify the hyperlink, click OK.

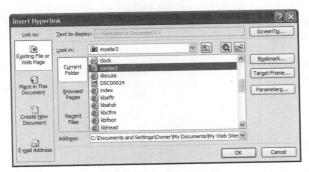

Figure 8-8 Use the Insert Hyperlink dialog box to specify the link for the hotspot.

4 Repeat Steps 2 and 3 to add more hotspots to the picture. When you are finished creating the image map, be sure to press Ctrl+S to save the page with your changes.

Moving, Modifying, and Deleting Hotspots

Editing hotspots after you've created them is easy, but not necessarily intuitive, if you haven't done it before. For example, you might need to change the position of a hotspot, resize it, modify the location to which it links, or delete it. Let's look at each of these tasks in turn.

Moving Hotspots

To move a hotspot, follow these steps:

1 Select the picture that contains the hotspot you want to move. The outlines of all the hotspots in that picture are displayed.

2 Position the mouse pointer within the hotspot, but not touching the outline of the hotspot.

3 Click and hold down the left mouse button, while moving the pointer to the desired location within the picture.

4 The hotspot moves with the pointer. When you are satisfied with the new position, release the mouse button.

Resizing Hotspots

To resize a hotspot, follow these steps:

1 Select the picture that contains the hotspot you want to resize. The outlines of all the hotspots in that picture are displayed.

2 Click within the hotspot or on the outline of it to display resizing handles.

3 Move the mouse pointer over a resizing handle. The resizing handle should appear as a small solid square on each of the corners and in the center of each side of the hotspot boundary.

4 Click and hold down the left mouse button, while moving the double-arrow pointer in the desired direction, to expand or contract the hotspot.

Changing Hotspot Links

To change the link associated with a hotspot, follow these steps:

1 Select the picture to display its hotspots.

2 Right-click the hotspot you want to work with, and then choose Hyperlink.

3 Use the Edit Hyperlink dialog box to specify the new location for the link, and then click OK.

Removing Hotspots

To remove a hotspot, select the picture that contains the hotspot you want to remove. Next, click anywhere within the hotspot to select it, and then press the Delete key.

Fast Wrap-Up

- Using photo galleries, you can create photo montages, albums, and slide shows for any pictures that you want to showcase.

- Photo galleries can even be used to highlight your organization's products or services.

- Another way to make a page stand out is to add a soundtrack or video clip.

- Soundtrack and video clips could be used to provide a recorded greeting from your organization's executive staff, or to have a product manager personally introduce your latest product or service.

- Sometimes you might want to create a visual menu, using an image map.

- With an image map, you can define clickable hotspots within a picture that are each linked to Web pages and resource files.

Working with Tables

9

10-Second Summary	
■	Create tables by drawing and inserting them
■	Customize the table's appearance using layout, sizing, and spacing techniques
■	Designate table headers, and add captions
■	Split, merge, and delete table cells

Working with tables is what this chapter is all about. Tables let you control the appearance of information you present. Most tables have rows of data organized into columns. The columns of data contain individual cells that are either header cells, which label the columns, or data cells, which contain the actual table information. Not only can you use tables to effectively organize information, such as sales records or performance statistics (as discussed in this chapter), you can also use tables to lay out the contents of your Web pages, as discussed in Chapter 11, "Advanced Layout with Tables and Layers."

Creating Tables the Easy Way

Whenever you want to create tables, you have several options. You can draw the table using the Table Draw tool, or you can insert a table with a specific size, layout, and style. Both techniques have their advantages and disadvantages:

■ **Draw Table** Draw Table is most useful when you want to create tables with *ad hoc*-sized rows and columns. If you want to create a table, but aren't really sure how many columns and rows you want to use, or how those columns and rows should be sized or organized, you might want to use the Draw Table tool. Also, if you want to create a table that has odd-sized cells, such as a cell that spans several rows or columns, the Draw Table tool might be best.

■ **Insert Table** Insert Table is most useful when you want to create a table with a specific layout, and a certain number rows and columns. If you know how many rows and columns the table should have, or, if you want the table to have a specific size, alignment and spacing within and between cells, you might want to use the Insert Table tool.

Regardless of which technique you use, you'll want to activate the Table toolbar by choosing View, Toolbars, Tables. Using the Tables toolbar, you can easily create and edit traditional tables (as discussed in this chapter), and layout tables (as discussed in Chapter 11, "Advanced Layout with Tables and Layers").

> **Aha!**   Dock the Tables Toolbar
>
> When you first use the Tables toolbar, it floats in the middle of the page, which can be annoying when you're trying to work. To get the toolbar out of the way, drag it to the top, left, right or bottom of the FrontPage window. When the toolbar is docked, it will change from a floating toolbar to a regular toolbar.

Going to the Drawing Board to Create Tables

One way to create tables is to draw them, using the Draw Table tool. With this tool, you can create tables with *ad hoc*-sized columns and rows. You can, for example, easily create unevenly-distributed rows and columns, and oversized cells. On the Table toolbar, you'll find two handy buttons (see Figure 9-1 and Figure 9-2) for drawing tables:

Figure 9-1   Draw Table changes the pointer to a pencil that lets you draw tables. Click and drag to draw.

Figure 9-2   Erase changes the pointer to an eraser that can erase table cell borders. Click and drag to erase.

Whenever you draw tables, you'll use Draw Table and Erase. The sections that follow discuss key table drawing techniques using these tools.

Getting Started Drawing the Table

As discussed previously, you'll draw tables with the Draw Table tool. Click Draw Table on the Table toolbar, and then follow these steps to draw your table:

1 Move the cursor to where you want the upper-left corner of the table to be.

2 Click and hold down the mouse button, then size the table by dragging the pointer down and to the right. Release the mouse button when the table is sized appropriately.

3 To add columns to the table, move the cursor to where you want to add the column. Click and hold down the mouse button; then drag the pointer down until the dashed drawing line extends to the appropriate row or table border.

4 To add rows, move the pointer to where you want to add the row. Click and hold down the mouse button, then drag the pointer left or right, until the dashed drawing line extends to the appropriate column or table border.

> **Aha!** Erase Your Mistakes
>
> Use the eraser to correct any drawing mistakes you make. Click Eraser on the Table toolbar. Position the pointer above, or to the left of the cell border to erase, then click and hold the mouse button while dragging down, or to the right. Release the mouse button when the cell border you want to erase is highlighted.

Resizing Tables You Have Drawn

Whether you are using the Draw Table or the Erase tool, you can resize tables and the rows, columns and cells they contain. Position the mouse pointer over the border you want to resize, click when the pointer changes to a double arrow, and then drag the mouse pointer in the appropriate direction. If you've selected a table, column or row border, the resizing affects the entire table, column or row with which you're working.

Avoid the Drawing Board by Inserting Tables

If the table is going to be simple, it might not be worth it to draw it. Instead, create the table using the insert table method. Simply position the insertion point where you'd like to insert the table, and then follow these steps:

1 Select Table, Insert, Table. This displays the Insert Table dialog box, shown in Figure 9-3.

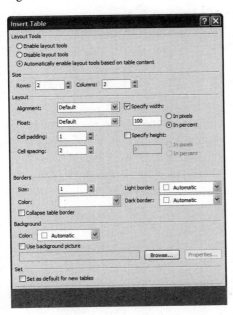

Figure 9-3 Use the Insert Tables dialog box to create tables with specific size, layout, borders and backgrounds.

2   Under Size, use Rows and Columns to set the number of rows and columns for the table.

3   To increase the spacing within and between table cells, you can use the Cell Padding and Cell Spacing settings. Cell Padding sets the spacing inside the cell. Cell Spacing sets the spacing between cells.

4   Under Borders, use Size to set the width of table borders, in pixels. If you set the border size to zero pixels, you remove the table border entirely.

5   Use Color to specify the border color to use. If you choose Automatic, the table is usually displayed with the same border color as the background color of the Web page.

6   To add shading to a border, you can set a different color values for the Light Border and Dark Border selection lists. The Light Border sets the color of the left and top borders. The Dark Border sets the color of the right and bottom borders.

7   Once you configure the table settings, click OK, and FrontPage will create your table. That's it. You'll find more specific information on sizing, layout, borders, and backgrounds throughout this chapter.

Customizing Table Layout, Size, and Appearance

Drawing or inserting tables is the easy part; getting tables so that they have the exact layout, size and appearance you want takes a bit more work. Don't worry, we won't leave you hanging without a few pointers—customizing your tables is exactly what this section is all about.

Positioning Tables Precisely for Alignment and Text Flow

Often a table you're creating will be a part of a larger document. For example, you may be adding a weekly sales record by region to a quarterly sales report, or you may be adding feature comparisons to your product page. In this case, you probably want to align the table so that it is centered, or on the left or right side of the page. You'll also probably want to specify how text or other page elements should flow around the table. For example, if a table has a left alignment, you might want text to flow around the right side of the table. Or you might want a table to be centered with no text to the left or right of it.

By default, tables are left-aligned and the flow is such that page elements are placed either above or below the table. You can change the alignment and flow of page elements around a table by completing the following steps:

1   Right-click anywhere in the table, and then select Table Properties from the shortcut menu. This displays the Table Properties dialog box, shown in Figure 9-4.

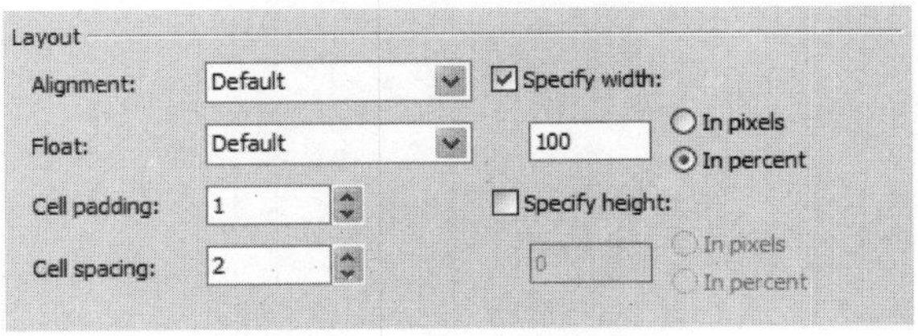

Figure 9-4 Use the options in the Layout panel to control the alignment and flow of text and other objects around the table.

2   Use the Alignment selection list to manage the alignment of the table relative to other objects. Select Left to left-align the table. Select Right to right-align the table. Or select Center to center the table on the page.

3   Use the Float selection list to manage the flow of text around the table. Select Left to left-align the table, and place text or other elements on the right. Select Right to right-align the table, and place text or other elements on the left.

4   Click OK to update the table's properties.

> **Note**   When the table alignment and float values are set to Default, settings of the user's browser determine the alignment and float that are used. In most cases, this means tables are left aligned and the flow is such that page elements are placed either above or below the table.

Sizing Tables Precisely

As with images, you can set table width and height settings in pixels or as a percentage of the current window size:

- When you size tables using pixels, you set a fixed table width, height, or both. For example, you might want a table to be precisely 300 pixels wide and 500 pixels in height.

- When you size tables as percentage of the current window size, you set width, height, or both, relative to the width and height of the browser window. For example, if you set the relative width to 75% and the browser window is 1024 pixels wide, the table will be 768 pixels wide. On the other hand, if the browser window is 600 pixels wide, the table will be 450 pixels wide.

More often than not, you will use relative sizing to allow readers' browsers to size the table. Sometimes, however, you'll need to use a fixed size for your table. You might, for example, need to ensure an image or text is positioned to the left of right of the table. Here, you would use a fixed size to get a specific result. If you decide to use a fixed size for a table, you should preview the page at various screen and display sizes to test the results. In most cases, you will want to design your page with 800x600 and larger display sizes in mind.

You can set the size of a table by completing the following steps:

1   Right-click anywhere in the table, and then select Table Properties from the shortcut menu.

2   Under Layout, select Specify Width. You can then:

●   **Set Fixed Width**   To set a fixed size, select In Pixels, and type a pixel size, such as 600, in the field provided.

●   **Set Relative Width**   To set table size relative to window size, select In Percent, and type a percentage, such as 90, in the field provided.

> **Note**   For a consistent look and precise flow, even when the page is viewed at different screen sizes, use a fixed width, such as 700 pixels. Keep in mind that 800x600 is a common screen size for most PCs. If you use a width larger than 800 pixels, users with smaller screen widths will have to scroll to view parts of the table—and most people hate to use horizontal scrollbars.

3   If you want to specify the table height as well, select Specify Height. You can then:

●   **Set Fixed Height**   To set a fixed size, select In Pixels, and type a pixel size, such as 600, in the field provided.

●   **Set Relative Height**   To set table size relative to window size, select In Percent, and type a percentage, such as 90, in the field provided.

4   Click OK to apply the changes.

Getting Creative with Table Borders and Formatting

When you create tables to organize facts, figures and other data, you'll usually want to have a border, both around and within the table, to delineate the rows and columns. By default, tables have borders, which are formatted as shown in Figure 9-5. Not very appealing, is it?

With the default settings, the border is a pair of lines, with the area between them painted the same color as the page background. You can get creative with the table border settings in a couple of different ways. One is to use the border size, color, and shading options of the Table Properties dialog box.

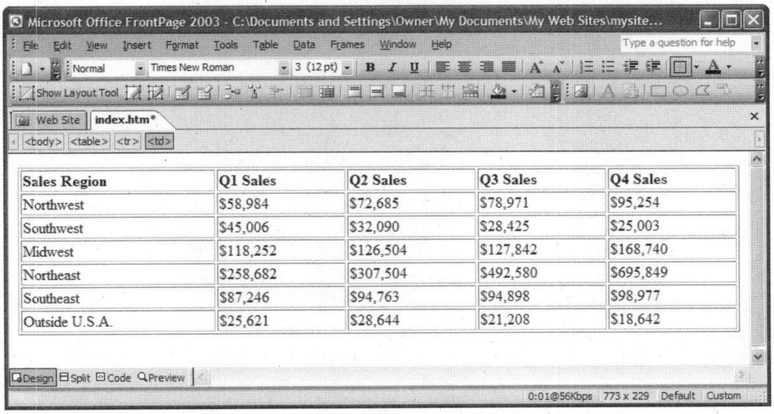

Figure 9-5 Most of the time, table borders are a pair of lines, with the area between the lines painted the same color as the page background.

Another fast way to change the look of the table is to use Table AutoFormat, which lets you apply any of over 50 ready-to-use formats. Styles available include simple, classic, colorful, grids, lists, 3D effects, contemporary, elegant, and professional.

To AutoFormat a table, follow these steps:

1 Click anywhere in the table, and then choose Table, Table AutoFormat. This displays the dialog box shown in Figure 9-6.

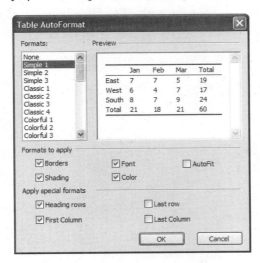

Figure 9-6 Use the Preview area to help you choose a format that you like.

2   Use the up and down arrows on your keyboard to move through the format list, until you find the format you want to use. In the Table AutoFormat dialog box, the style and layout of the currently selected table format is shown in the Preview area.

3   If a table format you want to use has special formatting that you don't like, use the options of the Apply Special Formats panel to change the format. Two options you might want to select or clear are:

- **Heading Rows**   Clear this option if you don't want to use shading, or other special formatting applied to the top row of the table. You'll also want to clear this option if your table doesn't have a heading row.

- **First Column**   Clear this option if you don't want to use shading, or other special formatting applied to the top column of the table. You'll also want to clear this option if your table doesn't have row labels in the first column.

4   When you're ready to format the table, click OK.

Adding Background Colors and Pictures to Tables

You can add background colors and pictures to an entire table, or to individual cells in a table. Figure 9-7 shows how you can use a background picture in a table. When you use colors and background pictures, you should preview the page afterward to make sure the text is readable.

If the text is unreadable, you'll need to change the background color or picture. For example, the table shown in the figure originally had black text, but after adding the picture, we had to change the text to white, so that the table data was readable.

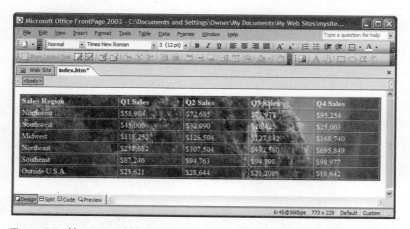

Figure 9-7   You can add background colors and pictures to tables; if you do, make sure the text is readable.

You can specify the background colors and pictures you want to use by completing the following steps:

1   Right-click anywhere in the table, and choose Table Properties.

2   Under Background, use the Color selection list to set the table's background color. If you use Automatic, the background color is set to use the browser default, which is usually the same as the background color of the page.

3   Select the Use Background Image check box, and then click the Browse button to find the background picture you want to use.

> **Note**   As with page backgrounds, the background picture for your table should be in GIF or JPEG format. If it isn't, however, FrontPage should convert it to either GIF or JPEG for you automatically, as discussed in Chapter 7, "Using Pictures in Web Pages."

4   Click OK.

Optimizing Cell Layout, Size, and Appearance

Just as tables have properties, so do the individual cells within them. Cell properties determine whether cells are considered data or header cells, the alignment of information within them, their width and height, and much more.

Designating Header Cells

When you create a table, its cells are designated as data cells by default. Typically, this means that the cells are left-aligned and not displayed in bold font. To designate cells as header cells and change their default formatting to bold, centered text, select the cells you want to work with, right-click, and then select Cell Properties. Then, in the Cell Properties dialog box, choose Header Cell under Layout.

Aligning and Sizing Table Cells

Table cells have several different properties that control their layout and size. These properties include settings for horizontal and vertical alignment of cell elements, row and column spanning options, and width and height settings. To set these table cell options, follow these steps:

1   Select the cell, or cells, you want to format. Then right-click, and select Cell Properties from the shortcut menu to display the Cell Properties dialog box, shown in Figure 9-8 on the following page.

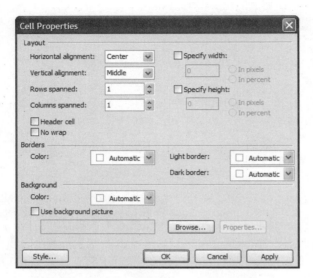

Figure 9-8 Use the layout options to align and size table cells.

2 Under Layout, use Horizontal Alignment to left-align, right-align, or center cell contents. You can also justify elements so that they are displayed with even left and right margins, if possible. Default sets alignment per the user's browser, which typically means data is left aligned.

3 Use Vertical Alignment to align cell contents with the top, middle or bottom of the cell. Default sets alignment per the user's browser, which typically means data is aligned with the middle of the cell.

4 If you want cells to have a specific width, height, or both, select and set values for the Specify Width and Specify Height as appropriate.

> **Note** Cell width and height can be set in pixels, or as a percentage of the window size. You may want to use a fixed size, when you are adding content of a specific size, such as a picture. If you don't have fixed-sized content for a cell, you'll probably want to use relative sizing (if you use any sizing options at all). With relative sizing, the browser sets the cell width, height, or both, based on the percentage of window size you specify.

5 Cells normally span only one row and one column. Use Rows Spanned and Columns Spanned as necessary to create cells that go across several rows or columns.

6 Click OK to update the layout of the select cell, or cells.

Setting Cell Border Style and Color

Cell borders are the borders within a table, not those on its boundaries. Normally, cell borders are displayed in the same way as the borders of the associated table. If you want table and cell borders to be displayed with a single solid line, rather than a double line with a colored border in between, right-click anywhere in the table, and select Table Properties. Then, on the Borders panel, choose Collapse Table Border. If you want to set cell borders differently from table borders, right-click anywhere in the table, select Cell Properties, and then use the options of the Borders panel to set the cell border colors.

Adding Background Colors and Pictures to Table Cells

Using the Cell Properties dialog box, you can also add background colors and pictures to cells. First, select the cells you want to work with and then display the Cell Properties dialog box by choosing Table, Properties, Cell.

Like the Table Properties dialog box, the Cell Properties dialog box has a Background panel. If you want to use a background color, use the Color selection list to choose it. If you want to use a background picture, choose Use Background Picture, and then click Browse to find the picture.

> **Note** As stated previously, the background picture should be in GIF or JPEG format. If it isn't, FrontPage will convert it automatically to either GIF or JPEG, as discussed in Chapter 7, "Using Pictures in Web Pages."

Essential Table Editing Techniques

Now that you've created a table, what's next? Well, you'll probably need to perform essential editing tasks, such as selecting table elements so that you can work with them, adding rows or columns, or filling in content, using existing data. You might also need to split, merge or delete table cells.

Selecting Cells, Rows, Columns, and Tables

Selecting tables and their contents is easy, but not necessarily intuitive, if you haven't done it before. With the mouse, you can select cells by clicking and dragging within the table. With the keyboard, you can hold down Shift, and use the Up, Down, Left or Right arrow keys.

You select rows and columns a bit differently, however. To select a row, move the pointer over the leftmost border of the row, and then click when the row selection arrow is displayed. To select a column, move the pointer over the topmost border of the column, and then click when the column selection arrow is displayed.

You can select a table and all its contents by clicking anywhere on the table and choosing Table, Select, Table.

Adding Rows and Columns to Existing Tables

You can insert rows and columns into tables by using the Insert Rows and Insert Columns tools on the Table toolbar. To add a row, position the insertion point in the row below the location where you want to add a new row, and click Insert Rows. To add a column, position the insertion point in the column to the right of where you want to add a new column, and then click Insert Columns.

You can also add a new row to the end of a table by pressing Tab in the last cell of a table.

Filling in Using Copies of Existing Table Data

You can use fill to repeat the content of one cell in multiple cells, without having to re-enter the content. When you fill cells, you copy the content of a cell (the *model cell*), to cells that are either in the row to the right, or in the column below.

To fill cells, follow these steps:

1   Start by entering content into the cell that you want to use for filling other cells.

2   Next select the model cell and the adjacent cells that you are going to fill.

- If these cells are in adjacent columns, select the model cell, and then drag the mouse to the right, selecting other cells in the row.
- If these cells are in adjacent rows, select the model cell, and then drag the mouse down, selecting other cells in the column.

3   Select Table, Fill Right, or Fill Down, as appropriate, and FrontPage will fill the contents of the other cells, based on the model cell.

Splitting Cells to Create Columns or Rows within Cells

You can split cells to create columns and rows within cells. Right-click the cell you want to split, and then select Split Cells. In the Split Cells dialog box, select Split Into Columns, or Split Into Rows, as appropriate, and then click OK. You've now added a column or row within the cell, and the table now has two or more columns or rows within that cell.

> **Note**   You can specify whether you want more than 2 columns or rows. After you select the Split Into option, use the Number Of Columns, or Number Of Rows field to set number of columns or rows into which you want the cells split.

Merging Cells, Columns, and Rows

You can merge two or more table elements into a single cell, column, or row. Select the cells, columns, or rows that you want to merge, and then right-click and choose Merge Cells. As a result of the merge, any data that was split between multiple table cells, columns, or rows is merged into a single element.

Deleting Cells, Columns, and Rows

You can delete cells, columns, and rows to remove these elements and their contents from the table. Select the cells, columns, and rows you want to remove. Right-click, and then choose Delete Cells.

> **Note**   Sometimes, you might want to use the deleted elements elsewhere on the page. In this case, select the elements to delete, then use Cut (Ctrl+X) to move the elements to the clipboard. You can then use Paste (Ctrl+V) to insert the elements where they are needed.

Fast Wrap-Up

- You can use the Draw Table tool to quickly create tables for use in Web pages.

- If you have more advanced needs, you can use the Layout Tables and Cells feature to create your tables.

- After creating a table, you can add text, color, and pictures.

- Table and cell properties can be configured separately. To customize the appearance of tables and table cells, you set table and cell properties.

- When you are editing tables, you can use fill, split, and merge techniques to help manage table cells and their contents.

Part 3
Advanced Web Page Techniques

Part 3, "Advanced Web Page Techniques," describes FrontPage's options for controlling the content and layout of Web pages. In Chapter 10, you'll learn about the many new tools available to help you write and edit clean HTML and XML code. Chapter 11, "Advanced Layout with Tables and Layers," examines features for designing pages that use tables and layers to create sophisticated layout and graphics arrangements. Chapter 12, "Adding Interactivity with Frames," covers FrontPage's ability to divide Web pages into frames, which add a new level of interactivity to a Web site.

Editing HTML and XML Markup

10

10-Second Summary

■ View both Web page code and visible design for a page with Split View

■ Write code faster and more accurately with Code IntelliSense

■ Store and re-use blocks of code from a library of Code Snippets

■ Search your Web page code to quickly update your Web site

■ Clean up your code to make your pages easier to load

Anything that makes your business look good, and your Web site function smoothly, builds trust among your customers—and that can directly benefit your bottom line. That applies not only to your Web site's public face, but to the underlying code that makes your site work smoothly and accurately process the orders placed online by your customers and business partners.

Back in the early days of theWeb, practically anyone could write HTML (and they *had* to work with raw HTML, before the development of user-friendly software like FrontPage). These days, the code that makes Web pages attractive and interactive is increasingly complex. The prospect of creating code that is not only clean and functional, but that works the same from browser to browser, and from one operating system to another, can seem intimidating. That is, until you begin to use the FrontPage features that make code more accessible and easier to work with. Clean code makes pages easier to revise, which reduces production time. This chapter gives you some hands-on experience working with FrontPage's tools for viewing, editing, and cleaning up your Web page code—features that not only enable you to write code faster and more efficiently, but also give you a jump-start on learning how to write HTML and XML correctly.

Lingo You probably know that *HTML* stands for HyperText Markup Language, the language originally used to mark up Web pages so their contents can appear correctly when displayed in a Web browser. You may be less familiar with *XML* or Extensible Markup Language. XML is another way of marking up Web pages that's not meant to replace HTML, but rather to complement it. In contrast to HTML, which contains a set of standard, well-defined tags for marking up text, images, and other contents, XML lets you create your own structured markup. By creating your own markup tags, you can focus on defining the way data is structured. XML is ideal for enabling database information to be exchanged between applications—for instance, between a Web browser and a data source. See Chapter 16, "Making a Site Database-Driven," for more information.

Revealing Markup Tags with Code View

If you've used a Web page creation progam before, you're aware that its primary purpose is to enable you to add images, format text, and design the overall look of Web pages, without having to enter Hypertext Markup Language (HTML) commands by hand. But FrontPage's Code View makes it easy to peek "behind the curtain" and work with the code that controls how Web pages (and Web sites) work. That includes not only HTML and XML, but Cascading Style Sheets (CSS) and advanced coding environments that FrontPage supports, like Active Server Pages (ASP), Active Server Pages .NET (ASP.NET), and scripting languages, such as JScript and VBScript.

Understanding Web Page Effects by Formatting Code

Whenever you want take a look behind the curtain, and examine the instructions that make text, images, colors, and other Web page contents appear the way you want them to, you need only to click the Code button beneath the page you are viewing and switch to Code View. The cursor is automatically positioned in the line of code that corresponds to the element where the cursor was last positioned when you viewed the page in Design View.

The ease with which you can switch to Code View means that, any time you are wondering what makes a particular Web page feature work, you can view the code to learn how to create the same effect the way a professional programmer would. Any time you select an image or other object, or position the cursor within a block of the text in the Web page you have under construction, you can instantly switch to Code View to examine the code that makes that element appear the way it does. Try it yourself: open a Web page that contains a table, and position your cursor within one of the table cells. Click Code, and you switch to Code View (see Figure 10-1), where you can view the attributes for that cell.

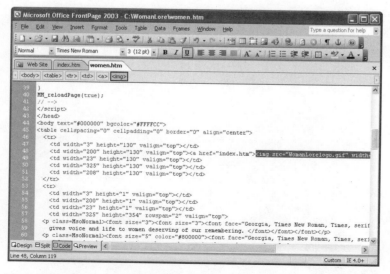

Figure 10-1   Learn how Web page effects are achieved with Code View.

By taking the time to customize the look of your page's code, you, or others in your company who are responsible for editing Web pages, can edit more easily later on. If you've been assigned to learn how scripts are used in Web pages, you can highlight them in a font or color of your choice. If you develop Web pages as part of a team, formatting your code makes it easier for your colleagues to edit or track down problems. The sections that follow suggest ways in which you can format your code.

> **Aha!**   Make Your Code Wrap
>
> You'll notice that, in Figure 10-1, the code extends off the screen to the right. You have to scroll to view it. You can change this by activating word wrap: choose Tools, Page Options, and then click the General tab. Check the box next to Word Wrap, then click OK. The General tab also lets you de-activate line numbers, the selection margin to the immediate left of the lines of code, and automatic indenting of scripts or HTML, so that new lines in the Code pane are aligned with the line above.

Customizing Code by Changing Colors

One way to customize the way FrontPage presents Web page code is to change the colors used to present various elements. Choose Tools, Page Options, then click the Color Coding tab to view the elements you can "colorize," which are summarized in Table 10-1:

Table 10-1 **Web page code elements you can format**

Element	Description
Background	Controls the background color against which the Web page code appears. You can make the code easier to read for everyone in your office.
Normal text	Controls the color of the body text that is contained on the current Web page. Changing the body text color enables you to highlight the contents that visitors to your Web site actually see.
Bookmarks	Controls the color of text, or other contents you have bookmarked, so that you can link to them.
Tags	Controls the color of HTML tags so that you can find and edit them quicker.
Attribute names/values	Controls the color of names and attributes that accompany tags.
Comments	Controls the color of comments that you or someone else has inserted into the Web page code.
Script elements	Controls the color of various parts of scripts that are contained within a Web page, such as Jscripts or VBscripts, so that you can edit them more easily.
DWT elements	Controls colors assigned to parts of Dynamic Web Templates that are contained on the current page.

Table 10-1   Web page code elements you can format

Element	Description
Layout elements	Controls the colors of Layout table tools such as borders, text, and labels.
Web part elements	Controls the colors of any Web parts that have been inserted in a Web page.

Suppose you need to leave messages for others in your company who will be editing the Web pages later. You'll make the comments easier to find by highlighting them in a special color. To change the color of comments, follow these steps:

1   Click the Code tool to switch to Code View.

2   Evaluate the current color used to display comments. Add your own HTML comment, as shown in the following example:

<!-- Created by IT Department 03-27-03. Review this page for possible revisions on 6-27-03 -->

3   Choose Tools, Page Options, and click the Color Coding tab.

4   Choose a color from the Comments drop-down list, as shown in Figure 10-2.

5   Click OK.

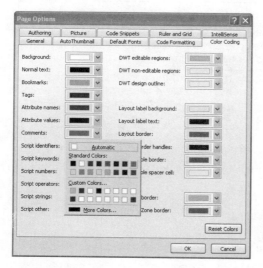

Figure 10-2 Change the color of comments or other code so that you or your coworkers can more easily find elements you need to revise.

> **Aha!** Create Your Own Colors
>
> If you don't like the colors that FrontPage provides by default, you can create your own in one of two ways. Click Custom Colors, and choose a color from the color wheel that appears. Or, you can clone a color from a Web page by clicking More Colors, Select, selecting a color with the eyedropper, and then clicking the color next to the element in the Color Coding tab to which you want to assign the new color. You can use the eyedropper to click not only a color in More Colors, but also in a Web page, or any other open window.

Change the Default Font

Courier is typically used to display Web page code because it's a monospaced font: adjacent lines of code line up, so they are easier to read. Unless you have a typeface preference, you should probably stay with Courier. But you can change the font by choosing a new one in the Code View section of the Default Fonts tab of the Page Options dialog box (see Figure 10-3).

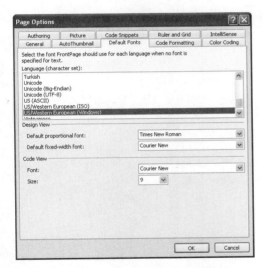

Figure 10-3 Change font selection and size to make Web page code more readable.

You may, for instance, change the size in which code is displayed to make it more readable. Choose a new font size from the Size drop-down menu list in the Default Fonts tab of the Page Options dialog box.

> **Note** Keep in mind, though, that the bigger the type, the more likely you'll have to scroll to read entire lines of code. For a long and complex Web page, this can be a lot of extra work for you, and for the other members of your organization's team of Web developers.

Change Other Formatting to Make Code Readable

Besides the font type, size, and color, and word wrap, the other attributes you may want to change in order to make your code more readable are are spaces and line breaks. The Code Formatting tab of the Page Options dialog box contains such controls:

- **Allow Line Breaks Within Tags**   Tells FrontPage to break lines, even if the break occurs within a tag, which might make code difficult to read. On the other hand, it means you won't have to scroll horizontally in order to read all of a page's code.

- **Tab Size And Indent**   Controls how much code is indented. Indenting makes it easier to read the attributes and values that follow a command.

- **Right Margin**   Specifies how much the code is indented from the right. A narrow column of code enables you to see other panes within the Front Page window, or other windows such as Web browsers.

- **Tags**   This box lets you apply line break settings to individual tags. Breaking a line of code after a tag doesn't affect the contents of theWeb page, but it helps you locate a particular segment of the page's code more quickly. For instance, breaking the line after the `<script>` and `</script>` tags lets you quickly see all of the code contained between them.

One of the most powerful controls on the Code Formatting tab enables you to base the formatting of all the code that FrontPage presents by basing it on the formatting of the current page. Once you have adjusted the code so that it looks the way you want it to, click the Base On Current page button to make the same settings apply to current pages as well. Such consistency enables you to instruct your co-workers to look for the same elements—"look for the green comments within the HTML code," for instance.

Previewing a Design in Split View

You already know that FrontPage's Design View lets gives you a WYSIWYG (What You See Is What You Get) view of a Web page—what you see in Design View is pretty much what you and your Web site visitors will see when they access the page online. But you'll edit more quickly if you can view the finished design and the code that underlies it simultaneously. Split View, one of FrontPage's most useful new features, splits the current page display into Code and Design View.

To switch from the current view to Split View (as shown in figure 10-4), press the Split button in the row of view buttons beneath the page display area. When the view splits, the Code View reflects where you are in the Design View, and vice-versa. The two views are, in fact, interactive: scroll down through the code, and the design view scrolls correspondingly, so that you can keep track of where you are in the code (or on the designed Web page). Move the drag bar up or down to resize the two views.

The big advantage of using split view is the ability to preview a change you make in the code for the current Web page. Once you make a change in Code View, you can see the effect instantly in Design View by pressing F5, or by selecting View, Refresh.

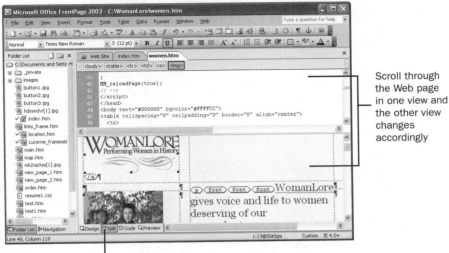

Scroll through the Web page in one view and the other view changes accordingly

Click here to toggle Split view on or off

Figure 10-4   Split view lets you check code changes in near-real time.

Creating and Editing Code

The more thorough your knowledge of HTML, XML, and XHTML, the better your ability to troubleshoot and adjust the Web pages you create. But that doesn't mean you have to know every last detail of such languages before you start. FrontPage provides you with a variety of features (some new, some improved) to help you generate code more quickly and accurately. If you're an aspiring code jockey, you'll find a variety of utilities that will help jump-start your syntax, as described in the following sections.

Learning Code More Quickly with Code IntelliSense

Errors in writing code, and subsequent debugging, can seriously slow down Web site development. To make sure you enter the right commands the first time, you usually need to refer to a bulky reference book as you type. No more: Microsoft IntelliSense technology provides an instant reference within the FrontPage interface to help you write code more easily.

IntelliSense is a great tool for learning code: you need only begin a tag or statement and, if you need a reminder of the options you can add to it, IntelliSense will complete the statement for you. You can take advantage of IntelliSense in one of several ways:

■   As you are typing code in Code View, IntelliSense presents you with lists of possible code elements you can add that correspond to the commands you are typing.

- Choose View, Toolbars, Code View to display the Code View toolbar, then click List Members, Parameter Info, or one of the options that appear in a drop-down list when you click the Options tool at the right-hand edge of the toolbar.

- Choose Edit, IntelliSense, and choose one of the four submenu options (List Members, Parameter Info, Complete Word, or View Code Snippets).

Here's an example of how the first button on the left, List Members, works: List Members acts like a programming tutor: if you're ever wondering about the correct attributes that can be applied to a tag or script command (or if you're simply wondering how to spell them correctly), place the cursor on the element in question, then click List Members. All the available code that you can use with that element appears in a shortcut menu (see Figure 10-5).

List Members button

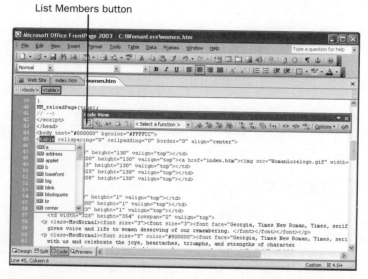

Figure 10-5   List members suggests possible code you can add to a tag or command.

The Code View toolbar and View Code Snippets are discussed in the sections that follow.

> **Note**   Code IntelliSense is available for HTML, CSS (cascading style sheets), XSL (Extensible Stylesheet Language), JScript, and ASP.NET.

Ensuring Accuracy with Typing Aids

Typing code is an unforgiving task. One typo, and an image doesn't appear, code instructions appear visibly on the page when they should remain invisible, or another effect doesn't work correctly. To make this exacting task go more quickly, FrontPage presents you with a variety of typing shortcuts. Some are available in the new Code View toolbar, while others are accessed by typing keyboard shortcuts in Code View itself.

Find Editing Tools Quickly with the Code View Toolbar

When you're working in Code View, you'll work more quickly if you have all of the relevant tools available. Many of those tools are located on the new Code View toolbar, which appears when you choose View, Toolbars, Code View.

The previous section explained how the first button in the Code View toolbar gives you a manual way to access IntelliSense code suggestions for what you're typing. The other commands in the Code View toolbar include:

- **Parameter Info**   If you are typing script in your Web page code and enter a command that can have more than one possible parameter (such as document. or window.), click the Parameter Info. button and FrontPage will prompt you with parameters you may want to add.

- **Complete Word**   Suppose you start to type a command, but you aren't sure how it's spelled. Click Complete Word, and FrontPage automatically completes the word for you.

- **List Code Snippets**   Displays bits of frequently used code that can be applied to the element at the insertion point. (See the section "Code Snippets" later in this chapter for more details.)

- **Go To Function**   This option is active only if the cursor is positioned within script that is governed by a function. Click it, and the function command is selected.

- **Function Lookup**   If the current page contains JavaScript or other functions, click here, and a shortcut menu appears with a list of those functions displayed. Select a function from the list, and it is highlighted. You and your co-workers can use the Lookup feature to learn how to write better code.

- **Toggle Bookmark**   Lets you create a temporary bookmark at the current insertion point, or remove a bookmark if one has already been created. These code bookmarks let you jump back and forth between portions of the Code pane— for example, between a script block at the top of a page and the script invocation at the bottom. Bookmarks enable you to direct co-workers to parts of the code they need to edit or proofread.

- **Next Bookmark**   Moves to the next bookmark on the current page.

- **Previous Bookmark**   Moves to the previous temporary code bookmark on the current page, if you have created any.

- **Clear Bookmarks**   Removes a bookmark if one has been selected.

- **Select Tag**   Selects the tag that controls the text where the cursor is positioned.

- **Find Matching Tag**   If you position the cursor in one part of a tag, such as <a>, click here to find the matching tag, such as </a>.

- **Select Block**   Selects a block of code that extends over multiple lines.

- **Find Matching Brace**   If you are in a script section, this causes the cursor to jump to the nearest matching brace.

- **Insert Start Tag**   Inserts the standard brackets, <>, so you can type a new start tag.

- **Insert End Tag**   Inserts the standard brackets, </>, so you can type a new end tag.

- **Insert Comment**   Inserts the <!-- --> commands so you can type a comment.

- **Options**   Lets you activate (or deactivate) word wrap, line numbers, the selection margin, or automatic indentation for the current code. You can select or deselect options in order to develop a "house style guide" that your company can use to create and edit Web page code consistently.

- **Microsoft Script Editor**   Launches the Microsoft Script Editor application, so that you can create or edit code you see displayed in Code View (see Figure 10-6). Advanced coders in your company will save time launching the Script Editor from within FrontPage.

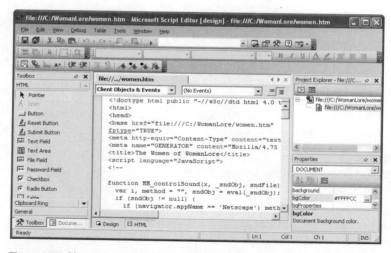

Figure 10-6 You can launch Microsoft Script Editor from the Code View toolbar if you want to edit some of the current Web page's code.

Keyboard Shortcuts

In a business environment, time is money. And chances are you're being paid, in part, to work quickly and accurately. Since you're creating code mostly by using your keyboard, it makes sense that you should have some keyboard shortcuts to make your typing go more quickly. Some of these are described in Table 10-2.

Table 10-2 Code View Keyboard Shortcuts

Type of Shortcut	Keys to Press	Description
Code Indentation	Tab	Indents selected block of code
	Shift+Tab	Reduces indentation of an indented block
Select Tag	Ctrl+;	Selects tag in which cursor is positioned
Find Matching Tag	Ctrl+:	When you select a tag (such as <head>) this finds the matching tag (such as </head>)
Select Block	Ctrl+'	Selects block of code in which cursor is positioned
Find Matching Brace	Ctrl+]	After you select one brace, you jump to the matching brace
Insert Start Tag	Ctrl+,	Inserts the <> characters
Insert End Tag	Ctrl+.	Inserts the </> characters
Insert Comment	Ctrl+/	Inserts the <!– –> characters

Suppose you're writing a long block of code, and you lose track of the end of the code. Just choose Edit, Code View, and press Ctrl+' (Ctrl and the ' key twice) to highlight the block of code from beginning to end. You can then scroll down to the end of the block to see what remains. You can even insert a bookmark at the end of the block of code so that you can jump to the end if you need to. You'll find a full selection of menu options and corresponding shortcuts for use in Code View when you choose Edit, Code View, and the shortcut menu appears as shown in Figure 10-7.

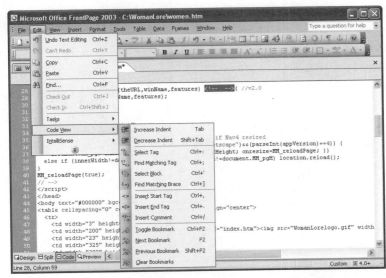

Figure 10-7 Keyboard shortcuts make your code creation go more quickly.

Find and Replace—With a Brain

When you need to make changes to all instances of the same tags or commands in the current page, Find And Replace can be a real time-saver. When you're in Code View and looking for code to find and replace, you can easily make queries that let you search the HTML code for the current page:

1   Choose Edit, Find, or press Ctrl+F.

2   When the Find And Replace dialog box appears, click HTML Tags.

3   Enter or paste the tag you want to find in the Find Tag box.

4   Choose an action from the Replace Action drop-down list.

5   Under Search options, choose All Pages if you want to search all pages in the current Web, whether they are open or not. Choose Open Page if you want to search only the pages that are open in FrontPage. Choose Current Page if you want to search only the currently displayed page.

6   Click Find Next.

After you find the tag, you can click Replace, or Replace All, to make changes. Suppose you expect to make the same search when you're working on other pages or Web sites. FrontPage enables you to set up rules, so you don't have to reconstruct the same search-and-replace criteria every time you want to make such changes. Your fellow Web page editors can use the same search-and-replace rules you do:

1   Choose Edit, Find, or press Ctrl+F.

2   In the Find What box, enter the text you want to find.

3   When the HTML Rules dialog box appears, click New Rule.

4   When the New Rule drop-down list appears, click Inside Tag if you want the rule to apply to the contents of the tag; otherwise, click Not Inside Tag.

5   Click New Rule beneath the rule you just created. When the next drop-down list appears, click the tag to which you want the rule to apply (see Figure 10-8).

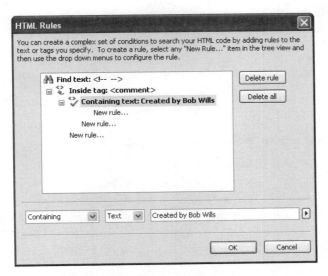

Figure 10-8 HTML Rules lets you set up rules that you can apply all at once to code searches.

The next time you, or one of your co-workers, open Find And Replace, your rule appears automatically. You can then perform Replace Actions in the Replace tab. You can also click Clear Rules to delete the rule and create new search criteria. Or, in the Find tab, you can click the right-pointing arrow next to the Find What box (see Figure 10-9) to display an extensive set of options for refining exactly what you want to locate.

Figure 10-9 You can search for specific attributes.

> **Aha!**   Edit Text Files
>
> You can import HTML, XML or other code files into FrontPage to edit with the typing tools described in this chapter. Pasting code into the Code pane now works the way a code developer would expect. The Code pane treats the pasted text as code, rather than body text.

See Also

See Chapter 3, "Maximizing Template and Wizard Options," for details on how to create Web page templates with FrontPage.

Speed Up Reusable Code with Code Snippets

When you're developing Web sites that contain dozens of pages, it's likely that many of those pages need to contain similar elements. After all, the consistent use of logos or navigation bars helps establish a corporate Web site's identity, and also makes it more usable. You don't want to have to type the code over and over. You could copy and paste the code from page to page, but you don't have to, because FrontPage goes a step beyond the clipboard. It makes reusable chunks of code available within the FrontPage interface itself in the form of *code snippets*.

Code snippets are chunks of frequently-used code that may need to appear in virtually every Web page. They can be chunks of HTML, CSS, JavaScript, or the other languages that FrontPage supports. You can also define your own snippets, or modify existing snippets, as described in Chapter 1, "Introducing Microsoft Office FrontPage 2003."

To add a code snippet to the code for the current page, position the cursor where you want the snippet to appear. You view FrontPage's predefined code snippets, shown in Figure 10-10, by pressing Ctrl+Enter. (A complete list of predefined snippets appears in Table 1-1 in Chapter 1.) Double-click a snippet from the list (or click a snippet and press Enter), and it is added to your code.

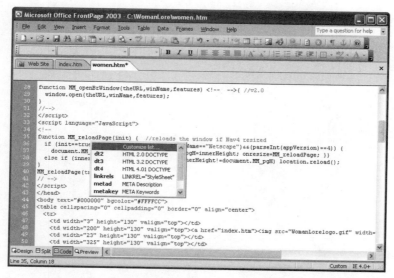

Figure 10-10 Add common code snippets while you type or edit your code.

Editing Faster with the Quick Tag Tools

In Chapter 1, "Introducing Microsoft Office FrontPage 2003," you got an overview of some of FrontPage's Quick Tag Tools (the Quick Tag Selector and Quick Tag Editor) that let you use Design View and Code View together to edit Web page content. Now you'll put these tools together in a way that streamlines your Web page code editing, while ensuring the accuracy that keeps everything on your page working right.

Speedier Editing with the Quick Tag Selector

First, display the Quick Tag Selector by choosing View, Quick Tag Selector. In Design View, position the cursor at the location on the currentWeb page where you want to edit text. Suppose you have a block of text that is flush-left, and you want it to be centered. The text, as shown in Figure 10-10, is formatted with the command:

<p class=MsoNormal>

When you pass your mouse pointer over this tag in the Quick Tag Selector, a drop-down arrow appears. Click this arrow and choose Tag Properties from the Quick Tag Editor list. When the Paragraph dialog box appears, choose Center from the Alignment drop-down list. The tag is automatically changed to the following:

<p class=MsoNormal align="center">

That's only one way to edit the tag by starting with the Quick Tag Selector. You can also use the Quick Tag Editor, as described in the next section.

> **Aha!** Match the Content to the Code
>
> When you pass your mouse pointer over the tags in the Quick Tag Selector, corresponding parts of the Web page displayed beneath it are highlighted. For example, if you're viewing a table and you pass your mouse over the <td> tag in the Quick Tag Selector, the corresponding table cell is highlighted, so you can be sure which part of the Web page you're editing.

Edit Code in Design View with the Quick Tag Editor

The Quick Tag Editor adds a new level of interactivity between the Design View for a Web page and its underlying code. Using the Quick Tag editor, you can insert or edit the tags in your document directly in the Design pane. You can select the text and edit the tags that surround it, wrap it in a new tag, insert new HTML, or remove a tag. As you learned in the preceding section, you can quickly edit tags by clicking the down arrow next to a tag displayed in the Quick Tag Selector, then choosing an option from the shortcut menu, as shown in Figure 10-11.

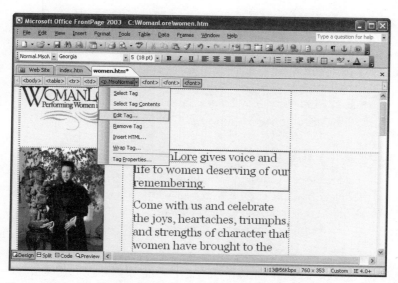

Figure 10-11   The Quick Tag Selector enables you to edit tags directly while still in Design View.

By selecting Edit Tag from the Quick Tag Selector's shortcut menu (as shown in Figure 10-11), you open the Quick Tag Editor, which enables you to edit tags quickly without having to open Code View. The drop-down menu on the left side of the Quick Tag Editor lets you perform three functions:

- **Edit Tag**   The tag appears in the box in the center of the Quick Tag Editor, where you can change it manually.

- **Wrap Tag**   Enter the tag within which you want to wrap the selected tag.

- **Insert New HTML**   Enter new HTML in the Quick Tag Editor box, without ever having to switch to Code or Split View.

When you're done making changes, click the green checkmark near the right-hand edge of the Quick Tag Editor (see Figure 10-12), to accept the changes and close the Quick Tag Editor.

Figure 10-12   The Quick Tag Editor lets you add or edit HTML, or wrap an HTML tag within another one.

Ensure Functionality by Cleaning Up Your HTML

If you have used FrontPage in the past, you may be aware that older versions of the software created HTML code that was difficult to scan, and contained plenty of unnecessary commands when you made changes to a page in Design View. You no longer have to worry about what constitutes "clean" HTML, or whether your HTML will be accepted by all browsers. FrontPage now cleans up the HTML that is automatically generated when you craft a page in Design View, or that you import from a Word file. You also have the ability to clean up your code, whether it's on the local version of your site or on a remote Web server. You can even identify individual tags, such as comments, attributes, or HTML white space, and have FrontPage clean it with just a few mouse clicks.

Keeping Your Local HTML Clean for Your Co-workers

Before you publish your Web site (a process described in Chapter 17, "Publishing Your Web Site"), it's a good idea to remove any unnecessary or unorthodox HTML commands that may have been introduced by other editors, or by programs like Microsoft Word, which may generate their own HTML. To clean up the HTML on the local version of your site (the files you maintain on your own computer, as opposed to the remote Web server), follow these steps:

1 Choose File, Save to save your changes on all the pages you have open in the FrontPage window.

2 Choose Tools, Optimize HTML.

3 In the Optimize HTML dialog box, select the HTML elements you want to remove, and click to deselect any that you want to maintain.

4 Click OK.

You might have to wait a minute or two as FrontPage automatically cleans up your code.

Synchronizing Your Code Edits on Your Remote Site

If you have cleaned up the HTML on the local version of your site, but you haven't cleaned up the published version on your Web server, don't worry. You don't need to re-publish all of your newly-optimized pages. Just tell FrontPage to clean up the remote version of your site by choosing View, Remote Web Site to switch to Remote Web Site View. Click Optimize Remote HTML. In the Optimize HTML dialog box, check the elements you want removed, then click OK.

> **Aha!**   Clean Up Your HTML Consistently
>
> Click Set As Default in the Optimize HTML dialog box to apply your HTML clean-up settings to your site whenever you publish it.

Fast Wrap-Up

- Code View includes features that make viewing and editing Web page code easier, including line numbers, color coding, and automatic indentation.

- FrontPage's new Split View lets you see both Design View and Code View at the same time; as you scroll through one view of a page, the other changes accordingly.

- Code IntelliSense provides useful tools for learning code and entering code accurately, such as List Members and Complete Word.

- Find And Replace lets you search for HTML tags, and set up rules so you can make repeated searches.

- Code Snippets help you save time by adding chunks of frequently used code that are predefined, or that you create yourself.

- The Quick Tag Selector and Quick Tag Editor let you view and edit HTML while you are still in Design View.

- FrontPage enables you to clean up unnecessary white space, or other HTML elements, both on the local and remote versions of a Web site.

Advanced Layout with Tables and Layers

11

10-Second Summary

- ■ Take control of your page's design with Layout Tables.
- ■ Duplicate precise graphic designs with tracing images.
- ■ Combine page elements in new ways with layers.
- ■ Automatically detect and edit layout tables.
- ■ Ensure that your layout works in a designated browser size.
- ■ Preview your page in multiple browsers for maximum visibility.

In a business environment, you are often called upon to duplicate a printed layout, or to create layouts that have to fulfill a complex set of requirements. Yet, it's often difficult to control the look of Web pages with great precision. Designers who are used to working in the field of traditional graphic arts are used to being able to position photos, headings, and other elements wherever they feel it suits the overall look of the finished page. You have to make "old school" graphic designers understand that, on the Web, pages appear differently depending on the viewer's browser, monitor, or operating system. Some colors, borders, and fonts don't appear at all, because the browser being used to display a page doesn't support them. But by using Microsoft Office FrontPage 2003's new design tools, including table layouts and layers, you quickly and easily gain a new level of control over the design of a Web page.

Enterprising Webmasters like you can use tables to satisfy the requirements of your company's managers and graphic designers. You can create tables that align photos and text, and add white space or spot color where needed. Layers enable you to move content around on the page dynamically, without having to fall into rows or columns. Once you have arranged your page's contents just the way you want, FrontPage gives you the ability to preview it in different browsers, and at different sizes, so you can ensure that the widest range of customers or business partners will be able to see your finished Web site just the way your company wants it to appear.

Crafting Page Design with Layout Tables

As you learned in Chapter 9, "Working with Tables," tables consist of rows and columns. Each row or column contains one or more cells. Each cell, in turn, has its own border, as well as the table itself. By default, the table borders are visible. However, by "turning off" table border display, your visitor sees only the text and images you've placed within the table cells, not the borders. The table thus becomes a tool for designing an entire Web page. The heightened level of control lets you precisely position elements in a way that helps boost your business's identity.

Templates Are for Tables Too!

If you want a jump-start in using tables for page layout, shop through FrontPage's page templates. Choose File, New to open the New task pane. Under the heading New Web Site, click More Web Site Templates. In the General tab, click Personal Web Site. When the Web site has been created, double-click index.htm. This page uses a table for layout (see Figure 11-1). You can use such a table-based template as a starting point for your own page, saving time in brainstorming layouts and in starting to execute them, too.

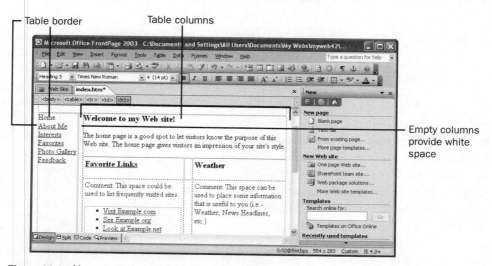

Figure 11-1   You can use a template as a starting point for creating a layout table.

Aha!   Editing Tables Is a Snap

Because borders aren't visible in a browser window, it's not always obvious whether a template, or other Web page you're viewing, was designed using tables. FrontPage makes it easy to edit tables, however, because borders are always visible in Page View. The dashed lines indicate that the table has been broken into cells (see Figure 11-1). You can also configure FrontPage to automatically activate table layout tools, if it opens a page that uses tables for layout, as described in "Perform Layout Detection" later in this chapter.

Creating Your Own Layout Table

FrontPage gives you several options for creating layout tables. If you love to draw and miss using pencil and paper to design pages, you'll love FrontPage's table pencil for instantly drawing tables (see "Going Back to the Drawing Board with Layout Tables" later in this chapter). You can insert a table from scratch using the Table menu, too. On the other hand, if you haven't used Web page tables very often, and you want a jump-start to create an effective layout quickly, the quickest and easiest way to use a table for page layout is by using the Layout And Tables task pane to insert a layout table.

Conveying a Message with a Pre-designed Layout Table

FrontPage gives you a selection of pre-formatted table layouts that provide you with a head start on your design. These table layouts enable you to choose and preview tables that have different background colors assigned to them. The type fonts also provide visual interest by conveying a particular impression (businesslike, high-tech, and so on). To insert a layout table and preview the available layouts, use the Layout Tables And Cells task pane. Just follow these steps:

1 Switch to Design View, if necessary, by clicking the Design button.

2 Position the cursor at the spot in the current Web page where you want the table to appear. If you want the layout table to control the design of an entire page, open a new blank page in Design View by clicking the Create A New Normal Page button.

3 Select Table, Layout Tables And Cells.

4 When the Layout Tables And Cells task pane appears, scroll down to the Table Layout section (see Figure 11-2).

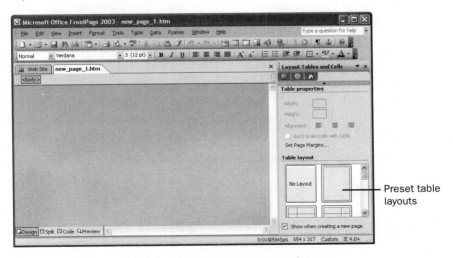

Figure 11-2 Choose a predetermined layout table template.

5 When the layout table templates appear, scroll through the miniature layout table templates.

6 Click a template to add it to the current page .

Controlling Layout by Creating a Table from Scratch

Of course, you don't need to use one of the pre-designed layout tables in order to design a Web page with a table. You might need to emulate the layout of your annual report or company newsletter, for instance, and you don't see a pre-designed layout table that does the trick. In that case, you can always create your own layout table from scratch by using aspects of the FrontPage interface you already started to use in Chapter 9, "Working with Tables." It's a good choice if you aren't comfortable with the table pencil icon for drawing tables (described in the following section), or if you want complete control over the arrangement of your table. Here's all you need to do:

1 Select Table, Insert, Table.

2 When the Insert Table dialog box appears (see Figure 11-3), select the option next to the Enable Layout Tools for this table.

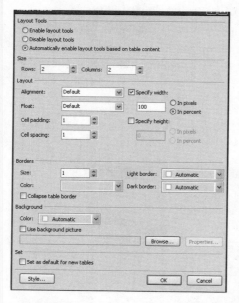

Figure 11-3 The Insert Table dialog box lets you create a table and activate layout tools.

3 In the Borders section of Insert Table, change the size to 0.

4 Set the number of rows and columns for your table, and specify other layout options such as the alignment of cell contents.

5 Click OK. The table appears in Page View.

Aha!   Add Extra White Space

If you want to create a layout table to design a Web page, you should not only set borders to zero, but you may also want to create columns or rows that are empty, except for a blank space. This creates space between columns that do contain content. You can also increase the amount of cell padding (the space between a cell's contents and its border) or cell spacing (the space between cells) in Table Properties to create more space between the contents of adjacent cells.

Going Back to the Drawing Board with Layout Tables

FrontPage gives you a way to create tables that's interactive and truly has a "hands-on" feel—you can draw tables directly in Design View by dragging a table pencil icon across the screen. One advantage of drawing a table is speed: you move your mouse a few times, and you have an instant layout table. Another is that tables and cells you draw with the table pencil have their border width set to zero automatically. Plus, it's fun to see the table appear as you draw it. You can draw a table or cell from one of two starting points, which are both depicted in Figure 11-4:

■ From the Layout Tables And Cells task pane, which appears when you select Table, Layout Tables And Cells.

■ From the drawing-specific Tables toolbar, which appears when you choose Table, Draw Table, or when you choose View, Toolbars, Tables.

In either case, FrontPage displays two table drawing tools. Click Draw Layout Table, then drag within Page View to create a new table. Click Draw Layout Cell, then drag within Page View to draw an individual cell within a table.

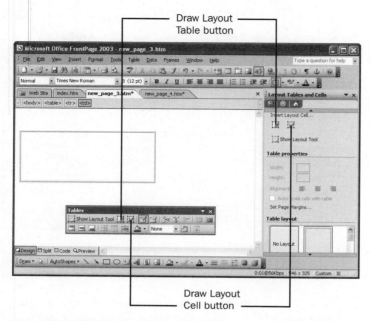

Figure 11-4   FrontPage's table drawing tools are found in the task pane or in the Tables toolbar.

Aha!   Sketch Your Table on Paper

Consider drawing a sketch on paper that indicates how you want your table to look before you start creating it from scratch. It's a good idea to sketch out on paper how you want your finished Web page to look. You'll know exactly how many rows and columns you'll need before you start filling in the table specifications in the Insert Table dialog box.

Once the Draw Layout Table and Draw Layout Cell buttons are visible, drawing a table is easy—so easy that it's worth trying it out a few times so you can get the dimensions just the way you want them. Let's say you want to create a layout table with two columns and one row, which is a common choice for designing a Web page. Follow these steps:

1 Switch to Design View, if necessary. Then click Draw Layout Table, in either the task pane or the Tables toolbar.

2   Pass your mouse pointer over Page View. Notice that the pointer turns into a pencil icon after you click on either Draw Layout Table or Draw Layout Cell. Click in Page View, hold down your mouse button, and drag down to the right. Release the mouse button, and a table with a green border around it is created (see Figure 11-5).

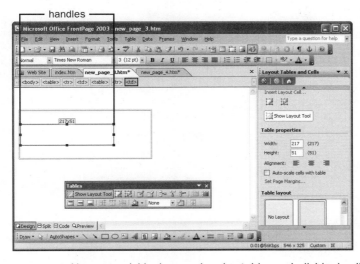

Figure 11-5 You can quickly draw and resize tables or individual cells.

3   Notice that, after you draw a table, four resize handles appear at the corners. Click and drag any of these handles in order to resize the table, in case you didn't draw it exactly right the first time.

4   Click Draw Layout Cell.

5   Click in the upper left-hand corner of the table you just drew. Drag down and to the right to draw a cell.

6   Release the mouse button. The cell appears outlined in color, with a white background (see Figure 11-6 on the following page). If you need to resize the cell, click and drag one of its handles.

7   Repeat steps 5 and 6 until you have drawn all of the cells you need.

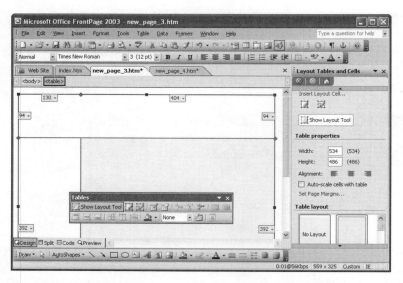

Figure 11-6 You can draw a layout cell within a table you have drawn.

You can now click within each of the cells you have drawn and insert text, images, and other contents as necessary.

> **Note**   If you click Draw Layout Cell before you have drawn a table, FrontPage automatically creates a table to enclose the cell that you draw.

Adapting to Content Changes by Adjusting Cells

Whether you draw or insert individual table cells, you may not always get it right the first time. One of your co-workers changes the size of your corporate logo, or an editor adds a few critical words. Not to worry: you can accommodate the changes by adjusting the cell properties with controls in the Layout Tables And Cells task pane. Follow these steps:

1   Make sure you are in Design View and that the Layout Tables And Cells task pane is visible.

2   Click the cell in the layout to highlight its border and resize handles.

3   Click Cell Formatting... in the task tane to display the dimensions and characteristics of the selected cells. The data appears under the heading Borders And Dimensions in the task pane (see Figure 11-7).

4   Change the data in the Size and Alignment boxes to adjust the cell. You can also click and drag any of the cell handles to resize the cell; the data in the Size And Alignment section of the task pane changes accordingly.

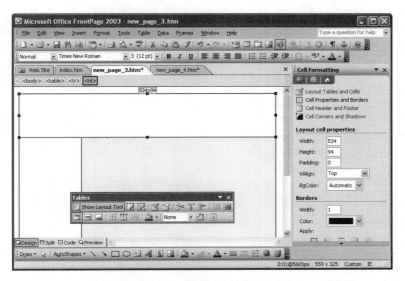

Figure 11-7 You can change cell characteristics from the task pane or by dragging cell handles.

Adding a Spacer

White space is essential in corporate communications. The empty areas on a page direct the viewer's eye to important words or images. White space is impossible to add on a Web page unless you add a spacer.

Lingo   A *spacer* is a table column or row, or a blank image—an image file, usually saved in GIF format—that has no contents. Spacers are commonly used by Web designers to add extra space between parts of a table, or parts of a Web page. Because spacer images, when created by graphics programs, can be assigned a specific height or width in pixels, they can give designers a great deal of control over the look of a page, especially one that has been designed using tables.

If you want to add just a few points or pixels of space, you can adjust cell spacing or cell padding. But to add large amounts of space, such as a quarter or half an inch, consider adding an extra column or row to the table as a spacer. FrontPage gives you the option to automatically add a spacer as part of its layout table tools, as described in the next section.

Ensuring Table Visibility by Autostretching

As you already know, the width of a table, or the cells within it, can be specified as either a fixed measurement, such as a definite number of pixels, or as a percentage of the width of the page or the table itself. Tables often need to be a constant width. One or more of the cells may contain a graphic image, such as a paid advertisement, that has to be displayed at the correct size. But using tables that have a fixed width is risky. Anyone who views the page that contains the table can resize his or her Web browser so that it's narrower than the table. As a result, the table's contents aren't completely visible, and the table itself may become distorted.

FrontPage's Autostretching feature enables you to change a table from fixed to variable width. Autostretching is the process of inserting a spacer image along either the bottom row, or rightmost column of a table. This last column or row is of variable, rather than fixed, width. Thus, it can change size, depending on the size of the browser window. To autostretch a table, follow these steps:

1   Create a layout table, either by drawing it or by using the Layout Tables And Cells task pane, as described earlier in this chapter.

2   Click Show Layout Tool in the Tables toolbar to display the layout tools. Click the size box next to the row or column where you want to add the spacer image, and choose Use Column (or Row) Spacer Image to add the spacer.

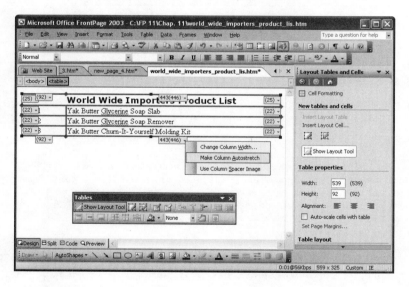

As you can see in the image above, the column on the right contains a small amount of text (a product number), and is wider than it needs to be. The column on the right needs to stretch to accommodate a narrow browser window. To make the column autostretch, click the size box for one of the cells in the column, and choose Make Column Autostretch from the short-cut menu. A new row containing two new columns appears at the bottom of the table. The columns aren't easy to see, because they are only three pixels in height (you can see this if you click carefully on the new column on the left, which contains a spacer image).

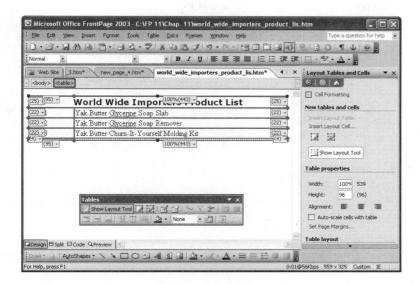

The column on the left has shrunk to fit the available text. If the viewer narrows his or her browser window, the table will stretch accordingly so all of the contents remain visible (see Figure 11-8).

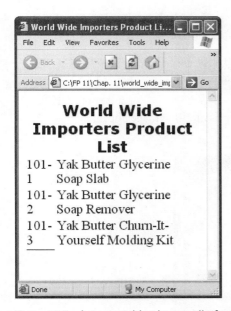

Figure 11-8 Autostretching keeps all of a table's contents visible, regardless of the browser window size.

Duplicating Precise Layouts with a Tracing Image

Suppose you need to duplicate the printed page's layout on the Web, or the layout of another Web page that's especially complicated. For layouts that are complex and need to be duplicated with precision, FrontPage gives you a powerful new tool. Now you can load an image of the layout you want to copy, and keep that image visible in the background while you reconstruct a new Web page "on top" of it. Such a procedure is called *image tracing*. A tracing image appears in the background of FrontPage's Display View, and you create the new page by manipulating elements in the foreground. The tracing image is only used during the Web page creation process, as a model you follow when working on a page. It doesn't show up in the final Web page. When you're finished, the Web page should represent a close approximation of the original design you were attempting to duplicate. Layout tools such as layout tables and layers (described in this chapter), should enable you to duplicate the design fairly closely.

Suppose you have an image that you want to "trace" in order to duplicate its layout. Microsoft's own home page provides a good example, because it uses a table layout with a complex arrangement of rows and columns, and embedded photos. The following steps assume that you have captured an image of the home page and saved it in one of the Web page formats supported by FrontPage (GIF, JPEG, or PNG):

1 Open a new blank Web page in Design View.

2 Select View, Tracing Image, Configure.

3 In the Image Tracing dialog box, either enter the path that points to the image in the File Name box, or click Browse and locate the file on your hard disk.

4 Move the Opacity slider to the left (say, to 30%) to reduce the opacity of the tracing image. The lower the Opacity setting, the fainter the image appears in the background.

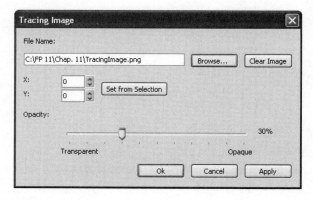

5 Click OK.

6 You can now use the Draw Table tool to create a table, as well as individual cells within it. Click View, Toolbars, Tables to display the Tables toolbar. Then click Draw Table.

7 Click and drag the table pencil over the appropriate segments of the Web page to duplicate the table cells, as shown in Figure 11-9.

Figure 11-9 Draw table cells and layers over the tracing image to duplicate the layout.

8 When your layout is complete and you no longer need the tracing image as a model, select View, Tracing Image, Configure. In the Tracing Image dialog box, click Clear Image, then click OK.

You'll notice that, if your tracing image extends to the edges of FrontPage's Design View, you won't be able to draw out to the edges. If that's the case, you can adjust the positioning of the tracing image within Design View: Select View, Tracing Image, Configure. Click the up or down arrows next to X and Y to move the X and Y coordinates of the tracing image. X moves the image from side to side, and Y moves the image up and down. Click Apply to adjust the image without closing theTracing Image dialog box, so you can continue to make adjustments if you need to.

> **Note**   The image you use for tracing can be in GIF, JPEG, PNG, TIFF, or BMP format. To obtain a tracing image, you can scan a printed booklet and save it in one of these formats. You can also use a graphics program to capture an image of a Web page and save it as a tracing image.

Understanding Layers

Tables give designers great control over the design of Web pages by enabling text and images to be positioned within rows, columns, and cells. But the contents of a cell cannot overlap one another, or extend to the edge of a table border. For the ultimate in control over Web page contents, you can use FrontPage to create layers.

A layer is a container that can enclose text, images, or other Web page contents. Layers are often called *dynamic* or *design-time*, because you can move them around freely on the page by simply clicking and dragging them. A layer can overlap another layer, or can be nested within another layer.

> **Caution**   Layers are flexible and advanced tools, but they have limitations. Some viewers who connect to pages that contain layers, and who have older browsers (Netscape Navigator 4 or earlier, or Microsoft Internet Explorer 4 or earlier) won't see anything at all, because those older browsers don't support layers. In addition, even if viewers have up-to-date browsers, don't expect pages that have been designed using layers to appear exactly the same from browser to browser, or from one operating system to another. You can alleviate these problems by converting layers to tables as described later in this chapter.

Working with Layers

Once you have worked with layout tables and cells as described earlier in this chapter, you'll have no problem working with FrontPage's layers. Layers give you the ultimate control over a Web page's contents, and traditional print designers love them. Each layer, in fact, appears like an individual table cell, with a box that displays the number of the layer on the page, and resize handles that you can click and drag to make the layer any size you want (see Figure 11-10). In addition, a list of all layers on the current page is displayed in the Layers task pane.

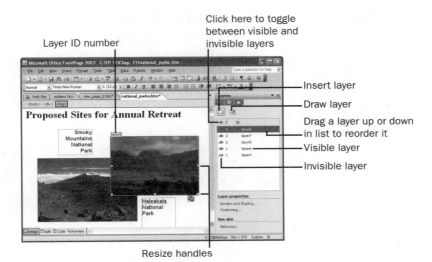

Figure 11-10   Layers give you maximum control over positioning of images and other Web page elements.

Once you have created a layer, click to position the cursor within it. You can then type text directly within the layer, insert an image by choosing Insert, Image, or paste text or an image within the layer. The layer's dimensions change automatically to accommodate the contents you add to it.

Streamlining the Process of Creating Layers

Designers in an office don't all work the same way. Some like to draw by hand, while others prefer to let computer software do the work. When you are ready to work with layers, you can add them to the current page in either of these two ways:

- Choose Insert, Layer to instantly add a layer to your page.

- Choose Format, Layers to display the Layers task pane, then click either Insert Layer, or Draw Layer. Insert Layer instantly inserts a layer on the current page; Draw Layer enables you to draw a layer directly on the page as you might a table or a cell.

When you are working on a Web page that contains one or more layers, you control whether or not they are visible, and which ones appear in front of others, by working with the controls in the Layers task pane. Layers in the panel are listed in "stacking order," whether they are actually stacked atop one another or not. Layer 1 is treated as being at the top of the stack, and the other layers follow beneath it. Such a list helps you keep track of, or select, layers in complicated layouts that contain multiple layers—some of the layers might be difficult to see because they are hidden beneath others. (It also provides you with a "roadmap" of the layers on a page that one of your colleagues has constructed and that you are assigned to revise.) You can alter the order of a layer in one of two ways:

- Click a layer in the Layers task pane list and drag it up or down to another position in the list.

- Click the layer's ID number in the Z column, and type a different number to move the layer higher or lower in the order.

You can change the visibility of all layers at once, by clicking on the winking eye icon at the top of the list. If the eye is "shut," all layers are invisible when the Web page is viewed in a browser. You can also click on a layer's eye icon to toggle between making it visible or invisible.

Positioning Layers

Once you have inserted a layer, you can move it anywhere you want on the Web page you're creating. This is the big advantage of using layers—you can click their ID number box and move them around the page with your mouse wherever you want, regardless of whether you are crossing table cells, horizontal rules, or images beneath them.

Often, though, you need to position layers with great precision in order to make them align with other elements on the page. You can precisely locate a layer by first clicking its border to select it, then clicking Positioning in the Layers Panel. The Position dialog box lets you control not only the location of the layer on the page, but also its size, and the way it interacts with any other Web page contents around it (see Figure 11-11).

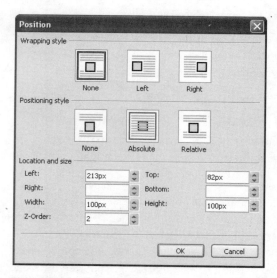

Figure 11-11   Use this dialog box to control position, size, and other features of layers.

> **Note** If the layers panel is not yet visible, just double-click a currently visible layer to open it.

In the Location And Size section of the Position dialog box, Left refers to the number of pixels from the left margin of the Web page you are working on; Top refers to the number of pixels from the top of the page, and so on. Z-Order refers to the selected layer's stacking order on the page. By carefully entering pixel values in the appropriate boxes, you can stack layers atop one another with 12 pixels of overlap, for example.

> **Note** By default, layer measurements are expressed in pixels, but you can change this if you're used to working with other units of measurement, such as inches or centimeters. Select Tools, Page Options, and click the Ruler And Grid tab. Then, choose an option from the Ruler And Grid Units drop-down list. You can choose Pixels, Inches, Centimeters, or Points. Table 11-1 compares the various measurement units.

Table 11-1 Web Page Measurement Units

Measurement	Abbreviation	Description
Pixels	Px	Used in computer graphics; one inch contains about 72 pixels
Inches	In	Common unit of measurement in the U.S.
Centimeters	Cm	One inch equals 2.54 centimeters
Points	Pt	Used in printing and graphic design; one inch contains 72 points

> **Note** Tables and layers share common characteristics: they can contain text and images; they can be positioned with precision; they can have their own background colors; and they can be used to control the design of Web pages. Layers and tables can be combined in order to create complex layouts.

Performing Layout Detection

You're likely to be called upon to edit any number of Web pages in the course of work or personal Web development. Many of those pages will use tables, which are increasingly popular tools for Web page layout. Some of those pages will have used FrontPage's layout tables feature, but many will have been created by more conventional means—and if someone else designed the page, you might not be sure what to expect. You can configure FrontPage to automatically detect any layout tables and automatically "turn on" layout table controls. To turn on layout detection, follow these steps:

1 Switch to Design View, if necessary, and position the cursor within the table. Then select Table, Table Properties, Table.

2 In the Table Properties dialog box, check one of the following:

- Select Enable Layout tools, in order to work with the layout table and cell controls for the currently selected table.

- Select Disable Layout tools, in order to "turn off" layout table and cell controls for the currently selected table.

- Select Automatically Enable Layout tool based on table contents, if you want FrontPage to enable any layout table controls for this table when you open the current Web page.

3 Click OK.

When you click on the table border to begin working on it, the layout tools will appear. Otherwise, they won't appear automatically when you click the table border.

> **Note**   The preceding steps only apply to the currently selected table—unless you select Set As Default for new tables in the Table Properties box. This enables you to turn on automatic table layout detection for any new tables you create.

Making Everything Visible by Targeting to Browser Size

You learned in the section on Autostretching that the size of the viewer's browser window has a bearing on whether or not all the flashy design elements you use to create a page, such as layout tables and layers, appear in their entirety in a browser window. Making sure your page will appear optimally in specific browser sizes is also a good idea for other reasons. Even though 19-inch and 21-inch monitors are becoming more affordable, you can't guarantee that all of the visitors to your Web site will have them. You should always assume that most of your visitors will have smaller monitors, with 17-inch, or even 15-inch screens. Also, while some of your viewers will have their monitors set to 800 × 600 screen resolution, others will be working at different resolutions.

FrontPage has the ability to target a Web page to a specific browser window size, or a specific screen resolution. This lets you evaluate how your site will look in different combinations of browsers and resolutions. To test a specific combination, click View, Page Size, and choose a resolution from the submenu that appears (see Figure 11-12).

Figure 11-12   Preview your page in different browser sizes and resolutions.

Aha!   Tables Versus Layers: Not an Either-Or Decision

You can add a new resolution or browser size to the submenu by choosing View, Page Size, Modify Page Sizes. When the Modify Page Sizes dialog box appears, click Add to add a new set of options.

Checking Your Layout by Previewing in Multiple Browsers

It's always a good idea to test a Web page in at least two browsers (if not more), because different browsers can display certain Web content very differently. To preview your page quickly in the default browser, select File, Preview In Browser, and choose a browser option from the submenu that appears.

Note   The browsers listed in the submenu are the ones you have currently installed on your computer, so you need to have two or more browsers installed in order to preview the page in two or more browsers.

Since you're pretty much certain to be checking your page in two or more browsers, FrontPage gives you a time-saver by including multiple browser options in the Preview in Browser submenu. FrontPage will prompt you to save your changes, if necessary. It will then launch Internet Explorer and the other browsers that are included in its browser list. Be sure to verify and edit the browser list before you choose one of the multiple browser options; otherwise, you'll spend unnecessary time and computer resources opening one browser program after another.

Fast Wrap-Up

- Layout tables enable Web designers to arrange an entire page's contents using tables.

- Layout tools include the ability to draw tables and table cells using an interactive table pencil tool.

- A spacer GIF image provides extra white space in layout tables.

- Autostretching enables a table to change width or depth along with the current browser window size, so that viewers have to scroll as little as possible to view all of the table's contents.

- FrontPage enables you to view a tracing image in the background of the Web page you are creating, so that you can duplicate a layout.

- Layers are interactive containers for text and images that can be moved freely around a Web page, and even stacked atop one another.

- FrontPage makes it easy to test your page, to make sure it appears optimally in multiple browser window sizes and screen resolutions.

Adding Interactivity with Frames

12

10-Second Summary

- Add interactivity to your Web site by creating framesets
- Save time by using predefined frame templates
- Reach all viewers by adding No Frames content
- Customize framesets to match your site's organization
- Target frames to respond to links in other frames
- Embed Web page content within an inline frame

Corporate Web sites that have been broken into multiple subwebs and contain many layers of Web pages can easily get complex, creating the need for a way of navigating the whole site easily. Frames provide a design team with one option for making complex business Web sites easier to navigate, while adding graphic interest and interactivity. Microsoft Office FrontPage 2003 enables you to easily divide a single Web page into two or more frames, each of which has its own URL. By dividing Web pages into frames, you can display multiple Web pages within a single Web page.

Frames are ideal for many business applications. Some frames are *static*—with content (such as your company's logo or a banner ad) that remains on screen as long as the viewer is on your site. Others are *dynamic*—their content changes when the viewer clicks on links contained in other frames. This chapter examines the various ways in which FrontPage makes frames easy to arrange and organize—which, in turn, makes your Web sites more usable.

> **Lingo** A *frame* is a subdivision of a Web page. Each frame contains a Web page and has its own properties, such as scrollbars and resizable borders. A *frameset* is a set of frames—the frameset page contains instructions that tell a browser how to present the rows and columns within the frameset and what properties (such as scrollbars) to display with each frame.

Avoiding Trouble by Understanding Frames' Bad Reputation

It might seem strange to begin a chapter about frames by first mentioning why many people dislike them. Remember the title of this book? In order to use FrontPage faster and smarter than ever before, you have to know the pros and cons of using all of its features. Frames have many advantages, but one big downside is their bad "rep." You don't want to look bad in the eyes of your customers or business colleagues by creating poorly designed frames-based Web pages. You should at least know why frames have a bad reputation, and how you can avoid the aspects of frames that irritate many Web surfers. Frames get criticized for many reasons. For one thing, they are frequently misused. What's the problem with frames, you ask? Here are some reasons:

- **Frames are easily misused**   Designers tend to put too many frames onto a single page. This confuses viewers, who lose track of where they clicked and what was supposed to change in response.

- **Frames aren't always supported**   Some older browsers don't support frames. While a small minority of viewers have such old browsers, they force the designer to come up with an alternate "no frames" layout for the page. Otherwise, non-frames browsers will display nothing at all.

- **Bookmarking can be difficult**   If a frames layout is not prepared correctly, visitors won't be able to bookmark a page that is contained within a frame—and won't be able to easily revisit your site in the future.

There's another, subtler reason why designers and Web surfers alike tend to look down on Web sites that are designed with frames. Frames aren't considered as elegant or trendy as other interactive tools, such as layers or tables. A Web site that is obviously set up using frames is suspect because it seems "clunky" and untrendy. But it doesn't actually need to be that way, especially if you use FrontPage to do a professional job of it.

> **Note**   There's an entire Web site called Frames Free! that's devoted to making frames obsolete. Before you prepare a frames layout yourself, it's a good idea to review what this site says about how *not* to use frames. Find out more at *http://www.noframes.org*.

Speeding Up Frame Design with Templates

Frames are one of those Web page features that are easier to understand when you actually see them and start working with them, rather than simply reading about them. One smart way to use frames is to start with a standard template instead of trying to create your own frames design from scratch. By setting up a frames structure for you, FrontPage lets you focus on the content you want to create. The easiest way to get started with frames is to open one of Front Page's predefined templates. Just follow these steps:

1 Choose File, New.

2 In the New Task Pane, under New Page, click More Page Templates.

3 When the Page Templates dialog box appears, click Frames Pages.

4 Click one of the layouts to select it, and read the description that appears on the right-hand side of the Page Template dialog box. (For this example, click Banner And Contents, a common frames arrangement shown in Figure 12-1.)

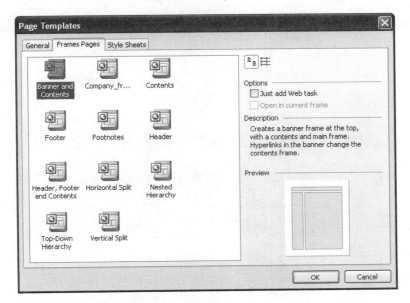

Figure 12-1 Speed up frames creation by choosing a predesigned template.

5 Click OK to open the layout in the FrontPage window (see Figure 12-2).

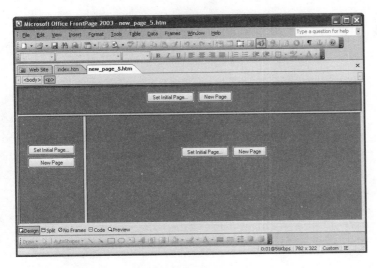

Figure 12-2 A frames template first appears with empty frames for you to fill with content.

When you insert a frames template, you might be confused as to what you're actually looking at. It appears as if you're viewing a single Web page that has been divided into three separate sections, each with its own borders. What you're actually looking at is a Web page that consists of a set of frames—a *frameset*. A set of frames contains a different set of elements than a single non-frames Web page, but the elements are ones that you're probably familiar with. There are many different kinds of possible frames layouts, but they all contain the standard elements shown in Figure 12-3.

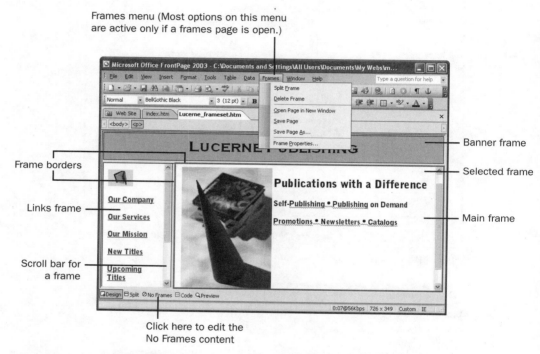

Figure 12-3   FrontPage gives you a Frames menu and other interactive tools for adjusting frames layouts.

Each frame can (and should) contain its own distinct Web page, but initially, it's empty. You need to insert Web pages into each of those empty frames, as described in the following section.

Aha!   Sketch Out Your Frames Beforehand

Before you choose a template, try sketching out your frames on paper. Determine what kind of content each frame should contain. When you browse through the templates, you'll be more likely to pick one that's just right for your site.

Understanding Frameset Structure: Rows and Columns

Rows are horizontal divisions of a frameset, and columns are vertical divisions. The example in Figure 12-2 contains two rows. The row at the top contains only one column; the row at the bottom of the page contains two.

Figure 12-4 shows some other variations on rows and columns that are available in FrontPage's frames templates:

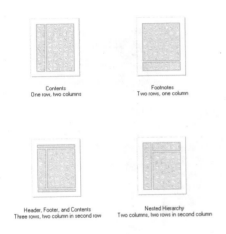

Contents
One row, two columns

Footnotes
Two rows, one column

Header, Footer, and Contents
Three rows, two column in second row

Nested Hierarchy
Two columns, two rows in second column

Figure 12-4   Framesets are divided into rows and columns.

Why is it important to know about rows and columns? If you need to make changes to a frameset, you need to understand what parts can be split into multiple frames. Understanding a frameset's structure also helps you sketch out frames, so that you can get an idea of what kind of arrangement best suits the needs of your business Web site.

Adding Pages to Frames

Once you create a set of empty frames, you need to fill each one with a Web page. While the need to create three separate Web pages for a set of three frames might seem like a lot of work, FrontPage streamlines the process considerably. Follow these steps for each frame in your frameset:

1 Click the New Page button in the frame you want to work on.

2 When the New Page and Set Initial Page buttons disappear, and your frame's background turns to white, edit the page as you would any other, adding text by typing, and adding images or other content with FrontPage's Insert menu.

3 When you're done editing, click New Page in the next frame in your frameset to begin editing it.

Once you have finished editing, you should save your changes, as described in the following section.

> **Aha!**   Open a Frame for Easier Editing
>
> Some frames are so small that they're difficult to edit. Click in the frame you're working on to select it, then choose Frames, Open Page in New Window. The frame opens in a new, bigger window so you can edit it more easily.

See Also You don't always have to add a complete set of frames using templates. You can add an inline frame at any time to an existing Web page; see the section on inline frames later in this chapter.

Saving Framesets to Preserve Your Page Layout

You can save a Web page that's inside a frame at any time. But the first time you choose File, Save when you're working on a frameset, you're working on a page that has been divided into frames—you'll notice two options under the File menu. Both options allow you to save the Web page you are currently editing, as well as the other frames in the same frameset. Just follow these steps:

1   Choose File, Save or File, Save All.

2   The Save As dialog box appears. The frame you have currently highlighted is selected, to indicate which frame's contents you are about to save (see Figure 12-5).

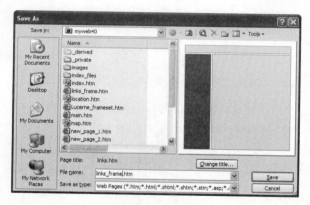

Figure 12-5 Save As highlights the current frame, so you know which one you're saving.

> **Note**   File, Save and File, Save All perform the same way when you're saving a frames layout for the first time: FrontPage prompts you to save all pages in the current frameset, one after another.

3   Assign the frame a name in the File name box. Be sure to give the frame you're working on a short but clear name that indicates its position in the frameset. Names like top_frame, left_frame, or links_frame make it easier for you to keep track of which frame you're working on.

> **Note** A good way to name frames so that you can easily remember the name of the main page in the set as well as the frame names is to use the form [mainpagename]_[framename], which helps you remember page names and frame names easily.

4 Click Save. The file is saved, and the Save As dialog box refreshes, prompting you to save the next frame in the frameset.

5 Repeat Steps 3 and 4 for all frames in the frameset. When you have saved the frames, the Save As dialog box opens again. The area around the page and the frame borders is highlighted, indicating that you should now save the frameset page. For clarity, you might want to save this page with the word *frameset* in the name—for example, *company_frameset*.

6 Click Save to save the frameset page.

Reaching All Viewers By Creating No Frames Content

If your Web site is intended to represent your company's public face on the Internet, or to generate sales through an online catalog, your goal is to reach as broad an audience as possible. You need to keep in mind that many older Web browsers don't accept frames. Your viewers might be coming to your page with a non-graphical browser such as Lynx; they might be browsing the Web with a handheld device or even a Web-enabled cell phone. To reach such users, you need to create an alternate version of your frames page—a "No Frames" page. FrontPage makes it easy to access the No Frames version of a page that uses frames. Open a Web page that has been divided into frames, and make sure you are in Design View. Click the No Frames button at the bottom of Design View.

Technically, you don't have to change the default "No Frames" content, which is the following single sentence:

This page uses frames, but your browser doesn't support them.

Such a page is likely to leave your visitors frustrated and clicking away to another site as quickly as possible. We strongly recommend that you provide at least minimal information about your site, and what the frames pages contain. At the very least, you should include the name of your company, a description of what you do, and some contact information. It's up to you how closely you want to duplicate your frames layout. You can, if you wish, approximate the frames design using tables, which are supported by a wider range of browsers than frames. An example is shown in Figure 12-6 on the following page.

Figure 12-6   You can approximate a frames layout using tables.

Customizing Frames to Match Your Design Needs

One of the useful features about frames is the extent to which standard arrangements can be customized to give your business site a unique look or to highlight content that's especially important. You can create a new frame to call attention to a sales promotion, or to present an advertisement so you can gain more revenue from your online presence. Two of the primary controls for adjusting the characteristics of individual frames are the Frames menu and the Frame Properties dialog box.

Viewing Frame Properties

When you need to control the attributes of frames in minute detail, you should display and adjust the properties of that frame. When you select an individual frame in a frameset by clicking within that frame, the borders are highlighted to let you know it has been selected. When you right-click within a frame, a shortcut menu appears. Choose Frame Properties, and the Frame Properties dialog box appears (see Figure 12-7).

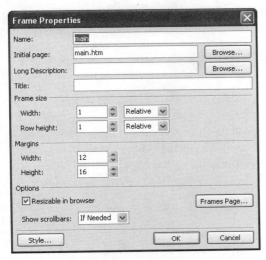

Figure 12-7 Change a frame's size, name, and other attributes using this dialog box.

The first thing you notice in the Frame Properties dialog box is that, in the box at the top, you are asked to specify a Name. Three boxes down, you can assign a Title. Both of these are different from the file name, which you assign when you save a frame. "What are all these designations?" you ask. The names are as follows:

- **Name**   When you target a frame so that its contents change when someone clicks a link in another frame, you use the name to identify the target.

- **Title**   This is the text that appears in the top bar of the viewer's browser window. Titles are important, because they are used by Internet search engines to index your pages. Pick a short, descriptive title that describes each page's contents.

- **File Name**   The file name is important, because others in your department might need to work on your pages. The filename should ideally describe the contents of the page and/or its position in the frameset.

- **Frame Size**   Change the frame's size by changing the Width and Row Height values. Use a specific pixel width if you want the frame to accommodate an item whose size you know, such as an image. Use a relative width if the contents of the frame (such as text) can change as the browser window is resized by the user.

- **Resizable In Browser**   Select this option if you want the viewer to have the ability to resize the frame by dragging its borders.

In a business environment, the Frame Name field is especially important. You need to keep all of a frame's names straight because the public needs to view your Web site without confusion, and other editors in the organization might work on the frames after you do.

> **Aha!**   Resize Frame Borders Quickly
>
> If the frame you're working on isn't the right size for the images, or other content you want, click and hold down on the frame border. Drag the border to reduce or enlarge the frame's size.

Showing or Hiding Frame Borders

You can streamline the appearance of a frames-based design by deciding to hide frame borders. Without borders, frames can be made to flow seamlessly into one another, and viewers can concentrate more easily on the contents of the frames, rather than the borders that separate them. Frame borders are displayed by default. To hide frame borders, follow these steps:

1   Right-click a frame and choose Frame Properties from the shortcut menu.

2   In the Frame Properties dialog box, click Frames Page.

3   In the Page Properties dialog box, click to deselect the Show Borders check box.

> **Note**   You can only hide or display frame borders for an entire Web page. You can't have some frames with borders showing, while other frames have no visible borders.

4   Click OK to close Page Properties, then click OK to close Frame Properties.

5   Click Preview to view the page without any visible borders.

> **Note**   Even if you make borders invisible on a frame, when you work on the page in the FrontPage window you can still see them—though the "invisible" frame border appears as a thin gray line that you can still drag if you need to resize the frame.

Changing Margins

Frames make Web pages more complex and content-rich. As a result, you may need to adjust the margins of your frames in order to make the contents more easily readable. The margin of a frame is the space between any one of the four borders and the text or images within them. By default, the left and right margins of a frame (the width) are 12 pixels. The top and bottom margins of the frame (the height) are 16 pixels. To adjust the margins, right-click the frame, and choose Frame Properties, then change the settings in the Margins section of the Frame Properties dialog box.

> **Note**   If you set a frame's Width or Height margins to 0, you make the frame's contents "bleed" to the border. This enables you to align images or text in one frame with images or text in another frame.

Adjusting Options

It's a good idea to put the viewer in control when it comes to frames. That way, they'll feel better about using the frames layout and overcome any of the "bad reputation" aspects of frames mentioned earlier in this chapter. The Frame Properties dialog box lets you change the following frame attributes to put viewers more in control:

- **Show scrollbars** The Show scrollbars drop-down menu in Frame Properties contains three options. If Needed means FrontPage will only display scrollbars if the text in the frame is longer than the frame can display in a single browser window. This option puts the viewer in control. The other two options do not: Always means the browser will display scroll bars whether the contents extend beyond the bottom of the frame or not; Never means the browser will not show scroll bars in the frame regardless of how long its contents are.

- **Resizable in Browser** Select this option in order to let the viewer resize the frame in order to make the frames more readable.

Adding Colors

Each frame within a frameset can have a distinct background color. By giving a frame a different color from those around it, you add visual interest to the Web page, while directing viewers' eyes toward the frame's contents. You might want to add color to a frame that contains special sales promotions or news about your company. Just follow these steps:

1 Click in the frame you want to adjust to select it.

2 Choose Format, Background.

3 On the Formatting tab of the Page Properties dialog box, click the Background drop-down menu, and select a background color for the Web page within the selected frame.

4 Click OK.

> **Caution**   Remember that you are only changing the color to the page that is *currently* displayed within the frame. If the frame's contents are meant to change because of hyperlinks clicked in other frames, you'll need to change the backgrounds of all the pages that might appear in that frame.

Splitting or Deleting Frames with the Frames Menu

You may need to adjust the number of frames in your layout in response to changes within your organization. FrontPage's Frames menu makes it easy. The options in the Frames menu become active when you have selected a frame. To split a frame, click anywhere within it to select it. Then choose Frames, Split Frame. The Split Frame dialog box appears (see Figure 12-8). Choose either Split Into Columns or Split Into Rows, then click OK to divide the frame into two equal size rows or columns.

Figure 12-8   Split a frame into two columns or rows using this dialog box.

To delete a frame, first select it, then choose Frames, Delete Frames. When a dialog box appears asking you to confirm that you want to delete the frame, click OK.

Targeting Frames

Frames pages really show their worth when you make them interact with one another. FrontPage makes it easy to target a frame, so that a link in one frame causes the linked content to appear in another frame. You only need to know which frame you want to target, and the name of the file you want to link to that frame.

Rename a Frame

1 Right-click the frame you want to target, then choose Frame Properties from the shortcut menu.

2 Type a new name in the Name box if you wish.

3 Click OK.

Make a Link to the Targeted Frame

1 Right-click the link that you want to "point" to the targeted frame that you named in the preceding set of steps.

2 Choose Hyperlink Properties from the shortcut menu. The Edit Hyperlink dialog box appears (see Figure 12-9).

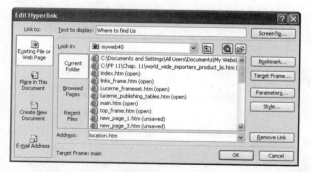

Figure 12-9 Choose the page you want to appear in the targeted frame.

3 Make sure the file listed in the Address box is the one you want to appear in the targeted frame.

4 Click Target Frame.

5 In the Target Frame dialog box (shown in Figure 12-10), click the frame where you want the linked file to appear.

6 Click OK to close Target Frame, and OK to close Edit Hyperlink.

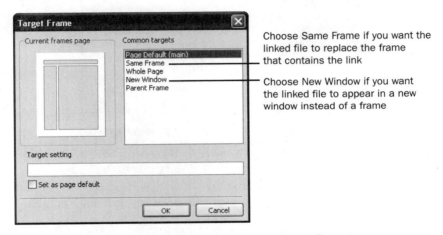

Choose Same Frame if you want the linked file to replace the frame that contains the link

Choose New Window if you want the linked file to appear in a new window instead of a frame

Figure 12-10 Identify the frame where you want the linked file to appear.

Dividing a Page with Inline Frames

In order to divide a Web page into two or more frames, you usually need to create a third, frameset page that contains the layout information for the frames. If you want to embed a small amount of information in an existing Web page, you can do it more quickly and simply by creating an inline frame. An inline frame is a frame that contains embedded content, as well as its own attributes, such as scrollbars. Inline frames are useful for adding a short fill-out form, a scrolling box with prices, or a set of examples that elaborate on the content in the rest of the Web page. First, you need to create the Web page that will be contained in the inline frame. (You can use an existing Web page as an alternative, however.) Then follow these steps:

1 Open the Web page where you want the inline frame to appear.

2 In Design View, position the text cursor at the spot on the current page where you want the frame to appear.

3 Choose Insert, Inline Frame to add the frame to the page (see Figure 12-11 on the following page).

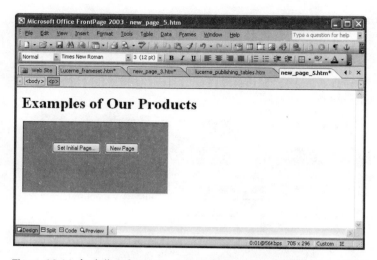

Figure 12-11 An inline frame is embedded within a conventional Web page.

4 If you want to use a Web page that you have already created, click Set Initial Page. Then select the page from the list that appears, and click OK. If you want to create a new page to insert into the inline frame, click New Page. Then create the page using FrontPage's usual tools for adding text, images, and other contents.

Once you have created the inline frame, you can adjust its properties by using the Frames menu options, the Frame Properties dialog box, and other approaches described earlier in this chapter.

Fast Wrap-Up

- FrontPage gives you a selection of predesigned templates for creating frames layouts quickly and easily.

- A No Frames version of a frameset enables users with older browsers that don't support frames to learn about content that is contained in the frames.

- The Frame Properties dialog box allows you to change characteristics of a selected frame, including its name, margins, or scrollbars, in order to make the frame easier for the viewer to use.

- The Frames menu gives you a quick and convenient way to split or delete frames in order to accommodate changes in content.

- You can make frames interactive by targeting a frame to display content in response to a link that is clicked in another frame.

- An inline frame enables you to embed a Web page within another one without having to create a frameset page.

Part 4
Making Your Web Site Interactive

Part 4, "Making Your Web Site Interactive," explores different ways to enrich a Web site with real-time content, and integration with other applications. In Chapter 13, you learn Web components, and how they can add dynamic effects, links, integration with components in the Microsoft Office System, and content to a Web site. Chapter 14, "Working With Forms," examines how FrontPage creates forms that enable you to interact with individuals who visit your site. Chapter 15, "Crowd Pleasing Form Extras," covers FrontPage's ability to add sophisticated features to forms, including validation, search results, and custom scripts. Chapter 16, "Making a Site Database-Driven," details how to make a Web site database-driven, drawing data from both Web-based and database application sources to give visitors up-to-the-minute information.

Using FrontPage Components

13

> **10-Second Summary**
> - ■ Make Web page elements interactive with dynamic HTML effects
> - ■ Make the current Web searchable
> - ■ Include Office spreadsheet and chart components
> - ■ Add pages, images, and other content
> - ■ Create link bars that make a Web site more easily navigable
> - ■ Add Top Ten lists and other interactive contents

FrontPage's basic set of tools is extensive, and will get the job done for just about all the basic Web site tasks you need—creating pages, working with images, formatting text, making links, and developing interactive page layouts. But when you take a step beyond the basics, and consider the more advanced utilities and business-oriented tools you can add to your FrontPage-based Web, you can quickly take your Web site to a new level of professionalism by adding Dynamic HTML (DHTML) effects and Web components. Without having to learn programming, you can achieve effects that used to be the sole province of Webmasters and programmers.

DHTML enables you to wow your Web site visitors by adding animation and transition effects to your pages. Web components are prepackaged programs you can add to a FrontPage-based Web to make it more functional and useful for your visitors. In this chapter, you'll learn how easy it is to add special effects and Web components to enable your site to interact with visitors, and give them a wider range of things they can do with your content. This chapter doesn't describe every possible component you can add; scroll through the lists in the Web Components dialog box to learn about all the options at your disposal for enriching your Web site without complicated programming.

Animating Your Site with Dynamic HTML Effects

FrontPage enables you to create some DHTML effects by adding them to your FrontPage-based Web as Web components. Web components automate many of the steps involved in creating animations or other features—many of which would require complex programming to achieve otherwise.

> **Caution**   If you have already formatted the current Web and added dynamic HTML effects or Web components like the ones discussed in this section, and you then change the status of the Dynamic HTML checkbox, some of the features on your Web site might become unusable. It's best to enable or disable DHTML when you first begin to work with the site.

Understanding DHTML

Dynamic HTML is a set of commands that enable Web pages to display animation of text, ads, images, marquees, buttons, and other Web page elements. DHTML can turn a static Web page into a business presentation, adding a feeling of professionalism to your Web site.

Typically, a DHTML effect starts with an event. You specify what event or action needs to take place for the effect to be displayed. You select the object that you want the user to act on. Then you choose an event from the first drop-down list in the DHTML Effects toolbar, as shown below in Figure 13-1:

Figure 13-1 Add interactivity by choosing special effects from this toolbar.

When you choose an event, the second drop-down list in the DHTML toolbar becomes active. You choose an option from this list to specify what should happen when the user performs the desired action. (The options vary depending on what event you specify.)

Then, you specify how you want the effect to take place. For instance, if you choose a wipe effect, you choose an option from the third drop-down list to describe how the page should wipe. You can apply a DHTML effect to images as well as text, encouraging visitors to focus on your most critical products and services.

Encourage Clicks with an Image Rollover Button

Rollovers are perfect for Web page buttons: the original button image changes in size or color, or turns into a complete different image that hints at where the browser will go when the viewer clicks on it. Each of these effects says to a visitor: "Click here!"

> **Lingo** A *rollover* is a Web page image that changes into something else—usually, a second image—when the viewer passes the mouse over it.

To add an image rollover button, follow these steps:

1   Open the Web page where you want to insert an image rollover button.

2   Position the cursor where you want the button to appear.

3 Click the Web Component button in the Standard toolbar.

4 In the Web Component dialog box (see Figure 13-2), click Dynamic Effects in the Component Type list.

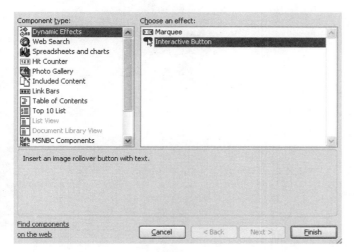

Figure 13-2 Add interactive content by choosing options from this dialog box.

5 Click Interactive Button in the Choose An Effect list, and click Finish.

6 When the Interactive Buttons dialog box appears (see Figure 13-3), scroll through the Buttons list of button styles, clicking on each to view a preview in the Preview box. Pass your mouse over the preview to see how it rolls over to a second image (usually with a different color).

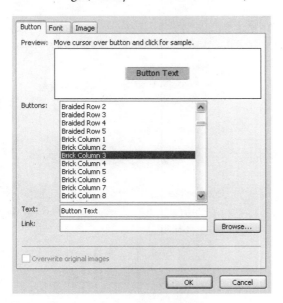

Figure 13-3 An interactive button changes appearance, inviting viewers to click it.

7 When you have chosen the rollover button you want, type the text you want on your button in the Text box (replacing the default Button Text).

8 In the Link box, enter the name of the Web page you want the button to link to (when a viewer clicks the button he or she will go to that page).

9 Click Text to change the style of the button text, the font color, or the alignment if you wish.

10 Click Image to change the color of the rollover image, make the image transparent, or change background colors if needed.

11 When you're done, click OK.

> **Aha!**   Change Your Button Properties
>
> Your first choices don't have to be the final ones. If you want to change an interactive button's text, color, effect, or other properties to fit your company's graphic identity, double-click it, then make your changes in the Interactive Button dialog box.

Grab Attention with a Marquee

A marquee is animated text that moves across a Web page and grabs a visitor's attention. Use it sparingly—when you want to announce an upcoming event or "breaking news" alert, for instance. Marquees are supported only by Microsoft Internet Explorer, and not by other browsers. If you want to add a marquee, you need to change the Authoring preferences for the current Web page:

1 Click Tools, Page Options.

2 Click the Authoring tab in the Page Options dialog box.

3 Choose Microsoft Internet Explorer only from the Browsers drop-down list, and click OK.

4 Position the text cursor at the location where you want the marquee to appear.

5 Click the Web Components button.

6 Choose Dynamic Effects, then choose Marquee.

7 Type the text for your marquee in the Text box of the Marquee Properties dialog box (see Figure 13-4).

8 Click Left or Right to specify whether you want the marquee to move to the right edge, or to the left edge of the page. Change other options (Speed, Behavior, and Repeat) as needed, and click OK when you're finished.

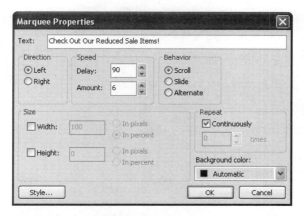

Figure 13-4 Use this dialog box to create moving marquee text guaranteed to grab a visitor's attention.

Adding FrontPage-Based Web Searches

The ability to search a corporate Web site's contents by entering terms in a search form is one of the features most highly desired by Web surfers. Many visitors immediately turn to a search form to find something, rather than clicking on links.

Normally, making a site searchable requires programming. FrontPage enables you to make your site searchable by inserting a Web component that indexes your site's contents, and then searches the contents in response to search queries. First, you create a simple form for searching the current FrontPage Web:

1 Open the Web you want to make searchable.

2 Position the cursor at the spot where you want to insert the search form.

3 Click the Web Component button.

4 Click Web Search in the Component Type list.

5 Click Current Web, and click Finish.

Aha! You Can Create a More Elaborate Search Form, Too

The Web Search component adds a search form to a FrontPage-based Web. If you are working on a SharePoint Web, the Full Text Search Web component becomes active in the Web Component dialog box. In either case, the form you add consists of one simple text box. You can create a more elaborate type of search form by choosing the FrontPage Search Page Template: choose Page Or Web from the New submenu of the File menu, click Page Templates in the Task Pane, and double-click Search Page.

When the Search Form Properties dialog box appears, you configure the Search Form and the results the user will receive:

1 Type a text label that will appear next to the search form.

2 Specify the width of the search form.

3 Type a label for the button users click to start the search.

4 Type a label for the button users click to clear the search box.

5 Click the Search Results tab.

6 Choose date and time formats for the search results the user will see after using the search form.

7 Select the Display Score checkbox, if you want the results to be ranked with scores.

8 Select the Display File Date and Display File Size checkboxes, if you want the results to display the file date and size. Click OK when you're finished to add the search form (see Figure 13-5).

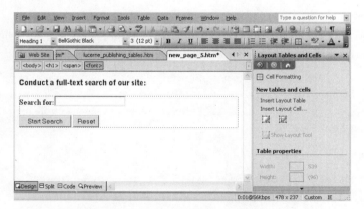

Figure 13-5 FrontPage makes it easy to configure the properties and search result options for this simple-looking search form.

> **Note** It's a good idea to provide your visitors with some information about file size and creation dates of the files presented in your search results. Such data helps the user know how current the document is, and how much information the file contains.

Including Spreadsheet and Chart Components

Some of FrontPage's Web Components enable you to include Excel 2003 and other documents in your FrontPage-based Web. Not only that, but your visitors can directly interact with the data contained in the documents. By embedding a spreadsheet or a chart in a Web page, companies can make data available to employees without requiring them to install the original applications—the Web browser becomes a uniform interface to databases, spreadsheets, charts, and many other types of information.

Add an Office Spreadsheet

By including a spreadsheet in a Web page, you not only save yourself a considerable amount of programming time, but you enable your visitors to interact with spreadsheets directly, without having to start up a separate Office application.

1 Open the page where you want to add the spreadsheet.

2 Click the Web Component button.

3 Choose Spreadsheets And Charts.

4 Choose Office Spreadsheet, and click Finish.

5 Click Commands and Options on the Office Spreadsheet's toolbar (as shown in Figure 13-6), if you want to import data from another file.

Figure 13-6 The Office Spreadsheet Web Component makes it easy to add a spreadsheet to a Web page.

6 Click Import, and type the location of the data in the URL box.

7 Check Refresh Data From URL At A Later Time, if you want to update your data whenever the spreadsheet loads.

You can also add content to a spreadsheet you add to a Web page by simply typing it, just as you would in Excel. Click in a cell and begin typing. You can also use the controls in the spreadsheet's own toolbar to format the data.

> **Aha!**   Link Your Spreadsheet to Live Data
>
> You can link your spreadsheet to a data source by clicking Commands And Options, then clicking the Data Source tab in the Commands And Options dialog box. Enter the URL of the data source in the Connection box.

You can also add an Office chart or a PivotTable to a Web page. Both options enable you to graphically present data contained in a spreadsheet or other data source. Proceed as if you were inserting a spreadsheet, then choose Office Chart or PivotTable in the Insert Web Component dialog box.

> **Caution**   Don't expect all of your visitors to be able to interact with spreadsheets, or other Office Web Components. In order to use the interactive data, they need to use Internet Explorer 4.01 or later, and have Microsoft Office Web components installed.

Keeping Track of Traffic by Counting Visitors

A hit counter is a utility that records the number of visits that are made to a Web page. They give visitors and site owners an idea of how much traffic a page is generating. FrontPage lets you add a counter to any page you want, in the form of a Web component. Just follow these steps:

1   Position the cursor at the spot in the Web page where you want the counter to appear (most counters appear at or near the bottom of a page).

2   Click Web Component.

3   Click Hit Counter, and click Finish.

4   Choose a style for the counter in the Hit Counter Properties dialog box (see Figure 13-7), and click OK.

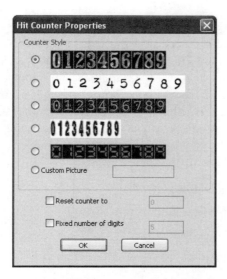

Figure 13-7 A hit counter tells visitors how much traffic your site is generating.

If you want to make changes to the counter, right-click it, then choose FrontPage Component Properties from the shortcut menu. The Component Properties dialog box lets you change the look of the counter as well as other characteristics:

■ Click Custom Picture, and enter a name for a custom counter image if you have a GIF image that includes the numbers zero (0) to nine (9), evenly spaced.

■ Select the Reset Counter To box, and enter a number that you want to start with.

■ Select Fixed Number Of Digits, and enter a number if you want to display a set number of digits. For example, if you enter 5, the number 1 will be displayed as 00001.

> **Caution**   Hit counters are not a perfectly accurate representation of how many unique visits you're getting to a page. Counters also record visits you make to the page to test and edit it. They also record visits by search engine programs that index Web pages to add them to their databases. Use them as a rough estimate of the number of visits, not an exact count.

Enriching Your Site with Informative Content

Any business Web site benefits by providing visitors with content that not only makes them stick around for a while, but also encourages them to return on a regular basis. Several of FrontPage's Web Components make it easy for you to add compelling content that supplements the information you create yourself.

Adding Top Ten Lists

You're already familiar with hit counters—utilities that display the number of times a Web page has been accessed. That's all the information a hit counter can convey. You can tell your visitors much more about how your site is being used, including the most popular pages and files, by adding a FrontPage Web component called a Top 10 List. When a visitor views a page that contains a list, live information is gathered from the Web server that hosts your site and is presented in the list. Top 10 lists can be invaluable to an internal audience of the co-workers in your organization who want to evaluate who is visiting your site, and what they are visiting most frequently. To add a list, follow these steps:

1 Open the page that you want to contain the list.

2 Position the cursor at the location where you want the list to appear.

3 Click the Web Component button, and click Top 10 List.

4 Click the list you want to add, and click Finish.

5 In the Top 10 List Properties dialog box (see Figure 13-8), customize the default name of the list if you want to.

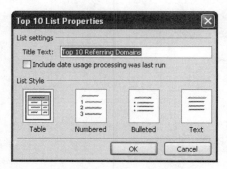

Figure 13-8 Top 10 Lists indicate how your Web site is being used.

6 Specify the graphic style for the list, click OK to add the list to the current page.

> **Note**   The ISP or Web hosting service that hosts your Web site should also provide you with statistics about how many visitors have come to your site, which pages are most popular, and so on. You may have to ask the host to start gathering such usage statistics—some hosts don't turn this feature on until you ask for it.

Table 13-1 Top 10 Lists You Can Add With FrontPage

List	What It Shows
Visited Pages	The top 10 most frequently visited pages on your site.
Referring Domains	The domains that users visit before they come to your site.
Referring URLs	The Web sites visitors came from immediately before they visit your site.
Search Strings	The most frequent keywords or phrases entered in search engines that display links to your pages.
Visiting Users	The computers that visit your site most frequently.
Operating Systems	The operating systems that your visitors use (such as Windows, Macintosh, or UNIX).
Browser	The Top 10 most popular browsers used to visit your Web site.

Help Customers and Clients Find You with a Map Link

It's often useful to provide visitors with maps to an event—or, if you're designing a business site, to your office. You can do it by adding an Expedia Web component to your site. You can either add a link to a map on the Expedia Web site, or a map to a specific location. Follow these steps:

1 Position the cursor where you want the map to appear.

2 Click the Web Component button.

3 Click Expedia Components.

4 Click Link to a Map, and click Finish.

5 The Link to a map Properties dialog box appears. Click Next, and follow the wizard through subsequent steps to add the map to your page.

> **Note**   You can also add an actual "static" map (a map whose contents don't change, unless you replace the map), instead of a link to a map. Click Web Components, click Expedia Components, and click Static Map. Click Finish, and follow the wizard through the process of adding the map. A static map works fine when the location you are highlighting isn't expected to change in the near future.

Making Your Site Newsworthy with MSN and MSNBC Components

News headlines are among the most popular kinds of content included on the home pages of many Web sites. So are search utilities that let visitors instantly search the entire Web from your site. By providing your visitors with the latest news, you give them another reason to remain on your site instead of going elsewhere. FrontPage gives you the ability to insert live news headlines from MSN and MSNBC—the information is gathered fresh from these news services whenever the viewer's browser accesses the page.

Help Visitors Locate Business Data with an MSN Component

The two Web components that come with FrontPage—a Web search box and a stock quote search box—adds functionality while helping keep visitors from leaving your site. They can search for the business information they need right from one of your own pages. To add an MSN component, follow these steps:

1 Open the page that you want to include the MSN component.

2 Position the cursor where you want the headlines to appear.

3 Click the Web Component button, click MSN Components.

4 Click the MSN component you want to add—a Web search box or a stock quote search box, click Finish.

Add an MSNBC Component

Adding news headlines can make your business look on top of current events, while helping visitors and employees keep track of what's happening in a particular field. If you work in the technology sector, add the MSNBC technology headlines Web component to your corporate intranet to keep your employees in the know; if you deal in agricultural futures or a travel-related field, the weather forecast component, or living and travel component can help you make critical business decisions. Here's how to add an MSNBC component:

1 Position the cursor on the Web page where you want the MSNBC component to appear.

2 Click the Web Component button.

3 Click MSNBC Components.

4 Click the type of MSNBC content you want to add (see Figure 13-9): business headlines; travel headlines; news headlines, sports headlines; technology headlines; or the weather forecast. Click Finish when you're done.

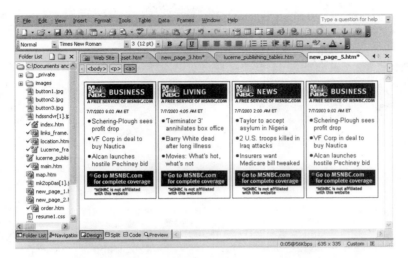

Figure 13-9 Help your employees stay informed with an MSNBC component.

> **Caution**   The danger with including a Web search box or any of the MSNBC components on your page is that visitors will leave your site as a result of a search, and never return. Be sure you want to include the search box before you actually include it.

Using Included Content Components

Maintaining a Web site can be time-consuming, and when you have lots of other work responsibilities to handle, it's to your advantage to automate as many of the processes as you can that involve adding and displaying content. The FrontPage included content Web components help you automate several tasks. You can insert standard bits of information, such as the name of the page's author, in multiple pages; you can also create a Web page with standard headers and footers that you can merge with existing pages.

Update Data Automatically with the Substitution Component

In order to convey a brand identity on the Internet, most companies develop standard Web page designs that consistently use standard elements. You can add a header or footer that you want to appear on multiple pages; you can include complete pages, or individual photos, as well. You can even schedule how long you want photos or other content to appear. You can also substitute content automatically when it changes—for instance, you can change an address or phone number when it is no longer valid, and have the Substitution Web component instantly update all of the pages where the content appears. Follow these steps:

1   Open the Web that you want to include the content that you include on one or more pages.

2   Position the cursor where you want to add the content.

3   Click the Web Component button, and click Included Content.

4   Click Substitution, and click Finish.

5   Choose an option from the Substitute With drop-down list (see Figure 13-10), and click OK.

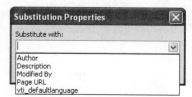

Figure 13-10 Add standard contents to Web pages using this component.

In order to have substituted content to insert on one or more Web pages, you need to first create that content. Along with the author information, you can add a description of the Web page, the name of the person who last modified the page, your company's name, address, or phone number.

> **Note**   The options initially shown in the Substitution Properties dialog box are default configuration variables. You can create custom variables in order to substitute content on one or more pages: Open the Web that you want to include substituted content, then choose Site Settings from the Tools menu. Click the Parameters tab. Click Add. Enter a name and value for the type of content you want to add. Click OK.

Merge Standardized Content with the Include Page Component

Another way to include content in a Web is to use the Include Page Component. This component doesn't just allow you to add an entire Web page. Use it when you want to create standardized headers, footers, or other contents that you want to merge into existing pages.

1   Open the page that you want to include header, footer, or link bar information from another page.

2   Position the cursor at the location where you want the included page information to appear.

3   Click Web Component, and click Included Content.

4   Click Page, and click Finish.

5   Enter the URL for the page you want to include in the Page To Include box, or click Browse to locate the file on your computer or network. Click OK.

Making Your Site Easier to Navigate

Several Web components help visitors to a Web site navigate—an important attribute for any business Web site that serves as a company's public face. By adding a link bar or table of contents to your page, you provide a way for visitors to get an overview of your site's most important areas of interest, and to move from one area to another any time they wish.

Linking Your Site with Link Bars

One of the easiest and most convenient tools you can give visitors for navigating the main areas of your Web site is a link bar. Normally, creating a link bar is a time-consuming process—especially if you're graphically challenged. FrontPage's Link Bar Web component, however, saves you the trouble of having to draw the link bar buttons and making the links.

> **Lingo** A *link bar* is a row of buttons, arranged either vertically or horizontally, that are linked to important pages on your site.

To create a link bar, just follow these steps:

1 Open the page that you want to include a link bar.

2 Position the cursor at the location where you want the link bar to appear.

3 Click the Web Component button, and click Link Bars.

4 Click Bar With Custom Links, and click Finish.

5 When the Create New Link Bar dialog box appears, enter a name for your link bar and click OK.

6 Click Add Link. In the Add to Link Bar dialog box, type the text to display for the link. The text you enter (such as Discussions, Documents, Lists, Images) should correspond to the type of content your site contains. Select the document in your site that you want to link to, then click OK. The link appears in Link Bar Properties (see Figure 13-11).

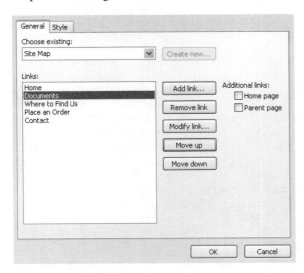

Figure 13-11 This dialog box leads you through the process of creating a link bar.

> **Caution** Make sure you link to files or pages that actually exist on your computer or network, and make sure the file names are accurate. FrontPage verifies the linked files' locations before it creates the link bar. If there's a mistake, the link bar won't be created, and you'll have to start over again.

7 Repeat step 6 for each link you want to add to the link bar.

8 Click Style.

9 Click Use Page's Theme if the current page has a theme applied to it, and you want the link bar to have the same theme.

10 Click a button style.

11 Specify whether you want the buttons in the link bar to be vertical or horizontal in orientation.

12 Click OK to add the link bar to your page (see Figure 13-12).

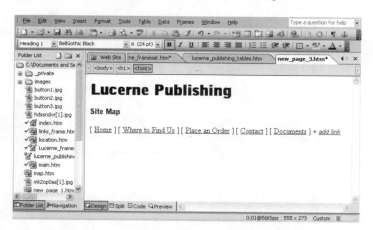

Figure 13-12 A link bar leads visitors to the main areas of your Web site.

> **Aha!** You Can Add Other Link Bars to Your Site
>
> You can also add a navigation bar to the current page as an included Web component. A navigation bar differs from a link bar in that it can be arranged to match the structure of the current FrontPage-based Web. Open the page where you want the navigation bar to appear, click Web Component, click Included Pages, and click Navigation Bar, and then click Finish. In the Navigation Bar Properties dialog box, you can then configure the bar to include different levels of Web pages on your site.

Adding a Table of Contents

In a FrontPage-based Web that contains many pages and categories (such as a Customer Support or Products and Services area), creating a Table of Contents makes it easier for visitors to find what they're looking for. The Table of Contents Web component creates a hierarchical set of hyperlinks to all of the pages in your site. Visitors can scan the links to get an overview of all of your site's contents, then click on the file they are looking for. Follow these steps to create a Table of Contents:

1 Position the cursor at the location where you want the Table of Contents to appear.

2 Click the Web Component button, and click Table Of Contents.

3 Click For This Web Site, and click Finish.

4 In the Page URL for the starting point of the table box, enter the URL of the Web page that will be presented on the left margin of the table of contents. Pages linked to this page will be indented.

5 Specify a font size for the heading that names the starting point page.

6 Select Recompute Table Of Contents When Any Other Page Is Edited if you want FrontPage to automatically recalculate the table of contents as you create or edit pages. Click OK.

> **Aha!**   Make Your TOC Your Startup Page
>
> If you want your table of contents to include your entire Web site, make your home page the starting point page. If the page that contains the table of contents is the same as the starting point page, the first link in the table of contents will be a link to the same page that is already displayed. You can avoid this confusion by excluding the starting point page from the table of contents: choose None from the Heading Font Size drop-down list in the Table of Contents Properties dialog box.

Copy and Paste Code with Advanced Controls

Typing Web page code from scratch is time-consuming, and a single typing error can force you to do more searching and debugging than you'd like, just to track it down. Inserting one of the FrontPage Web components that allows you to copy and paste HTML, Java, ActiveX, or other objects into Web pages can save you from having to type them from scratch. The Web page code controls are found by opening the Web Component dialog box, clicking Advanced Controls, and choosing one of the following options:

■ **HTML**   When you choose this control, and click Finish, the HTML Markup dialog box appears. You can then type or paste in some HTML code to add. If you have some standard code that you need to appear on each Web page (such as the comment <--! Created by John Miller of Web Team 3-26 -->), you can paste it here.

■ **Java Applet**   Java is a powerful programming language that lets you add sound, animations, and many other interactive features to Web pages. When you click Java Applet, and then click Finish, the Java Applet Properties dialog box appears. You use this dialog box to identify an applet: a small, self-contained program written in Java. You can specify the size and alignment of the area on the Web page where the applet will execute—as well as a message for users with older browsers that don't support Java, to tell them what they're missing.

■ **Plug-In**   One of the most common plug-ins is Acrobat Reader, which displays Adobe Acrobat PDF files in a Web browser window. Choose Plug-In, then click Finish to display the Plug-In Properties dialog box. Use this dialog box to set properties for a plug-in you want to process a file on the current Web page.

Lingo A *plug-in* is a player or reader application that works within a Web browser to process content that the browser can't handle directly.

■ **Confirmation Field**   This Web component is used to send a confirmation page to a user who successfully fills out and submits a form. Confirmation tells the individual that the data was received. Use this component when you are creating a form, as described in Chapter 14, "Working with Forms."

■ **ActiveX Control**   Use this Web component to add one of a set of common objects that are installed when both FrontPage and Microsoft Internet Explorer 5.5 or later are present on your system. The objects let you perform a variety of functions, for example:

- ActiveMovieControl: Plays a video file you have linked to the current page

- Calendar Control: Adds an interactive calendar to the current page

- Microsoft Office Chart: Creates charts and graphs from data sources you identify

- Microsoft WindowsMediaPlayer: Plays an audio file

■ **Design-Time Control**   Use this component when you need to add an ActiveX component or Java applet to the current page.

■ **Flash**   If you have created an animation with the popular application Macromedia Flash and you want to add it to the current page, use this component to insert it.

Lingo *Design-time controls* (DTC) give Web page designers the ability to easily embed pre-written HTML or other code within a Web page. A design-time control can take one of two forms. It can be an ActiveX component or Java applet embedded within a Web page. Or, it can be a control that is usable only while the page is being designed—in other words, at design time.

Web components and DHTML effects add a new degree of interactivity to a FrontPage-based Web. Many business Web sites include among their most important goals the ability to connect with, and find out about their customers and visitors. The most detailed and direct way to solicit information—creating a Web page form—is examined in the next chapter.

Fast Wrap-Up

- DHTML effects allow you to create "wipes" and other events without programming.

- Image rollover buttons encourage visitors to click by changing appearance at mouseover.

- Web search components help visitors find what they're looking for through a keyword search.

- Spreadsheet and chart components enable you to integrate Excel and other documents into your Web pages.

- Hit counters keep track of how many times a Web page has been visited.

- Included pages, MSN and MSNBC components, and Top Ten Lists help make a site content-rich.

- Link bars and Table of Contents pages make it easier for visitors to navigate your site.

Working with Forms

14

10-Second Summary

- Jump-start Web form creation with FrontPage templates and wizards
- Create List Forms that enable your coworkers to share information
- Create text boxes, file upload controls, check boxes, and other elements that help users fill out forms
- Help users choose from a list by creating drop-down boxes
- Enable users to send you information by creating push buttons
- Store form results in the right format and location so you can interpret the information you receive

Forms add a new level of interactivity to a Web site. They turn a Web site from a one-way to a two-way communication medium. Usually, Web surfers find out about you when they visit your site; you don't learn too much about who they are, unless you give them a form to fill out.

The ability to help users create forms that actually work has always been one of FrontPage's strongest features. Microsoft Office FrontPage 2003 not only streamlines the process of creating the data entry part of a form—the text boxes, buttons, and other elements that the user fills out—but it also provides the computer programs that process the information someone sends you, and presents it in a form you can read and use, such as an e-mail message.

In this chapter, you learn how forms work, and about the individual elements that the user sees. You learn about the different options for creating forms, starting with how to use the shortcut methods, the templates and wizards. You get detailed instructions on creating individual parts of a form. Then, you learn about the options FrontPage gives you for processing the information you receive from your visitors, or (if you create an e-commerce Web site) your customers.

Creating a Form with Time-Saving Shortcuts

Web page forms are commonly used to register visitors for services, or to give them a chance to voice their opinions. Common Web page forms include a guest book, where visitors can post their names and comments on a Web page, and feedback forms, where visitors can submit their comments to the Web site owner. FrontPage 2003 gives you templates, which enable you to create both types of forms instantly, without having to create each data entry element from scratch. Your job is to customize the form's contents according to your own requirements.

Jump-Start Your Form by Choosing a Template

FrontPage includes three Web page templates that are intended for soliciting specific kinds of information from visitors.

■ The User Registration form enables a business to register users, so that they can access restricted pages, or so that they can simply keep track of who visits the site.

■ The Guest Book (see Figure 14-1) is perfect for a business that wants to hear from its customers about how well its Web site is operating, but does not need to identify those individuals by name. Other customers can view previous visitors' comments, and respond with their own opinions.

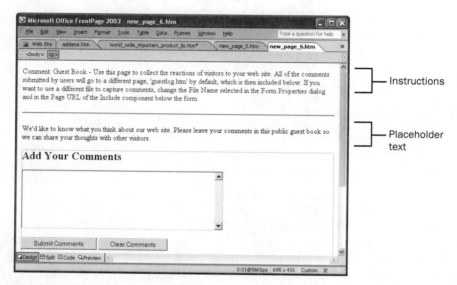

Figure 14-1 Templates help you create interactive forms quickly.

■ The Feedback Form invites comments from the site's visitors, while giving them a place to identify themselves by name. Use the Feedback Form when you want to gather contact information from your visitors or customers, so that you can get in touch with them later on.

Choose one of FrontPage's templates when you want to include a standard feedback element on your Web site, and you don't need to customize the form extensively. (If you want more flexibility, use the Form Page Wizard, as described in the next section.) To quickly create a form from a template, follow these steps:

1 Open the Web that you want to contain the form.

2 Choose File, New.

3 Click More page templates in the New page section of the Task Pane.

4 Click one of the form templates in the Page Templates dialog box, and click OK.

5 When the page appears, read the instructions that appear in purple. Click the placeholder text (which appears in black) and replace it with your own content.

> **Caution**   Unless you use a custom script (a computer program written in a language such as Perl or C++) to process the information submitted from a Web page form when it is sent to your Web server, you need to have the FrontPage Server Extensions or Microsoft SharePoint running on the server that hosts your site. Otherwise, you won't be able to use one of FrontPage's form handlers to process the information that comes to you from a Web page form. Ask your ISP or network administrator whether SharePoint or the server extensions are available. Once your Web form has been published to a Web server running SharePoint or the FrontPage Server Extensions, you can test the form yourself by clicking Preview In Browser.

Tailor Your Form with the Form Page Wizard

Any business Web site needs a variety of forms that elicit more than feedback comments from customers or other visitors. Forms that invite users to submit their names, addresses, and other contact information have great value as marketing tools. FrontPage's Form Page Wizard will help you design a form for any purpose. Let it lead you step-by-step through the process of creating a registration, purchase, or service request form. The Wizard enables you to tailor the form to your own needs, while including your name and contact information, and also attaching the proper form handler. Just follow these steps to start using the Form Page Wizard:

1 Open the Web that you want to contain the form.

2 Choose File, New.

3 Click More page templates in the New page section of the Task Pane.

4 Double-click Form Page Wizard to open it.

5 Read the first page of the Wizard, and then click Next.

The subsequent screens of the Wizard lead you through the process of designing a Web page form, without having to create each of the input boxes and buttons laboriously, one at a time.

Specify the Information You Want

First, the Form Page Wizard helps you identify the information you want visitors to submit when they fill out the form.

1 Click Add to add a question or prompt that invites users to fill out your form.

2 Specify the type of information you want the form to gather (see Figure 14-2 on the following page).

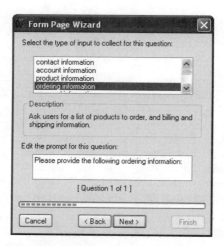

Figure 14-2 The Form Page Wizard helps you gather many types of business information.

3 Review the prompt for the desired information, then click Next.

4 Specify the kinds of data you want to collect for the type of information you specified (see Figure 14-3), and click Next.

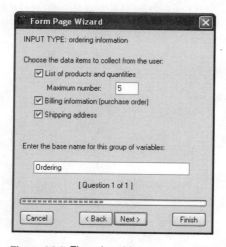

Figure 14-3 The wizard lets you identify specific kinds of data to collect.

5 Repeat Steps 1-4 for each field you want to add, and click Next.

The final screens of the Wizard let you control what's usually the most technical and difficult part of creating a Web page form: specifying the way you want to receive information, so that you can work with it easily when it arrives.

> **Caution**   Limit the personal information you want the user to submit to a minimum. Many Web surfers are put off by forms that ask them to reveal a lot about their personal lives. Some may skip filling out your form altogether if they feel their privacy is being invaded.

Configure How You'll Receive Information

Whether you'd rather receive a text file that you can open in a word processing document, or a Web page you can view in your browser, the Wizard lets you specify how the form information is processed by the server. Just follow these steps:

1   Specify how you want the form information to be formatted when it is presented to the user, and click Next.

2   Specify whether you want the results to be sent you in the form of a Web page, or a text file, or whether you have a custom script available to process the information (see Figure 14-4).

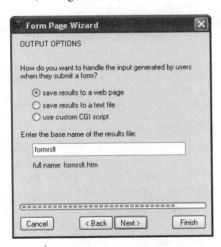

Figure 14-4 This simple-looking screen lets you control some complex form processing.

3   Click Next. (This is the last screen that asks you for information. In the last screen, click Finish.) The finished form appears in the FrontPage window (see Figure 14-5 on the following page).

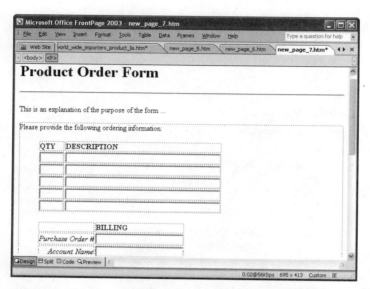

Figure 14-5 The Form Page Wizard enables you to painlessly assemble a form with multiple data-entry fields such as this.

Lingo The term *CGI script*, which appears on one of the Wizard screens, refers to a program that uses the Common Gateway Interface (CGI), a way for Web servers and client programs to communicate with one another.

The Parts of a Form

Every form has two parts: the data-entry elements (shown in Figure 14-6), and the script, which processes the data that the user submits. The part you create (either from scratch, or with the help of FrontPage's Form Page Wizard or templates), are the text boxes and buttons the user fills out. Some of the data-entry elements are shown below.

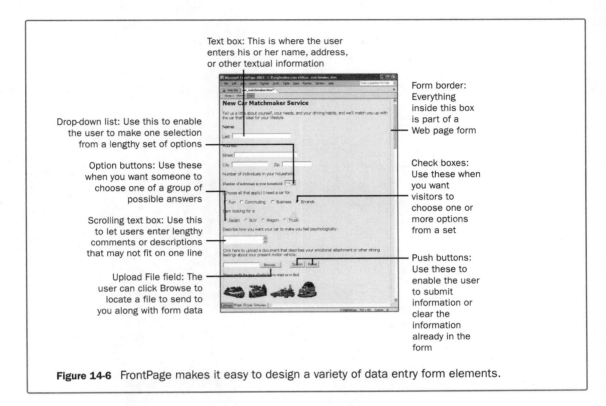

Figure 14-6 FrontPage makes it easy to design a variety of data entry form elements.

Text box: This is where the user enters his or her name, address, or other textual information

Form border: Everything inside this box is part of a Web page form

Drop-down list: Use this to enable the user to make one selection from a lengthy set of options

Check boxes: Use these when you want visitors to choose one or more options from a set

Option buttons: Use these when you want someone to choose one of a group of possible answers

Scrolling text box: Use this to let users enter lengthy comments or descriptions that may not fit on one line

Push buttons: Use these to enable the user to submit information or clear the information already in the form

Upload File field: The user can click Browse to locate a file to send to you along with form data

Help Your Co-workers Share Information with List Forms

A list form is a form that you place in a document library or interactive list on your Web page. It differs from traditional Web page forms in that it enables members of a workgroup to share ideas and submit information that they can then access and view. List forms are part of Microsoft SharePoint Team Services—they require that the page which contains the form be published on a server that is running SharePoint Team Services. To add a list form, follow these steps:

1   Open the page where you want the list form to appear.

2   Choose Insert, Form, List Form.

3   Select the kind of form you want to add from the drop-down list at the top of the List or Document Library Form dialog box (see Figure 14-7 on the following page).

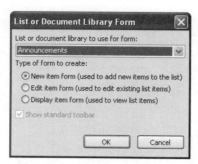

Figure 14-7 You can identify a list or document library to use for a list form.

4 Choose the type of form you want to create:

- Click New Item Form if you want visitors to add items to the list form.

- Click Edit Item Form if you want visitors to be able to edit items in the list, or change their own responses.

- Click Display Item Form if you want visitors to be able to view responses to a survey.

5 Click OK, and click Save to name and save your page on the SharePoint server (see Figure 14-8).

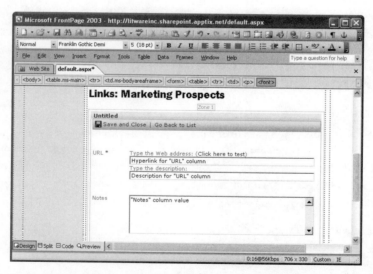

Figure 14-8 List forms give colleagues a way to submit and share ideas.

You can create the following kinds of list forms: Announcements, Contacts, Document Library, Data Sources, Events, General Discussion, Links, Shared Documents, and Tasks. However, each Web page can contain only one list form.

A list form, like other Web page forms, contains one or more fields. A field is a data entry element that gives the user a place to enter information. A text field, for instance, might include a first name or last name. Once you create a SharePoint list form, it's easy to modify the form, so that you and your colleagues can enter exactly the information you want to share. Here's how to add a list field:

See Also For more information about creating interactive lists and document libraries, see Chapter 18, "Working Collaboratively."

1 Right-click the list form, and choose Customize SharePoint List Form from the shortcut menu.

2 Once the form has changed to layout customization view, right-click anywhere in the form and choose Insert List Field from the shortcut menu.

3 Choose the field you want to display from the Field To Display drop down list (Figure 14-9).

Figure 14-9 This dialog box makes it easy to add list fields to a list form.

4 Specify whether you want to show only the name of the field, or the field data—in other words, the field itself. Click OK.

5 Right-click the form and choose Revert SharePoint List Form to view the form with the new field.

> **Caution** If you want to add a new field to your list form, don't right-click on an existing field when you choose Insert List Field. If you do, you'll replace the existing field with a new one. Right-click a part of the form that doesn't yet contain a field.

Letting Users Fill Out Text Boxes and Areas

The text box that enables the user to enter a single line of text (no more than a word or short phrase, depending on the size of the box) is probably the single most common data entry element used in Web page forms (although Submit or Clear buttons are virtually universal as well). They're pretty much indispensible for enabling visitors to send you their names, addresses, and other important information. Whether you're creating your own form from scratch, or editing an existing form, FrontPage makes it easy to create the box and control its size. First, you create a form:

1   Open the page that you want to include a form.

2   Position the text cursor where you want the form to appear.

3   Choose Insert, Form, Form.

4   Press Enter a few times to make some space above the Submit and Reset buttons so that you can enter a text box (see Figure 14-10).

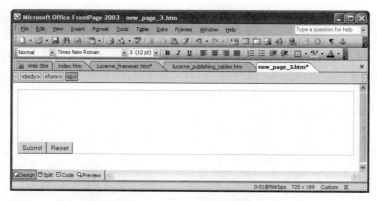

Figure 14-10 First, create a form so that you can add text boxes and other data-entry elements.

Aha!   Create a Form Instantly

You don't have to insert a form before you create a form field. If you insert a form field without first creating a form, FrontPage will create a form for you automatically.

Insert a Text Box

Once you have a form defined on the current Web page, it's a matter of a few steps to create a box into which a visitor can enter the necessary information:

1   Enter text that explains the purpose of your form, and format it as you would any other text.

2   Enter a label for the text box you want to create, and press the spacebar once or twice.

3   Choose Insert, Form, Textbox.

Aha!   Drag Your Text Box to Give Users More Room

Give your users enough space in which to type. The text box created by FrontPage won't accommodate more than 20 characters. Most street addresses (and a few proper names) will need more space. You can drag the box's right edge to provide more room.

Invite Extended Comments with a Text Area

Sometimes you want to invite viewers to submit extended comments—about your site, your business, or your level of customer service, for instance. You can indicate that extensive comments are invited by creating a Text Area box—a text box that has a scrollbar so users can enter multiple lines of text. Just follow these steps:

1 Enter some text that prompts the user to enter some information in the text box.

2 Position the cursor at the location in the form where you want the text area (a scrolling text box) to appear.

3 Choose Insert, Form, Text Area.

Aha! Label Your Form Box Clearly

Right-click a text box, or other field, and choose Form Field Properties from the shortcut menu to change the field's properties. The Name field becomes important when you receive and process the information you receive from the form. The data entered in the box will be presented next to the box's name, in a form such as "Lastname=Holden." Make sure the Name box contains a clear indication of the field's contents, so that you can process the information more easily. The Initial Value box in Text Box Properties enables you to specify some text that the box will contain when the user first views it, even before entering any data in the box.

Let Visitors Transmit Files with File Upload Controls

You want to make it easy for your viewers to send files to you—as easy as it is to fill out one of your forms. If your visitors have files they want to submit to you along with their form information, you can insert a special file upload control to let them do so from inside the form. That way they don't have to e-mail you an attachment or transfer the file to you by File Transfer Protocol (FTP). Just position the cursor at the spot in the form where you want the file upload control to appear, and choose Insert, Form, File Upload.

Letting Users Make Choices with Check Boxes and Option Buttons

Many Web page forms give users the ability to select one or more selections from a group of options by clicking on boxes or option buttons. Such boxes help users along by providing them with possible selections.

The big difference between check boxes and option buttons is this: check boxes give users the ability to select more than one option, or all options, while option buttons enable users to select only one choice from a group.

Enabling More than One Choice with a Check Box

When you want users to make more than one choice from a group, create a set of check boxes. Just follow these steps:

1 Position the cursor at the spot in the form where you want the check box to appear.

2 Choose Insert, Form, Checkbox.

3 Type a label for the check box.

4 Choose Insert, Form, Checkbox and type labels for other check boxes you want to add (see Figure 14-11).

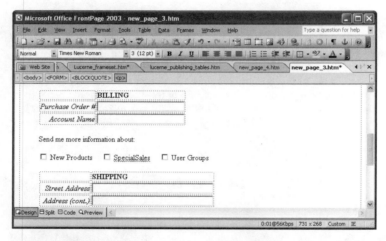

Figure 14-11 Insert check boxes when you'd really like viewers to choose more than one option.

Aha!   Set a Box's Initial State

If you think one of the choices in a group of option buttons or check boxes is likely to be selected more often than the others, you can set its Initial State to be selected. Right-click the button or box, and then choose Form Field Properties from the shortcut menu.

Providing a Single Choice with an Option Button

Sometimes, only one choice is possible from a group of options. When you want your visitors to choose only one option from a group, add option buttons by following these steps:

1 Position the cursor at the location in the form where you want the option button to appear.

2 Choose Insert, Form, Option Button.

3 Type a label for the option button.

4 Choose Insert, Form, Option Button and type labels for other option buttons you want to add (see Figure 14-12).

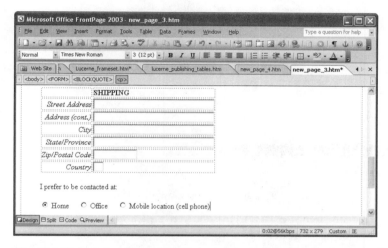

Figure 14-12 Insert option buttons when you want viewers to choose only a single option.

> **Note** As you can see, the first option button in a series of buttons is already selected. You can unselect the button by right-clicking it, choosing Form Field Properties from the shortcut menu, and then selecting Not Selected in the Option Button Properties dialog box.

Presenting a Group of Choices with a Drop-Down Box

If you want to give your visitors the chance to choose one option from a group of options, while enabling them to scroll through a list of possible responses, create a drop-down box. Drop-down boxes are ideal for long lists—the obvious example is a list of all 50 states in the U.S., from which the user has to make a selection to identify where he or she lives. To create a drop-down box, follow these steps:

1 Position the cursor at the location in the form where you want the group box to appear.

2 Select Drop-Down Box from the Form submenu of the Insert menu.

3 Right-click the drop-down box, and then choose Form Field Properties from the shortcut menu to display the Drop-Down List Properties dialog box (see Figure 14-13 on the following page).

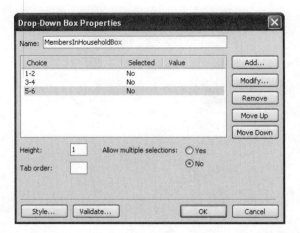

Figure 14-13 Name your drop-down box and add contents using these options.

4 Type a short but descriptive name for the drop-down menu in the Name box.

5 Click Add. (For any item you want to include in the list, you need to click add, and then follow steps 6 through 7 below.)

6 Type the name of the first item you want to list in the Choice box in the Add Choice dialog box.

7 Check Selected if you want the list item to be selected initially, and click OK.

> **Aha!**   When you type a name for the drop-down menu in the Name box, be sure to type one word, with no blank spaces. (Blank spaces can interfere with the form handler that processes the form results.) This applies to all form field names, not just drop-down menus.

Enabling Users to Send Data with Buttons

When users have finished filling out your form, they need to submit the information to you. Usually, they do it by pressing a button labeled Submit, Send or something similar. Clicking a submit button sends the user information to the form handler that has been associated with the form, so that you can receive the data and make use of it. Clicking Reset tells the user's browser to reset the buttons to their original values. Your job is to make the buttons that appear on your form clearly visible and easily identifiable.

Adding a Push Button So Users Can Submit Data

A push button is a button labeled Submit, Reset, or another designation of your choice that the person who fills out a form clicks to perform actions. To create a push button, position the cursor in the form where you want the button to appear, and choose Push Button from the Form submenu of the Insert menu.

> **Aha!**   Before You Add that Button...
>
> The Submit and Reset buttons are added by default when you insert a form.

Adding More Information with an Advanced Button

An advanced button is a button you can customize to provide more information or graphic interest than a simple one-word label. The surface of an advanced button is an open area that you can "fill" with a graphic image, a paragraph of text, or another bit of content. Use an advanced button when you want the user to get a graphic preview of what will happen when they click it, or when you want to present detailed instructions.

1 Position the cursor at the location in the form where you want to add an advanced button.

2 Choose Advanced Button (shown in Figure 14-4) from the Form submenu of the Insert menu.

3 Type a label for your button immediately to replace the highlighted label Type Here, and then click elsewhere in the form to make the label change.

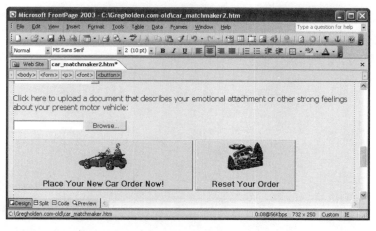

Figure 14-14 Advanced buttons can include graphics and formatted text.

> **Aha!**   Adding Text to a Button Label
>
> To change advanced button label text, click the inside surface of the button (not the edge of the button or you'll select the button itself), scroll across the placeholder text to highlight it, type the text you want to enter, and then format the text, using the options on the Formatting toolbar.

Storing Form Results

Simply creating a form's "public" face is one thing, but the next phase is equally important: telling FrontPage what needs to happen with the data the form collects. Processing data submitted via Web page forms is an area where FrontPage really shines. Rather than having to use a program called a Common Gateway Interface (CGI) script to process the data, you can use FrontPage's built-in components to do the work for you. For some forms, you'll want to save the results to a file in your FrontPage-based Web, so that you can work with them later. If the amount of data you're collecting is small, you can also have the results sent to you in the form of an e-mail message.

Saving Form Results in a File

One of the most straightforward ways of handling form data is to save the information to a file so that you can open it and work with it. FrontPage enables you to specify that the data be saved as an HTML file you can open in your Web browser, or as an ASCII text file you can open in any text editor. Just follow these steps:

1 Right-click anywhere in the form.

2 Choose Form Properties from the shortcut menu.

3 Click Send To to send the results to a file on your Web site (see Figure 14-15).

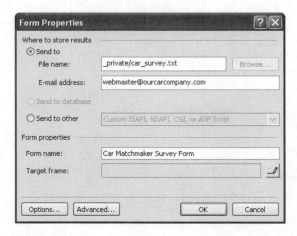

Figure 14-15 Use this dialog box to save form results to a text file.

4 Enter a new file name or folder name if you wish to.

5 Click Browse to locate a folder on your Web site where you want to store the results, instead of the default _private directory.

6 Click Send To Database to store the results in a database file.

7 Click Send To Other if you have a custom script you want to use to process the data.

8 Enter the name of the form in the Form name box, and click OK.

> **Caution** The form results are sent, by default, to the folder _private on your Web. This folder cannot be browsed by your visitors, so it makes sense to store form results there because it helps protect the privacy of anyone who fills out the form. Storing it in another publicly accessible folder on your Web can cause big privacy problems that you want to avoid, especially if you're in business. Keep the results in _private, unless you have a compelling reason to put them elsewhere.

Having Form Results E-mailed to You

Another convenient way to save form data is to have the results e-mailed to you. That way, you can access them from any computer that's online, and you can send an e-mail response immediately.

1 Right-click anywhere in the form, and choose Form Properties from the shortcut menu.

2 Click Send To to send the results to a file on your Web site.

3 Delete the contents of the File Name box if you want the results to be only e-mailed to you, and not saved in a file as well.

4 In the E-mail Address box, enter the e-mail address where you want the form results to be sent, and click OK.

> **Aha!** Make Your Form Results Easier to Recognize
>
> It's a good idea to change the default file results file name (form_results) to something more specific, so that you know exactly what the file contains when you want to view it.

Gaining Control By Specifying Form Results

Simply specifying whether FrontPage should save form data as a text or HTML file, or as an e-mail message doesn't give you a lot of options. Once you begin to receive form information from your visitors, you'll probably want to customize the results, so that the information comes to you in a clearer way. Even if you've already saved the form, identified the form handler, and published the form, you can still customize the form results at any time to make the form more useful. By controlling form results, you make FrontPage a front-end tool for presenting the data you need to keep your organization running smoothly.

Name and Format the Results File

Sometimes, you want to have form data presented in chronological order. Other times, you'd rather see the most recent information presented first. Changing such options gives you the ability to view form data the way you're going to work with it in preparing projections, budgets, or marketing proposals.

1 Right-click anywhere in the form you want to edit, and choose Form Properties from the shortcut menu.

2 Click Options.

3 Click the down arrow next to the File Format drop-down list, and choose the format in which you'd like to receive the data (see Figure 14-16).

Figure 14-16 FrontPage gives you many options for saving form data.

4 Check Include Field Names if you want the file to include the names of each field, as well as the data.

5 Click the Optional Second File section of the File Results tab, and fill out the File Name box, if you want to specify a second file to receive the results—to present one set of results in a plain-text document and another in HTML, for instance. Click OK.

> **Aha!** Prioritize Your Form Results
>
> If you check the Latest Results At End box on the File Results tab of the Options For Saving Results dialog box, FrontPage will put the most recent results at the end of the file. Otherwise, you'll see the most recent results at the beginning of the file.

Adding Flexibility by Saving Form Results as XML

Extensible Markup Language (XML) enables you to use HTML-style markup tags to identify data elements. You can create tags that identify the data you have received from the form. By saving form results in XML format, you can easily open and work with them in other applications that support XML.

To save form results in XML format, follow steps 1 to 3, as presented in the preceding section "Name and Format the Results File." Then choose XML from the File Format drop-down list.

> **Aha!** Test Your Form Handler
>
> The utility that processes your form results is called a form handler—a program that runs on the Web server that hosts your site. Be sure to test your form, and the form handler, before you open your Web site to the public. You should be the first one to fill out the form and send yourself some test results, so that you can see if the form handler works correctly.

Organizing Your E-mailed Form Information

Having form responses e-mailed to you is convenient, but in a business environment where you might receive dozens of e-mail messages per day, you need to get all the help you can when it comes to organizing your e-mail and responding to it efficiently. FrontPage can help in several ways. You can have the program alert you to the message's conents, and even configure a filter that can automatically file the message for you. Just follow these steps:

1. Right-click the form that has been set up to e-mail results to you, and choose Form Properties from the shortcut menu.

2. Click Options, and click E-Mail Results.

3. Click the down arrow next to the E-Mail Format box (see Figure 14-17 on the following page), and choose a formatting option for the e-mail messages.

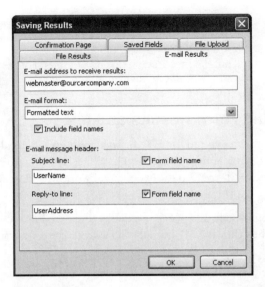

Figure 14-17 Use these options to define the format of e-mailed results.

4 Enter a subject line for the e-mail messages you receive in the Subject Line box, if you want FrontPage to include the subject line in the form results, to remind you exactly what is being submitted. This is especially important if you have several forms on your Web site, and visitors submit information on a wide variety of topics. Including the subject line enables you to use your e-mail program's Filters option to automatically file the message in a predesignated folder if you wish to.

5 Enter information in the E-mail message header section of the a standard subject line for messages you send in response to users who submit form information to you. Click OK.

Aha!   Enter a Reply-To Line

The ability to pre-enter a reply-to subject line for e-mailed form results gives you a great deal of control. Enter a reply-to line if you expect to be replying to many or all of the individuals who fill out your forms, and you want to give them a standard response.

Learning More by Saving Additional Information

When you save form results, you normally save only the fields that you have included in the form. But you can learn even more about the data that was submitted by taking advantage of FrontPage's ability to let you save additional form information. The additional information can prove useful when you analyze the results. Follow these steps:

1 Open the Saved Results dialog box for the form (see Steps 1 through 3 under "Organizing Your Emailed Form Information").

2 Click Saved Fields.

3 Check one of the options in the Additional Information To Save section (see Figure 14-18) if you want the form results to include the name of the user's computer, the username of the individual who filled out the form, or the user's browser type.

4 Specify a Date format or time format in the Date And Time section if you want to save the date and time the form data was submitted. Click OK.

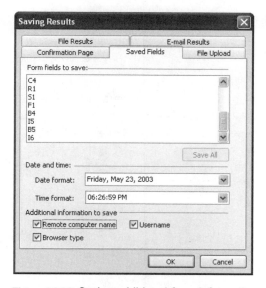

See Also One of this book's authors, Greg Holden, explored the ins and outs of setting up an e-commerce Web site with FrontPage in the book *E-Commerce Essentials with Microsoft FrontPage*, also published by Microsoft Press.

Figure 14-18 Saving additional form information can help with analysis.

Setting Up a Web Store

A Web store—Web site that is intended to sell goods or services to the general public—has goals that are different than informational or community-building Web sites. You need to make it as easy as possible for customers to locate what they want. You then have to present sales items in an attractive way. Sales information must be backed up with high-quality customer service. It's important to market your site so that it will reach a well-defined target audience. You need to be able to process transactions online as well.

Many of those goals can be achieved by creating Web page forms. Forms are needed to enable your prospective customers to make inquiries, and to enable your actual, current customers to select items and submit shipping and payment information. For instance, one of the most important forms on any e-commerce Web site is one that the customer fills out after making a purchase. It enables the customer to submit payment and shipping information to the store's site. In order to protect customer information, you should store credit card information, addresses, and other personal information, on a secure server that encrypts data using Secure Sockets Layer (SSL), a set of technologies that is designed to protect information transmitted over the World Wide Web. Microsoft bCentral enables you to use FrontPage to create such forms, and store them on Microsoft bCentral's own secure server. You can also create Web pages that include Buy buttons, which allow customers to store selections in an electronic "holding area" called a shopping cart, until they are ready to be purchased. Find out more about Microsoft bCentral at *http://www.bcentral.com*).

One thing you can use to help create Web store forms is Microsoft bCentral, Microsoft's hosting service for Web-based businesses. bCentral provides its customers with a variety of services for setting up Web stores. One of those services, Customer Manager, includes forms that help you receive and track information and inquiries submitted by the customers who visit your site. bCentral integrates with FrontPage through a utility called Microsoft bCentral Customer Manager.

Fast Wrap-Up

- FrontPage's templates and wizards provide you with shortcuts to creating feedback and other forms.

- List forms enables a workgroup to share ideas or information on a SharePoint Team Services Web site.

- Text boxes, text areas, and scrolling text boxes enable visitors to send you essential business information.

- File upload controls give visitors a way to send you files.

- Check Boxes and option buttons enable users to make choices from a group of alternatives.

■   Drop-down boxes let users make a single choice from an extensive group of options.

■   Buttons—whether standard push buttons or advanced buttons—enable users to submit their information to you.

■   The information you receive from individuals who fill out your forms can be saved as text files, HTML or XML documents, or e-mail messages sent to you.

Form results can be customized to make information easier to work with.

Crowd Pleasing Form Extras

15

10-Second Summary
- Make Web forms more interactive by adding images and labels
- Set form validation rules to get the information you need
- Make search forms work properly by adjusting results
- Send a confirmation page to your visitors
- Add extra form information with a hidden field
- Create registration forms so your visitors can access special content

---

Once you start to use forms, you'll realize that the amount of information you receive from visitors, and the way the information is presented, is critical to your business operations. By getting your visitors to send you the information you need, in the correct format, you can easily use the form as a front end to a database that you can use for marketing and analysis.

In this chapter, you'll learn about different ways in which Microsoft Office FrontPage 2003 can help you create forms that provide the information you need—and are easy for your visitors to fill out. You'll learn how images and shortcuts can make forms more "clickable" by giving users keyboard shortcuts. You'll learn how to control the way user information is sent to you through forms validation. And you'll learn how to set up search forms, confirmation pages, hidden fields, and registration forms, all of which help you and your visitors interact more effectively through forms.

Improving Clickability with Pictures and Labels

Web page forms don't have to be limited to text and data entry elements. You can add pictures as well. The pictures can encourage users to click, and help them make selections accurately, which is very important if you're running an online store and want to reduce returns.

A label is text that appears next to a check box, option button, or other form field. Labels also make a form more clickable. By having FrontPage designate a word or phrase as a label, the user is able to click, either on the label or the field next to it, in order to perform an action. Once you create a label, you can designate a keyboard shortcut, so that a user can select the form field with the keyboard as well as with the mouse.

Adding Graphic Interest by Inserting a Picture

To insert an image that can give your form more graphic interest, just follow these steps:

1   Position the cursor in the form where you want to add the picture.

2   Choose Picture from the Form submenu of the Insert menu.

3   Select the picture you want to add, and click Insert.

Improving Interactivity by Adding a Clickable Label

You can't predict how much experience the visitors to your Web site are going to have when it comes to using browsers and filling out forms. Beginning-level users (not to mention those who have trouble manipulating a mouse) might not know exactly where to click when they need to make a selection. FrontPage can help by streamlining the process of creating interactive labels. A label is a clickable word or phrase next to a form field; users can click either on the label or the field to make a selection. To create a label:

1   Select both the field and the text that you want to convert to a form label. For instance, click an option button or a check box to select it; then hold down the Shift key, and position the cursor after the text to select it as well.

2   Choose Insert, Form, Label to create the label.

3   Once you create a label, you can create a keyboard shortcut within the label by selecting a character and pressing Ctrl+U, or clicking Underline in the Formatting toolbar. The character that is underlined is automatically converted to a keyboard shortcut (see Figure 15-1).

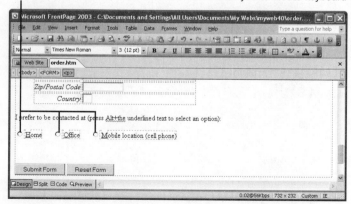

Figure 15-1 Labels make a form more clickable and enable you to create keyboard shortcuts.

> **Note**   Make sure you don't have any blank spaces (not to mention paragraph returns or line breaks) after the field when you select it and the accompanying text. If you select the blank space by mistake, you won't be able to create the label.

Setting Validation Rules to Ensure Correct Data Entry

Creating an effective Web page form is a balancing act: you want the form to be easy for your users to fill out. But you also want the information to be useful to you, and you want to control how users fill out the form, so that they give you the information you are looking for. If you're running a business on the Web, it's critical that your customers fill out registration, purchase, and shipping forms accurately.

FrontPage can help you create validation rules that give users the freedom to submit the data they want while ensuring that the data is transmitted in the form in which you need it. By taking a little extra time to set up rules that users need to follow when they fill out forms (also called forms *validation*), you enable the process of verifying that the forms have been filled out accurately and completely.

Setting Validation Rules for Text Boxes

Text boxes and text areas are among the most frequently used form input elements. They are used to hold such important contact information as names, addresses, and phone numbers, and such important product ordering information as credit card numbers and product numbers. It pays to set rules for validating user input, so that the information comes to you correctly, and you don't lose orders, or have to delay shipping to verify data that wasn't submitted the right way to begin with. To validate text box input, follow these steps:

1   Right-click the text box for which you want to set rules, and choose Form Field Properties from the shortcut menu.

2   When the Text Box dialog box appears (see Figure 15-2), click Validate.

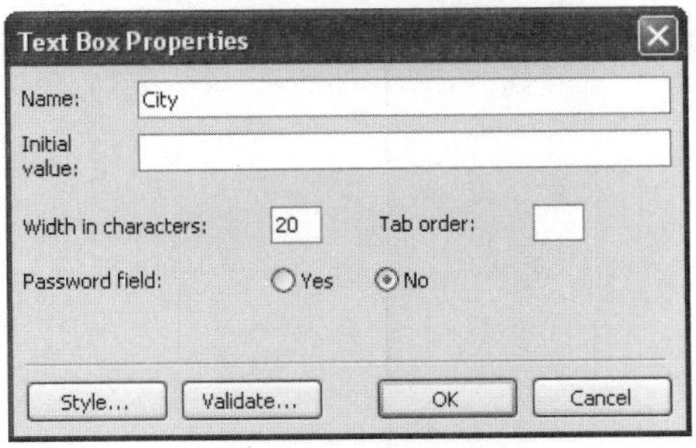

Figure 15-2 Use this dialog box to set validation rules and other properties for text boxes.

3 Choose an option from the Data Type drop-down list to constrain the type of content that can be typed in the text box. By default, the option is set to No Constraints. However, you can specify text, integer, or number constraints.

4 Type a name for the field in the Display Name box (see Figure 15-3). Enter a name that describes the type of data you want users to enter. The name you enter appears as a prompt if the user attempts to leave the field blank.

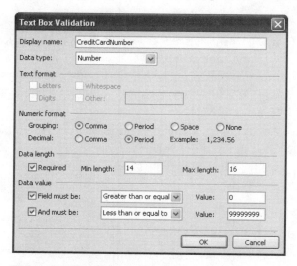

Figure 15-3 This dialog box lets you specify validation rules, so that users enter the text box data you want.

> **Note**   A field's display name becomes visible to your users when you set up rules for the fields in your form. When you use rules, FrontPage uses a field's name, and displays it to a user if that person has filled out a field incorrectly. (When the user presses the Submit button, the form is validated, and a message is displayed listing any fields that haven't been filled out correctly.) Because field names are visible when you set up rules, you should make sure your fields have clear, understandable names, instead of abstract codes.

5 If you choose text, select the kinds of text content that the user can enter in the Text Format area. (Or, if you choose Number or Integer as a Data Type, specify additional options in the Numeric Format area).

6 Check Required if you want this field to be a required field. (Otherwise the user doesn't have to fill out this text to complete the form.)

7 Specify the minimum or maximum number of characters or numbers the text box can contain.

8 Click OK to close Text Box Validation, and OK to close Text Box Properties.

> **Aha!** Set an Initial Value
>
> You can help ensure that your visitors fill out text boxes or other form fields correctly by suggesting a response in the Initial Value box in the Text Box Properties dialog box.

Set Rules for Drop-Down Boxes

You may create a drop-down box with a set of options to choose, but without validation, there's no guarantee that users will choose the right option, or any option at all. Often, drop-down boxes contain a prompt, such as Choose One or Make a Selection, as the first option. Validation ensures that users won't leave this option selected, but instead, will choose one of the options you do want them to pick. Just follow these steps:

1 Right-click the drop-down menu list that you want to have rules, and choose Form Field Properties from the shortcut menu.

2 When the Drop-Down Box Properties dialog box appears, click Validate.

3 When the Drop-Down Box Validation dialog box appears (see Figure 15-4), click Data Required if you want this to be a required field in your form.

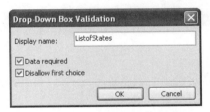

Figure 15-4 Validating drop-down boxes ensures that users will make a choice from your list of options.

4 Enter a name in the the Display Name box—it will be used to prompt users if they don't make a choice from this list.

5 Click Disallow First Choice, if you want to use the first item in the list for instructions (such as "Choose One").

6 Click OK twice to close the Drop-Down Box Validation and the Drop-Down Box Properties dialog boxes.

Set Rules for Option Buttons

The problem with option buttons is that one choice is often preselected by default when the form is designed. Since only one button in a set of option buttons may be selected, it's possible that someone will leave the default option selected—that is, unless you remove the default selection, and then set up validation for the option buttons in the group:

1 Right-click any one of the option buttons in a set. If any of the buttons is preselected, right-click it instead.

2 Choose Form Field Properties from the shortcut menu.

3 If you right-clicked a pre-selected button, when the Option Button Properties
dialog box appears, click Not Selected to remove the default option.

4 Click Validate.

5 When the Option Button Validation dialog box appears (shown in Figure 15-5),
check Data Required to require that the user select one of the buttons in the set.

6 Type a display name for the option button, so that users see it as a prompt if they
do not make a selection from the group, and then click OK.

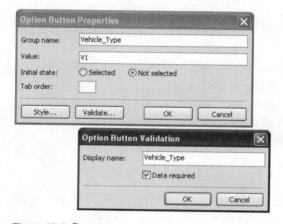

Figure 15-5 Remove any default selections, then activate validation for the option
buttons.

Aha! You Only Need to Activate Validation Once

When you add rules to any option button in a group, the rules apply to all buttons in
that group. Only set rules for one of the buttons, and don't worry about the others.

Optimizing Search Forms and Search Form Results

In Chapter 13, "Using FrontPage Components," you learned how to make a Web searchable
by using FrontPage's built-in Web Search component. FrontPage makes it easy to go a step
or two beyond the default search options to fine-tune the way search input is presented, as

well as how search results appear. Customizing the search form or the search results makes sense when you want to limit the part of your Web that is "searchable," or when you want to cut back on the amount of information your visitors receive. Follow these steps:

1 Right-click anywhere within the search form, and select Search Form Properties.

2 In the Search Form Properties tab, adjust the data input fields as needed:

- Enter new text in the Label For Input box if you want to provide users with a more personalized, playful, or specific label—such as Search Our Web or Search The Catalog—than the default Search For Label.

- Enter a different number in the Width In Characters box if you want to give users more room (or less room) to enter search criteria. Adding more room might be useful if you want to give customers the option of searching by lengthy product names and product numbers, for instance.

- Change the label for the Start Search button box to something more personal and unique than the generic Start Search text. If your Web site is youth-oriented, for instance, you might change the label to Find It! or Go For It!

- Change the label for the Reset Button box to something different only if you feel Reset isn't specific enough—you might change it to Start New Search, for instance.

3 Click the Search Results tab (see Figure 15-6), and change one of the options that determine how search results are presented:

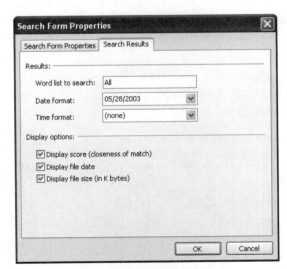

Figure 15-6 Specify how search results are presented to the viewer using this dialog box.

- Change the default term All in the word list to Search Box if you don't want visitors to search all files in your Web (except those in hidden folders). If you want visitors to search only a sales catalog, for instance, enter the name of the folder that contains the catalog files instead.

- Change Date Format or Time Format to another format—or to (None)— if you don't want date stamps or time stamps to be presented.

- Select Display Score (Closeness Of Match), if you want visitors to see a score along with each file listed in the search results; the scoring mechanism assigns a numeric value to the result according to how relevant it is to your search criteria.

- Deselect Display File Date or Display File Size, if you don't think visitors need to know the date a file was created or last updated, or how big the file is in kilobytes. Most search results don't include the file size, and deleting it keeps the search results simpler.

A way to gain an even greater degree of control over search forms and results is to create the form from scratch, and use a custom script to process it, as described in the following section.

Using Custom Scripts with Forms

FrontPage's built-in form handlers are sufficient for most simple forms. But to create forms that return catalog Web pages, or detailed information about the type of browser and connection the visitor is using, or other post-submission processing, there's no subsitute for a custom script. Custom scripts open a two-way communications channel with your visitors, providing a response when searches are made, or when someone logs in to a restricted area of your Web site.

Traditionally, custom scripting is performed by experienced computer programmers. But you may not need to hire someone or learn a programming language to make use of a custom script. Plenty of ready-to-use scripts can be found on the Internet, and often you can find prewritten programs to meet your business needs.

> **Lingo** A *custom script* that processes form data is an external computer program that is designed to accept the information entered into a form's date-entry fields and process them. Such a program is likely to take the form of a Common Gateway Interface (CGI) script or Active Server Pages (ASPs).

While it's beyond the scope of this book to discuss how to create a custom script from scratch, FrontPage does make it easy to associate a custom script with a form that you have designed. Just follow these steps:

1 Right-click anywhere within the form, then choose Form Properties.

2 When the Form Properties dialog box appears, click Send To Other, and choose Custom ISAPI, NSAPI, CGI, or ASP Script from the drop-down list.

3 Click Options. When the Options For Custom Form Handler dialog box appears (see Figure 15-7), enter options for the Action, Method, and Encoding Type Fields:

- Action specifies the action that you want the custom script to perform when form data is submitted by the user. You can specify a URL leading to a custom script, so the data can be processed by it (for example, an absolute path leading to the script might be: *http://www.myfrontpageweb2.com/ cgi-bin/inquiry.pl*. A relative path might be *../inquiry.pl*). You can also send the data to an e-mail address using the mailto action (for example, *mailto:account@myfrontpageweb2.com*).

- Method describes the way the form will submit data to the server. The two options are GET and POST. POST is the preferred method, used by FrontPage by default. POST transmits data in a separate stream to the custom script or form handler. GET adds the data to the URL of the custom script; the number of characters you can send using GET is limited to 4096, and you should only use GET with forms that are certain to solicit only a small amount of data.

- Encoding Type specifies the Multipurpose Internet Mail Extensions (MIME) content type used for encoding the form data before it is passed tothe server. Form data needs to be encoded so that data input fields can be matched to key values. When you use a custom script, you don't have to set a value in the Encoding Type field, but you could use the default value *x-www-form-urlencoded*.

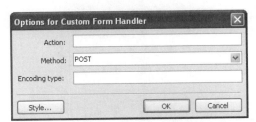

Figure 15-7 if you have a custom script available to process form results, use these options to specify how the script should work.

Lingo MIME stands for *Multipurpose Internet Mail Extensions*, a standard way of designating file types so that they can be processed by browsers, other applications—or in this case, custom scripts.

Keeping Visitors Informed by Sending a Confirmation Page

After your visitors send you the information they requested, they'll naturally want to know if their data was received by you successfully. Every bit of interaction and courtesy you can provide them will improve your image and, hopefully, your public relations. To let them know their submission was successful, and (if necessary) that you'll be responding shortly, you can use FrontPage to identify a confirmation form. When the form results arrive at the Web server, the form handler automatically sends this page to the sender, acknowledging the receipt. FrontPage includes a confirmation template that makes the task a breeze:

1 Open the Web that contains the form you've created.

2 Choose Page or Web from the New submenu of the File menu.

3 Click More Page Templates in the New Page section of the Task Pane.

4 Click Confirmation Form, and click OK.

5 Customize the confirmation form by adding your own content.

6 Right-click any fields you want to customize, and choose Confirmation Field Properties from the shortcut menu (see Figure 15-8).

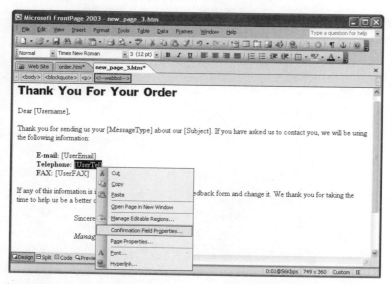

Figure 15-8 This template helps you create a confirmation page.

7 Enter a new name for the field in the Name Of Form Field To Confirm box, and click OK.

> **Aha!** Improve Accuracy with the Confirmation Page Template
>
> There are two advantages to using FrontPage's Confirmation Page template instead of creating your own page. First, you save yourself some work. Second, FrontPage automatically sets up the confirmation page so that the user's message and contact information are displayed. That way, the user can make sure the correct information was submitted to you.

Gathering Extra Information with Hidden Fields

A hidden field is something the user doesn't actually see when filling out the form you've created. Sometimes, hidden fields are essential to provide information that a script, database, or file needs to process the form information. A hidden field can also serve as a note to you, visible when you receive the data from the file. When you create a hidden field, you can leave information about the name of the form, the place it was published, or the version number of the form.

A hidden field contains two attributes: a Name (a keyword associated with the field), and a Value (the version number, date, or other information contained in the field). To create a hidden field, follow these steps:

1 Right-click anywhere in the form, then choose Form Properties from the shortcut menu.

2 When the Form Properties dialog box appears, click Advanced.

3 When the Advanced Form Properties dialog box appears (see Figure 15-9), click Add.

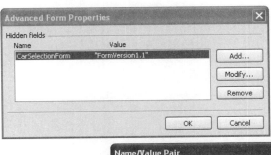

Figure 15-9 Hidden fields automatically submit background information that can help you process form data.

4 Enter a name and value for the hidden field, and click OK.

> **Aha!**   Place a Hidden Field Wherever You Want
>
> Since you don't actually see the hidden field in the FrontPage window, it doesn't matter
> where you place the cursor before you create the field. In order to modify or remove
> hidden fields, right-click the form, then choose Form Properties from the shortcut
> menu. In the Advanced Form Properties dialog box, select the field you want to
> change, and then click Modify or Remove.

Registering Your Visitors

One effective strategy for finding out who is visiting your Web site is to create a registration
form. Giving users the option to log in to your site with a username and password has
advantages for both site owners and visitors. Visitors who register can subscribe to publications, or access "premium" content you create just for them. With the user information
you receive from registration forms, you can tailor your site to address your visitors' needs,
and make it more effective.

Creating a Password Field

A password field is a text box in which a user enters a password. When you create such
a text box by right-clicking it, and choosing Form Field Properties, you click Yes next to
the Password field option. This allows the password that is entered to appear in the form
of asterisks, rather than text characters, so unauthorized users cannot determine the
password while it is being typed. Together with a text field that captures a user's login
ID, a password field can be used to validate that the user has access to a protected area
within your Web site (see Figure 15-10).

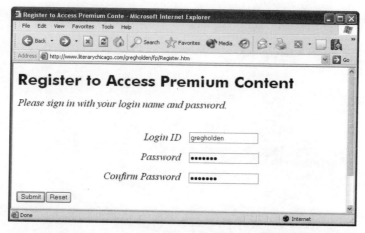

Figure 15-10   Password fields help register users to enter a restricted area of a Web site.

Enable Registration Quickly with the User Registration Template

Password fields can be combined with User IDs and other information to create a registration form. Such a form provides an entry point for users who want to access restricted or premium content online. FrontPage comes with a User Registration Template that makes it easy to create such a form.

In order for the registration form to work, you need to prepare the target Web to use the Registration Form Handler, which creates accounts for new users. To prepare the Web, open it in FrontPage, and choose Tools, Server, Permissions. (You can't do this on a file-based Web.) When the Permissions Administration form appears, click Change Permissions. When the Change Subweb Permissions form appears, click Use Unique Permissions For This Web, then click Submit. Turn off anonymous access for the subweb on its Site Administration form. Then you can create the user registration form as follows:

1 Choose File, New.

2 Click More Page Templates in the New Page section of the Task Pane.

3 Click the General tab.

4 Click User Registration, and click OK.

5 Replace the placeholder text in the registration form (see Figure 15-11) with your own text.

6 Click Save and save the file in the root directory of your FrontPage-based Web.

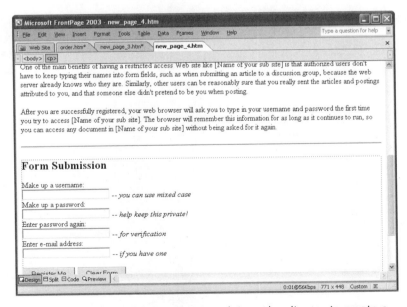

Figure 15-11 The User Registration template makes it easy to create a registration form.

The registration form must be saved to the root Web, not the Web site itself. For example, if the protected web site is *http://Root/Subweb*, the form must be saved in Root.

> **Note**   When FrontPage creates the user registration form, read the comments at the top of the form carefully. The first comment explains that some servers do not permit users to register themselves—specifically, servers running Microsoft Windows 2000 or NT do not permit this. Ask your network administrator or Web host if the server that hosts your site allows user self-registration.

Customize the Registration Results

Once you create a registration page, you need to configure FrontPage's Registration Form Handler so it will work on your Web. Follow these steps:

1   Right-click anywhere in the registration form.

2   Choose Form Properties from the shortcut menu.

3   Make sure Send To Other is selected.

4   Make sure Registration Form Handler is displayed, and click Options.

5   Click the Registration Tab, and type the name of your Web in the Web Name box (see Figure 15-12).

Figure 15-12 Point the Registration Form Handler to your user registration Web.

6   If you want the user to verify a password by entering it twice, type a name for the confirmation field in the Password Confirmation Field box.

7 Enter the URL of a custom page to be displayed in case registration fails, if you want to create your own page (otherwise FrontPage supplies a default page). Click OK.

8 Click the File Results tab, and type the URL of the file that you want to receive the registration data that the user submits.

9 Choose a desired format for the registration information from the File Format drop-down list.

10 Click Saved Fields, and check one of the Additional Information To Save check boxes, if you want to collect additional registration information from your visitors. Click OK.

Caution The name you type in the Web Name box must match the name of your Web exactly, including any hyphens or underlines, or the registration form handler will not process your registration form data. The safest way to get the name exactly right is to click the Open Web button and locate the Web on your computer or network to double-check the correct name.

Fast Wrap-Up

■ Images add graphic interest to Web page forms, while labels make a form more clickable, and enable you to create keyboard shortcuts.

■ Validation rules enable you to control how visitors fill out a form, so that you get the results in a format you can process and use.

■ Search form input fields can be optimized so that forms more clearly reflect your site's "personality." Search results can be adjusted to give users only the information they really need.

■ Custom scripts open a two-way communication path with visitors, providing responses when form data is submitted.

■ Confirmation pages let visitors know their information was received successfully, which improves their level of satisfaction with your site.

■ Hidden fields enable you to gather more specific information, such as version numbers, that can help you make use of forms data.

■ Registration forms give you a way to let users register themselves, so that they can gain access to restricted content.

Making a Site Database-Driven

16

10-Second Summary
- Work with live data on a Windows SharePoint Services Web site
- Create Data Views that let users easily post to a database
- Format Data Views the quick way by implementing preformatted styles
- Create, edit, and add databases with the Data Source Catalog

In the business world, accurate and up-to-date information is the key to success. When it comes to creating a Web site, publishing the most accurate information you can, and getting it online as quickly as possible, keeps customers satisfied. By linking your site to live data sources held in databases, you ensure that your visitors get current information instantly—and once you set up the system, with the help of Microsoft Office FrontPage 2003, the information is generated "on the fly" in response to requests. The Web browser becomes a database client, and a Web server a database server.

FrontPage has always made it easy to save form results to a database or make connections to existing databases through its Database Interface Wizard and Database Results Wizard. Now, FrontPage makes working with live data easier than ever. By combining FrontPage 2003 with a Microsoft Windows SharePoint Services Web site, you can use FrontPage as a complete interface for working with databases. You can present a variety of live data, including Web services, XML services, and OLE database data sources. This flexibility lowers the cost of creating and maintaining your Web site. Support for standards like Extensible Markup language (XML) and Extensible Stylesheet Language Transformations (XSLTs) gives your co-workers the ability to post to the Web, using only their Web browsers.

This chapter focuses on FrontPage's newest tools for working with data. You'll learn how to view data, format it, sort it, and connect one data source to another, all from within the same tool you use to create the Web pages on which the data appears.

Making Your Content Up-to-Date With Live Data

Live data is data that you view on the Web that is not static, but drawn from a database, and presented on a Web page in response to your request. You get a view of the data on the Web page, and the part of the Web page on which the data appears is called a Data View. The source of the live information you view is a database, which is called a Data Source. These two elements—Data Views and Data Sources—are illustrated in Figure 16-1:

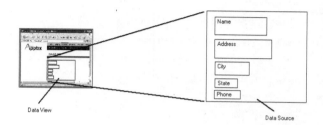

Figure 16-1　When you add a Data View, you present live content drawn from a Data Source.

FrontPage gives you lots of ways to view live data. You can:

- Create data-enabled Active Server Pages (ASP)

- Create an ASP.NET site. A Web site based on ASP or ASP.NET can use a data source such as Microsoft Office Access 2003.

- Create a data-driven Web site using Windows SharePoint Services

You then run either the Database Results Wizard or the Database Interface Wizard to create Web pages that present the database contents online and let you interact with them. The option you choose depends on which technology is available on your Web server.

The best way is to use a site based on Windows SharePoint Services. This enables you to access a wide range of data sources, including desktop-based and server-based databases, XML files, Web services, and SharePoint lists. When you create a data-driven Web site, you select data sources from a data source catalog and use Data View Web Parts to present data. Data View Web Parts render data by using Extensible Stylesheet Language Transformation (XSLT).

> **Note** All of the options related to Data Views, Data Source Catalogs, and Web Parts presented in this chapter require your Web site to be hosted on a server that makes use of Windows SharePoint Services. The following technologies are required on your Web server: Microsoft Windows Server 2003, Standard Edition, Enterprise Edition, Datacenter Edition, or Web Edition; Microsoft Internet Information Services (IIS) 6.0 in IIS 6.0 worker process isolation mode, and ASP.NET. Check with your ISP or Web host to make sure these services are available.

Presenting Live Data by Inserting Data View Web Parts

The first step in creating a Web page that is designed to present live data is to create a Data View. A Data View performs two functions: it displays data on the current Web page, and also provides other members who have access to the Windows SharePoint site to post their own data by filling out the simple form that appears in the Data View when the page is viewed with a browser.

> **Lingo** The term *Data View* is actually short for *Data View Web Part*. A *Web Part* is a modular unit of information that makes up part of a SharePoint Web page. Multiple Web Parts can be enclosed within an area called a *Web Part Zone* that is invisible when the page is viewed in a browser but that appears as a dotted line in the FrontPage window.

The advantages of using Windows SharePoint and FrontPage are speed and convenience: you only need to choose a single menu option to make a link between the current Web page and a data source. Without SharePoint, you need to create the data source, create a database connection to the data source, and then create the Web page that is designed to display the data. Rather than having to follow all of these steps, you only need to:

1 Open the Web page on which you want to present the Data View. Make sure you are in Design view, and that you are in a Web site that uses Windows SharePoint Services.

2 Position the cursor where you want the new Data View Web Part to appear. If you position the cursor beneath the current Web Part Zone, it will be in a separate zone. If you click the label Left at the top of the Web Part Zone to select the Zone itself, you can add the new Data View Web Part to the current zone.

3 When you are ready, choose Data, Insert Data View.

4 When the Data Source Catalog task pane appears (see Figure 16-2 on the following page), make a selection from the set of data sources: SharePoint Lists, SharePoint Libraries, database connections, XML data sources, and more. (See the section "Working with the Data Source Catalog" later in this chapter for more information.)

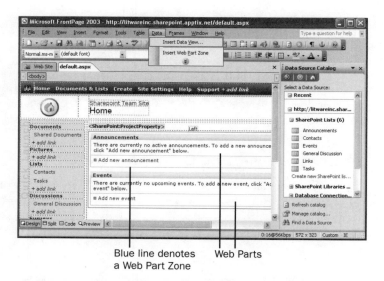

Blue line denotes   Web Parts
a Web Part Zone

Figure 16-2 The Data View menu option and Data Source Catalog task pane are available when you are working on a Windows SharePoint Services site.

Once you add a data view, you can format it as described in the following section.

> **Caution**   Each Data View Web Part within a Web Part Zone is enclosed by an orange box when you view it in FrontPage Design View. The Web Part Zone itself is enclosed by a blue box. Don't select an existing Web Part Zone when you create a new one— you'll delete the previous Web Part Zone when the new one is inserted.

Speeding Up Formatting by Inserting Data View Styles

One of the advantages of using Data Views is the ability to make data look the way you want from directly within FrontPage, and see exactly how it will look in a Web browser. Rather than having to launch and use a database application, you can format a Data View using FrontPage's formatting options: right-click the Data View, choose Web Part Properties, and change the formatting options in the properties dialog box that appears (see Figure 16-3).

Figure 16-3   You can change a Data View's visual appearance by choosing from these options.

Browse through Preset Data View Styles

You gain a lot more control over formatting, as well as a preview of how the elements within a Data View are arranged, by applying a preset style. Follow these steps:

1   Single-click the Data View you want to format to select it.

2   In the Data View Details task pane, under the heading Manage View Settings, click Style.

3   When the View Styles dialog box appears, scroll down the list of layout options in the HTML view styles box. Click each option to read about it under the heading Description (see Figure 16-4).

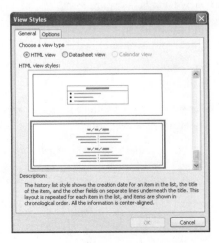

Figure 16-4 Preview and quickly choose a layout style for a Data View from this list.

4   When you've chosen an option you like, click to select it.

5   If you want to add a toolbar to a Data View that enables your co-workers to perform functions such as posting or sorting items, click the Options tab, and select the box next to Show Toolbar With Options For.

6   When you're done, click OK.

> **Note**   It's worth taking a detailed look through all of the styles to find the one that's right for you. Don't overlook the ones at the bottom of the lengthy list. The History option, for instance, is especially good if you have a lot of events or comments posted, and you want to arrange them chronologically.

Applying Conditional Formatting

Dynamic conditional formatting enables you to change the visual characteristics of data, if certain conditions are met. It's the feature to use if you want your Web site to highlight information, so that you and your co-workers can make decisions based on important criteria. Apply conditional formatting when you need to be alerted to anomalies within a set of values. In a set of sales figures, you might want to highlight particularly good results. For example, you can display values that are less than $100 in red and values greater than $1000 in green. You can also decide whether to show or hide items, based on conditions such as their value, or their position in the data view. To apply conditional formatting to a Data View, follow these steps:

1   Click to select the element in the Data View that you want to format.

> **Note**   Click carefully: Selecting the entire Data View does not display the Conditional Formatting option in the task pane. Rather, you need to select an individual field within the Data View that you want to format.

2   Click Conditional Formatting in the Data View Details task pane.

3   When the Conditional Formatting options appear in the task pane, click Create, then choose one of the three options that appear (see Figure 16-5).

- Choose Show Content if you want the conditions to cause the content to be visible when the Web page is viewed in a browser.

- Choose Hide Content if you want the conditions to cause the content to be hidden when the Web page is viewed in a browser.

- Choose Apply Formatting if you want special formatting (such as a color) to be applied when the conditions are met.

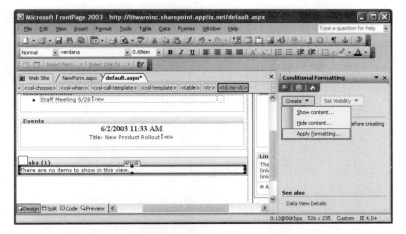

Figure 16-5 Conditional formatting can cause content to be shown, hidden, or appear in a special way.

4   When the Condition Criteria dialog box appears (see Figure 16-6), click Click Here To Add A New Clause.

5   When a drop-down list appears under Field Name, choose Rows or Status.

6   When a drop-down list appears under Comparison, choose one of the list options (Equals, Greater Than, Contains, Does Not Contain, and so on.)

7   When a drop-down list appears under Value, either select a value from the list, or choose the blank option at the bottom of the list and type your own content. For this example, type the word **Announcement**. Click OK when you're finished.

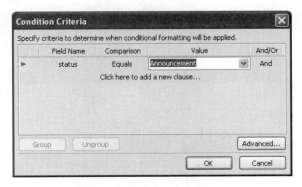

Figure 16-6 Establish the criteria for the formatting you want to apply.

8   When the Condition Criteria dialog box closes, the Modify Style dialog box automatically appears. Click Format, and choose an item (Font, Paragraph, Border, Numbering, or Position) that has the formatting you want to apply.

For instance, if you want to format the word *Announcements* in red and all caps when it appears, click Font. When the Font dialog box appears, choose red from the Color drop-down list, select the box next to All Caps, then click OK. Click OK again to close the Modify Style dialog box.

When you're done, the conditional formatting you have specified appears under the heading Existing Conditions in the Conditional Formatting task pane. You can modify the conditions, or add new ones, if you wish. Click Set Visibility if you want to change the formatting immediately by making it visible or hidden.

Sorting, Filtering, and Grouping Data

Anything you can do to analyze data more quickly will boost your productivity and enable you to create more accurate reports. Sorting, filtering, and grouping are three basic ways of analyzing data; FrontPage gives you the ability to perform such analysis without having to launch a separate database application:

- Sorting enables you to find the highest or lowest data value in a set of records, or rank values in order.

- Filtering displays only data that matches the filter condition—perfect for focusing your attention on specific records within a data source.

- Grouping enables you to view a set of records that are in proximity to one another—all the cells in a row, for instance.

Sorting, grouping, and filtering gives you the ability to help your colleagues by allowing them to see only the information that is most relevant or urgent. By editing your SharePoint Services site's contents, you make the site more useful, and increase the chances that your colleagues will actively participate by sharing their own information. Just follow these steps:

1 Right-click the Data View you want to format, and choose Data View Properties from the shortcut menu.

2 When the Data View Details task pane appears, click Filter.

3 When the Filter Criteria dialog box appears, click Click Here To Add A New Clause. See Steps 4 through 8 in the preceding section on Conditional Formatting to learn how to set the criteria; the process is basically the same.

4 When you're done filtering, click Sort And Group in the Data View Details task pane.

5 In the Sort And Group dialog box (see Figure 16-7), select options from the Available Fields list. (These are the fields that are contained in the Data View you are formatting.) Click Add to move each to the Sort Order column.

6 Click each of the items you have moved to the Sort Order column, and click
Move Up or Move Down to change the order. Click OK to close Sort And Group.

7 When you're done, click OK.

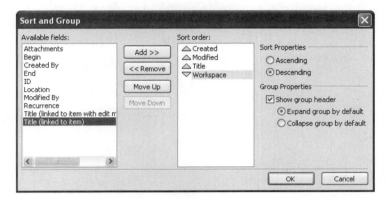

Figure 16-7 Sort and group items in a Data View, so that you and your colleagues
see only the most important contents.

Connecting Web Parts

By default, a Data View that you add to a SharePoint Services Web page is a standalone Web
Part. When someone adds a link, announcement, task, or other bit of information to share
with the other members of the workgroup, the contents of that Web Part alone change. Any
other Web parts on the page stay the same.

Web Part pages become more interactive and useful when they are connected—the contents of one part change in response to a change in another part. Connecting Web Parts
enables you to create sophisticated scenarios on a single Web page. One part can contain a
"master list" of categories or topics (for example, a list of employees), and when the viewer
chooses one of those items, the corresponding details appear in another Web Part (such as
a set of contact information for the selected employee). To connect one Web Part to
another, follow these steps:

1 Right-click one of the Web Parts that you want to connect, and choose Web Part
Connections from the shortcut menu.

2 When the Web Part Connections Wizard appears, make sure Provide Data Values To Another Web Part is chosen under Choose The Action on the source Web
Part To Use For This Connection, then click Next.

3 When the next screen of the Wizard appears, choose to connect to either a Web
Part on this page or in the current Web. If you choose a Web Part on another
page, click Browse to locate the page. Then click Next.

4 When the next screen of the Wizard appears (see Figure 16-8), choose the Web
    Part to which you want to connect from the Target Web Part list. Then, choose
    an action from the Target Action list, and click Next.

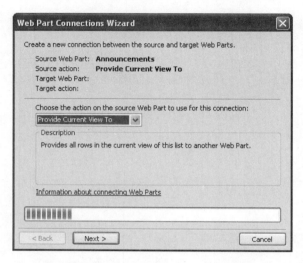

Figure 16-8 You can make a change in one Web Part affect the data in another
Web Part.

5 In the next screen of the Wizard, select the columns containing data that will
    change in the two Web Parts that you want to connect. Click Next.

6 In the next screen of the Wizard, create a hyperlink connecting one part to the
    other. Click Next, then click Finish to establish the connection.

Once you have connected the two Web parts, it's a good idea to click File, Save to save your
changes, and then preview the Web page in a browser, so you can test the connection to see
if it works the way you want it to.

Creating a Web Part Zone

Web Parts can stand by themselves on a Web page. But when you group them with other
Web Parts in a container, called a Web Part Zone, you give your co-workers added functionality. By creating a Web Part Zone, you give users the ability to click on a Quick Launch,
or similar link, in their browser window to automatically load a Web Part into the Web Part
Zone without having to use FrontPage. To create a Web Part Zone:

1 Choose Web Part Gallery from the drop-down list at the top of the task pane.

2 Scroll down to the bottom of the Web Part Gallery options, until the New Web
    Part Zone button is visible.

3 Click to position the cursor in a part of the current Web page that is not already part of a Web Part Zone, then click New Web Part Zone.

4 Select a Web Part from the list displayed in the Web Part Gallery Task Pane, then click Insert Selected Web Part to add it to the Web Part Zone you just created.

By default, the Web Part Zone is given a generic name such as Zone 1, Zone 2, and so on. However, you can change the name by right-clicking the zone, and entering a new title in the Zone Title box in Web Part Zone Properties.

Working with the Data Source Catalog

Sales catalogs gather a variety of items in a single location, so that you can browse through them quickly and make selections. The Data Source Catalog that becomes available when you use FrontPage on a Windows SharePoint Services Web site does much the same thing. It collects all of the data sources that already exist on your Web, from Access or SQL data-bases to XML files and SharePoint libraries, so that you can add them as needed. If you work in an environment in which more than one person may be responsible for designing pages and creating data sources, having all of them accessible in an easy to use Data Source Catalog can save you time searching for information.

The Data Source Catalog doesn't just help you locate data sources, however. You can use it to configure new data sources that you want to incorporate into your Web, as well as to change the properties of data sources. The following sections provide you with an overview of the different kinds of data sources you can work with as part of the catalog.

Connecting to SharePoint Data Sources

One of the advantages of working with a SharePoint Services Web site is the fact that data sources you can add to data views are not limited to just database files. You can add any SharePoint element to a Data View. These include Announcements, Contacts, Events, General Discussion, Links, and Tasks.

If none of those options fits your workgroup's communications needs, click Create New SharePoint List beneath the list of SharePoint data sources in the Data Source Catalog task pane. The SharePoint List dialog box appears. Click New List Wizard to create a custom SharePoint list, and choose the selection that best fits your needs, such as: Custom list, to create a new list completely from scratch; Custom List in Datasheet View, to create a list in the style of a spreadsheet; or one of the more specific SharePoint list options shown in Figure 16-9 on the following page.

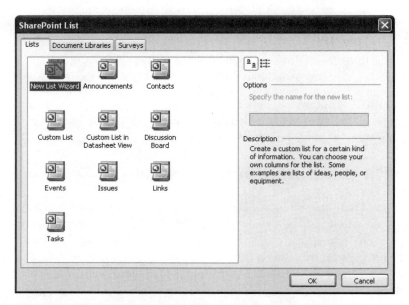

Figure 16-9   You can use the Data Source Catalog to create a new SharePoint list or document library that you can add to a Data View.

Not only that, but you can also add SharePoint Libraries in much the same way. Select a document library from the list shown in the Data Source Catalog. If you don't see a list that meets your needs—for instance, if you want to create a library of Active X Controls or databases, click Create New Document Library. The SharePoint List dialog box appears, with the Document Libraries tab selected, so that you can create a new library with the New Document Library Wizard, or select one from the options presented (Document Library, Picture Library, or Form Library).

Connecting to XML Data Sources

Support for XML throughout the Microsoft Office System is one of its strongest features. That support extends to the Data Source Catalog, where you can select an XML file or service to add to a Data View. The XML file you select does not have to be in the form of a Web page. FrontPage enables you to add Microsoft Word files, as well as URLs that are configured to return Web pages written in XML.

To add an XML file, click the plus sign (+) next to XML Files, and make a selection from the list of files that appears.To add an XML file to the Data Source Catalog, click Add To Catalog under XML Files, then locate the file in the Data Source Properties dialog box.

Connecting to Web-Based Data Sources

XML Web Services are sources of information that you can add to applications or Web pages in order to make them more valuable to your visitors. Examples include stock quotes, the latest news headlines, or financial reports. If you have an XML Web service, you add it by clicking the plus sign (+) next to XML Services, and choosing an option from the list that appears. When you click Add To Catalog under XML Web Services, a special, extra-detailed version of the Data Source Properties dialog box appears that lets you specify not only the location of the service, but also exactly what parameters are needed to connect to it (see Figure 16-10).

Figure 16-10   Use this dialog box to specify connection parameters for an XML Web service that you want to add to a Data Source Catalog.

Connecting to Microsoft SQL Server Data Sources

No database connection tool would be complete without support for Microsoft SQL Server databases. Click the plus sign (+) under Database Connections to identify any existing databases already on your SharePoint Web. Click Add To Catalog to add a database that's not yet been added to the Web.

Fast Wrap-Up

- FrontPage lets you make a site database-driven by drawing information from a Data Source and presenting it in a Data View.

- A Data View displays data on the current Web page, and enables SharePoint Services team members to post their own data, using only a Web browser.

- Apply conditional formatting to a Data View when you want to hide, show, or highlight information that meets criteria you specify.

- Sorting, Filtering, and Grouping data highlights information, so that your colleagues can identify the most important data and work with it more quickly.

- Web Parts can be connected, so that a change in one Web Part can automatically change the contents in another one.

- FrontPage's Data Source Catalog enables you to quickly identify and add database connections, SharePoint Lists, and a variety of other data sources.

Part 5
Administering and Updating Your Web Site

Part 5, "Administering and Updating Your Web Site," describes how to get your Web site before the eyes of others, and how to keep the site running smoothly once it goes online. In Chapter 17, "Publishing Your Web Site," you learn how to transfer your Web page files from your own computer to a server, where others can see them, and make use of the content you've worked hard to prepare. Chapter 18, "Working Collaboratively," examines the benefits of working with a Microsoft SharePoint Team Services Web site, where workgroups can post and share information. Chapter 19, "Administering Web Sites,"covers FrontPage's ability to keep a Web site running smoothly: producing clean HTML, following task lists, and making sure hyperlinks work correctly. Chapter 20, "Customizing and Maintaining FrontPage 2003," details how to make FrontPage fit your preferred working style, by personalizing toolbars, configuring editors, and using the built-in Detect and Repair utility when problems occur.

Publishing Your Web Site

17

> **10-Second Summary**
> - Preview your Web site to check functionality before it goes online
> - Publish your Web site files to a Web or FTP server
> - Publish to a server that supports WebDAV (Web-based Distributed Authoring and Versioning)
> - Get the whole picture with FrontPage's new remote site view
> - Synchronize Web site files so that both local and remote sites are up to date

The term *publishing* tends to make getting a Web site online sound complex and difficult. But Microsoft Office FrontPage 2003 takes publishing sites out of the province of Webmasters, and puts it squarely in your hands. Publishing refers to the process of transferring your files from your local, disk-based Web (the one you maintain on your own computer) to a remote Web site. The remote Web site can be a location on a SharePoint or other Web server, where others view the site with their browsers. It can also be a file system on your own computer, a shared network folder, or another computer on your network that others on the local network can view, or that can function as a backup. This chapter explores some of the many ways FrontPage enables you to publish sites. There are a number of different server types out there—FTP, SharePoint, WebDAV—and FrontPage makes it easy to work with any or all of them, depending on your needs.

Verifying Your Web Site's Functionality by Previewing Pages

One of the most important aspects of managing a Web site is previewing pages before they go online and become visible to outsiders. Previewing gives you a chance to verify that your pages look and behave the way you want them to—that your images all appear in their entirety, your hyperlinks take visitors where you want them to go, and so on. FrontPage not only makes it easy to preview pages in different browsers, but also enables you to quickly choose a specific browser window size, which is essential, if you want to make sure large images, tables, or frames-based pages appear the way you want them to at various sizes.

Checking Pages Quickly with Preview View

FrontPage gives you two ways to preview pages. The first way (a quicker option than previewing in a browser, which is described below) is to click the Preview button beneath the page editing view. This allows you to preview the page as it would appear in a Web browser, but still remain in FrontPage. Use Preview view when you're in the process of working on the page, and you want to check it quickly before making changes.

Testing the End Result by Previewing in a Web Browser

Once you've finished editing a page, and have saved your changes, you should go a step beyond Preview view, and click Preview In Browser to launch your default browser, with the current page displayed. Previewing in a Web browser enables you to see a Web page just as the visitors to your Web site will see it.

FrontPage provides you with a convenient list of all the browsers you have installed on your filesystem, which enables you to test a page in more than one Web browser. This lets you evaluate your site, using the software that the maximum number of your visitors are likely to use. One of the best new FrontPage features enables you to preview a page in a specific browser window size, without ever having to leave Design view. Here's how to do that:

1 Open the page you want to preview, and click Save on the Standard toolbar to save your pages.

2 Click the Preview In Browser button on the Standard toolbar, or press F12 to open the page in your default browser.

3 After checking the page in your default browser, click the down arrow next to the button to choose a browser or browser size from the list of browsers available on your system (see Figure 17-1). Or choose File, Preview In Browser, Multiple Browsers to view the current page in multiple browsers in succession.

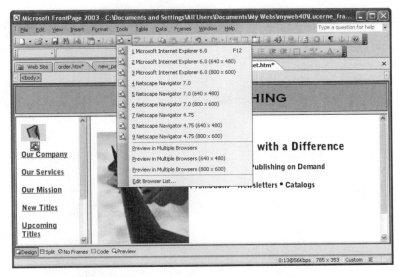

Figure 17-1 FrontPage makes it easy for you to open files in more than one Web browser.

Aha!   Save Before You Preview

If you haven't saved your page before you choose Preview In Browser, FrontPage prompts you to do so. Clicking Automatically Save Page Before Previewing in the Edit In Browser dialog box will prevent this prompt from reappearing whenever you want to preview a page.

Keeping Up with New Software by Adding a Preview Browser

New versions of Web browsers appear on a regular basis, each with a new set of features. You need to add browsers to FrontPage's Preview In Browser list, to make sure you can check your pages in the latest and greatest software around. To select a default browser, add a new browser, or delete a browser from the list, follow these steps:

1 Choose File, Preview In Browser, Edit Browser List.

2 Click Add to add another browser to the list (see Figure 17-2 on the following page).

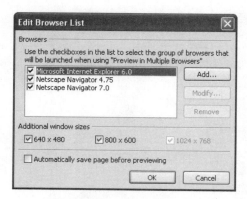

Figure 17-2 Use this dialog box to add or remove browsers from FrontPage's Preview In Browser list.

3 When the Add Browser dialog appears, enter the name of the browser in the Name box.

4 Click Browse, and use the new Add Browser dialog box to locate the browser on your filesystem.

5 Click OK to close both dialog boxes and return to Edit Browser List.

6 Click one of the Window Size buttons to specify a default browser window size.

7 Click OK to add the browser to the Preview In Browser list.

> **Caution**   Don't use FrontPage's Preview In Browser function as the final preview for your Web pages. After your pages are published, you need to check them all by opening them in one or more browsers. Checking them over a "live" Internet connection rather than open pages on your own file system will show you whether your site takes too long to open. You can also make sure all the image and text files you need to display were actually published, or whether some are missing.

Going Live: Publishing Your Web Site

When you're finished creating content, previewing pages, and verifying hyperlinks (see Chapter 19, "Administering Web Sites"), the time comes to move your pages from your own computer to a Web server, where they can be accessed by other Web surfers. This process is called publishing your Web site. FrontPage makes it easy to publish to a server that is running the FrontPage Server Extensions or SharePoint Team Services (an extended server, in other words), as well as FTP or WebDAV servers.

Publishing a Web to an Extended Server

If you are using a server that supports the Microsoft FrontPage Server Extensions or SharePoint Team Services, FrontPage makes the publishing process a matter of a few mouse clicks. The advantage of publishing on one of these "extended servers" is that you can create advanced features, such as feedback forms and discussion Webs, and also take advantage of the collaboration tools on a SharePoint site. You first need to set up the properties of the extended server that will host your Web site:

1 Click View, Remote Web Site.

2 When the message Click "Remote Web Site Properties..." appears, look in the toolbar immediately above FrontPage's Design view, and click Remote Web Site Properties (see Figure 17-3).

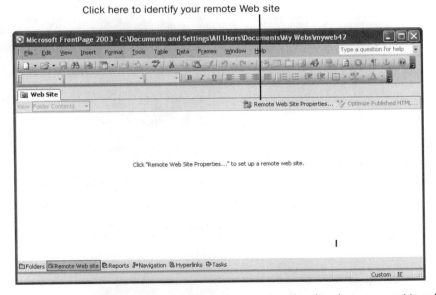

Figure 17-3 Click Remote Web Site Properties to set up the site where you want to publish.

3 When the Remote Web Site Properties dialog box appears (see Figure 17-4 on the following page), select the publishing method that applies to your own Web server setup:

- **FrontPage or SharePoint Services**   Choose this option if your Web server has one of these sets of server extensions installed.

- **DAV**   Choose this option if your server supports Distributed Authoring and Versioning, a standard that allows workgroups to collaborate on shared files.

- **FTP**   Choose this option if you use File Transfer Protocol to publish files from your local computer to the Web server.

● **File System**   Choose this option if you are going to publish your site to a location on your own computer or on a shared network folder.

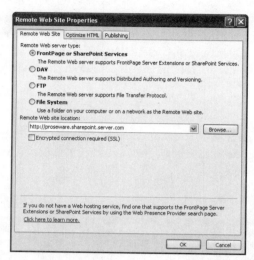

Figure 17-4 Select the type of server that will hold your Web site, and enter its URL.

4 Enter the URL of the Web site in the Remote Web Site Location box. Click OK.

FrontPage immediately connects to the remote Web site, and displays both the Local Web Site and Remote Web Site contents (see Figure 17-5). Once you are connected, select Local To Remote under Publish All Changed Pages, then click Publish Web Site to move your pages from your local site to the remote location.

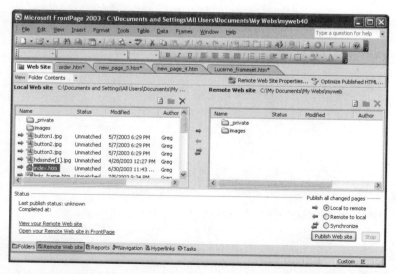

Figure 17-5   FrontPage displays both the local and remote versions of your Web site.

Gaining Flexibility by Publishing with FTP Server View

File Transfer Protocol (FTP) servers are typically provided by Internet Service Providers (ISPs) to give their customers Web server space for their personal or business Web sites. There are other reasons why you might publish using FTP, however. For instance, different workgroups may be creating content and editing your Web site. This might happen with a large organization that has different branch offices. Some offices might use FrontPage to create Web content, while others might use a tool like Macromedia Dreamweaver. When you can't predict how files will be created, opt for flexibility by publishing to an FTP site.

> **Lingo** *File Transfer Protocol (FTP)* has been around longer than the Web itself. It's a communications method intended solely for moving files from one computer to another on a network.

When you publish to an FTP site, you'll need the server name, username, and password from your Internet Service Provider, as well as the name of the directory where your Web site files are stored. Once you have this data close at hand, follow steps 1 and 2 from the preceding section. When the Remote Web Site Properties dialog box appears, click FTP, and enter the URL for the FTP site. Then click OK. When the Name And Password Required dialog box appears (see Figure 17-6), enter the name and password needed to connect to your FTP server, then click OK.

Figure 17-6 FrontPage enables you to enter the password and username required to connect to an FTP server.

> **Caution** When you enter the URL of your Web site in the Remote Web Site Properties dialog box, be sure to include the protocol (in this case, *ftp://*). The URL should take the form *ftp://ftp.myftpserver.com*.

Maintaining Functionality by Publishing a Web to Local File

Publishing doesn't have to take place over the Internet. It's a good idea to create a backup of a Web site, either on your own computer or, better yet, on a shared folder on another computer on your local network. In case your own machine experiences serious damage, you can use the backup version to update your site as needed. You might wonder why you would want to publish a Web site, rather than simply copying the Web site's files and folders from one location to another. Publishing ensures that you don't forget any files you need, and that you maintain your Web site's structure. It also ensures that any FrontPage Web page components you've included on your pages will actually function.

See Also See Chapter 13, "Using FrontPage Components," for a detailed examination of Web components you can add to your site with FrontPage.

To publish your site to a local folder, open The Remote Web Site Properties dialog box as explained in preceding sections. Then:

1 Select File System.

2 In the Remote Web Site Location box, enter the UNC form (such as \\server\folder\subfolder) of the path leading to the web you want to publish. Or click Browse if you need to locate a server on your local network. Click OK.

> **Caution**   Make sure there aren't any blank spaces or capital letters in the name of the folder to which you are going to publish your files. UNIX or UNIX-style Web server operating systems don't work well with blank spaces or capital letters, and in the interest of compatibility, FrontPage doesn't allow you to use them either.

3 Enter the username you use to access your Web server, if one is required, and then enter your password.

4 Select Save This Password In Your Password List, if you want your password to be automatically entered for you in the future. Click OK.

5 Once the local site appears in Remote Site View, select Local To Remote under Publish All Changed Pages, then click Publish Web Site to move your pages from your local site to the remote location.

Lingo *Universal Naming Convention (UNC)* is a way of locating a file on a filesystem that is machine-independent. Rather than specifying a drive letter and path (such as C:\Program Files\folder\subfolder), UNC uses the form \\server\share\path\filename.

Controlling Document Changes by Publishing with WebDAV

If the server to which you publish your site exists on a corporate intranet, it may support an advanced protocol for collaborative document authoring called WebDAV. FrontPage 2003 now supports publishing to servers which use this Web content management framework, allowing files to be locked, so that they can't be overwritten (if you and coworker are both working on the same document, you won't undo one another's changes). WebDAV uses XML, which enables you to save metadata about a file (such as its author, title, subject, and creation date) along with the file's actual contents. This allows you to search for files created by a particular author, or edited on a specific date.

Lingo *WebDAV (Web-based Distributed Authoring and Versioning)*, is a protocol developed by the World Wide Web Consortium, designed specifically for publishing and maintaining files on the Web. It allows information about a file to be stored in such a way that editors/authors can make changes to the file, or its properties, without overwriting changes that other editors/authors have already made to the file.

Publishing to a WebDAV server is pretty much the same as publishing to an FTP server: open the Remote Site View Properties dialog box, as described in preceding sections, select DAV, enter the URL of the server in Remote Web Site Location (which will probably include your username, or directory name), and click OK to display the server's contents in Remote Site View. Select Local To Remote under Publish All Changed Pages, then click Publish Web Site to move your pages from your local site to the remote location.

See Also If you want to find out more about WebDAV, you'll find an excellent introductory article on the subject at *http:// ftp.ics.uci.edu/ pub/ietf/ webdav/intro/ webdav_intro.pdf.*

Synchronizing Local and Remote Sites

If you are the only person who creates and updates your Web pages, you're not likely to get confused about which version of your site—the local version or the remote version—has the latest files, and which files need to be updated. You can, after all, update pages, either on the local or remote site, using FrontPage. After you revise a file, you copy it to the other location, so that both versions of the site are up to date. But in a corporate environment, Webmastering is seldom done in isolation. If two or three people have recently updated pages, they either need to keep meticulous records about where the latest files are, or do the efficient thing, and let FrontPage handle the synchronization of local and remote sites.

Synchronizing Files with Remote Site View

FrontPage's new Remote Site View is easy to use, especially if you're used to working with FTP software to move files from one location to another. When FrontPage connects to a remote location, it compares the files displayed in both Remote and Local Site View. The Status column, which appears in both views, gives you an indication of whether a file in one view is matched in the other view. If you see a file that is in Local view, and listed as unmatched, that means that the file does not exist in Remote view. If you publish that file by clicking on one of the three controls between Remote and Local views, the file is moved from one site to another, and its status becomes Unchanged. The Unchanged status turns to Changed when you edit the file. See Figure 17-7 on the following page for an example.

Click here to move selected files from Local to Remote Web site

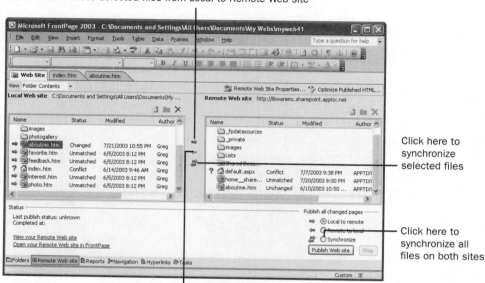

Click here to synchronize selected files

Click here to synchronize all files on both sites

Click here to move selected files from Remote to Local Web site

Figure 17-7   FrontPage makes it easy to synchronize files located on one site with the contents of another site.

Synchronizing files means you make sure the latest versions of the files on one Web site (whether local or remote) are matched on the other Web site. If you have updated only a few files, and want to save time, you can synchronize only those files by selecting them in either the Local or Remote Web Site window, then clicking the bottom-most of the three buttons between the two Web site views. If you want to make sure all the files on both sites match exactly, click Synchronize under Publish All Changed Pages, then click Publish Web Site.

Speeding Up Revisions by Publishing Only Updated Pages

Once you are familiar with the steps involved in setting up a remote site and opening its contents in Remote Site View, it's easy to publish only the pages you've updated most recently by opening the Web you want to publish in Remote Site View and doing one of the following:

- Select the files in Local or Remote Site View that you want to publish: use Shift+Click to select contiguous files, and Ctrl+Click to select discontiguous files. Then click Publish Selected Files from the Local (or Remote) Web Site to the Remote (or Local) Web Site.

- Select either Remote to Local, or Local to Remote under Publish All Changed Pages, then click Publish Web Site.

You can control the way files are published to the remote Web site by opening Remote Web Site Properties, and clicking the Publishing tab. Under Publish, select Changed Pages Only, if you want only to move files that you, or others, have edited (see Figure 17-8).

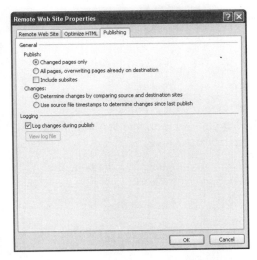

Figure 17-8 Use these settings to specify whether you want to publish all files, or only those that have changed.

> **Aha!** Make Sure You Publish What You Need
>
> You might want to click All Pages, Overwriting Pages Already On Destination, if you aren't sure what has been changed, and don't have a lot of files to transfer. Click Log Changes During Publish, if you want to keep a record of what you published, and when it was published in a log file.

Opening a Web Site So You Can Update It

A FrontPage-based Web, like any Web site, is an ongoing project. You need to keep updating and correcting your pages to provide visitors with the most current information available. It's also important to update your Web site, in order to delete files you no longer need. This can reduce the amount of server space your Web site consumes, and if your ISP limits the amount of space you have, file management is especially important. You can open a Web site to update it by clicking File, Open Site, or by clicking the down arrow next to the Open button, and choosing Open Site. If the Web is on your local computer, locate the Web by clicking the Look In drop-down list. If the Web is on another computer, enter its URL in the Web Name box.

Aha!   If you are reopening a Web that you opened recently, choose the Web's name from the Recent Files submenu of the File menu. FrontPage will connect to the Web automatically, without making you locate it in the Open Web dialog box.

Fast Wrap-Up

- FrontPage lets you verify that your pages look and function the way you want, in Preview view, or by previewing in one or more Web browsers.

- Publishing on an extended server (one that supports the FrontPage Server Extensions, or SharePoint Team Services) lets you add form handlers and other Web components, and take advantage of collaborative tools.

- Publishing to an FTP site gives you flexibility: you can publish to the same site from different locations, using different Web page creation software.

- Publishing to a location on your local network, or on your own filesystem, gives you a backup version of the site, in case you need it.

- FrontPage streamlines the process of synchronizing either selected Web page files, or all files, on both the remote and local versions of a site.

Working Collaboratively 18

10-Second Summary

- Learn how Microsoft Windows SharePoint Services fosters collaboration on shared projects
- Assemble the system and database software required to install Windows SharePoint Services
- Add users and assign access levels, using HTML administration pages
- Back up and restore the collaboration database, in case of system failure

All groups of employees need a place where they can share ideas, send messages to one another, and exchange files so they can complete projects more efficiently. When I worked as a newspaper reporter, in the days before computers took over newsrooms, we used to assemble in a room, where we would put the paper together after the stories were written and typeset. Each of us took a set of pages to paste up, and we would take galley proofs of stories from a pegboard, where they had been hung after coming off the typesetter. That way, we could keep track of which stories had been used, and which remained. Along the way, we would ask questions and provide information to one another about the stories we had written.

A Windows SharePoint Services Web site provides the same sort of collaborative environment, but alleviates the need for co-workers to be physically present in the same place, or at the same time. The work gets done, but files are retrieved electronically. Team members can provide information to one another through their Web browsers, track jobs by following lists to which they all have access, and update lists as tasks are completed. This chapter introduces you to Windows SharePoint Services, and explains how to get up and running with this collaborative environment, which is closely integrated with Microsoft Office FrontPage 2003.

Introducing Windows SharePoint Services

In Chapter 16, "Making a Site Database-Driven," you learned about Windows SharePoint Services, and how it can make a Web site database-driven. But what is SharePoint, and how can it help you create and administer sites faster and smarter? SharePoint is a collaborative environment that is especially designed to work with Microsoft Windows Server 2003, and the Microsoft Office System. It provides a group of individuals with a place on the Web where they can view documents, post information, and track ongoing jobs—all through a Web browser. Whenever you need to get people together for a discussion, to take a vote, or to share comments on documents, consider using SharePoint to give them a place to work together from their individual locations, without having to arrange meeting times and travel routes.

Getting Acquainted With SharePoint Standard Features

A SharePoint site enables you and your co-workers to use lists and other shared documents to complete projects collaboratively. You set up a meeting workspace, invite your co-workers to your site, and work on the document or project together at the same time. You might be discussing the project on the phone, while editing it in the online workspace through your Web browsers. SharePoint also provides document checkout and versioning, which helps co-workers track when a document has been changed.

A Web page on a SharePoint site has standard features, such as those illustrated in Figure 18-1.

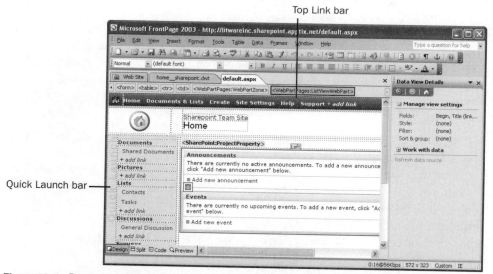

Figure 18-1 Pages on a SharePoint site present team members with navigation elements that make shared documents easy to find.

When you open a SharePoint site in FrontPage, you can customize the standard navigational elements: add custom pages, or change the order of the items contained in the Quick Launch bar, or Top Link bar. If you want to make the pages match the look of your corporate Web site, add a corporate logo or a theme that includes your company colors.

Understandng What You Need to Do to Install SharePoint

FrontPage enables you to create SharePoint Web sites on a Web server that operates Windows Server 2003. Windows SharePoint Services, in fact, is being advertised as a part of Windows Server 2003. What if you don't have Windows 2003 Server installed yet?

You can gain access to SharePoint by installing the predecessor to Windows SharePoint Services, SharePoint Team Services (STS). You can find STS on the Office XP CD, for instance. (However, keep in mind that SharePoint Team Services is only included with the Developer edition of Office XP.) One advantage of using STS is that it will run on Windows 2000 servers. Another is that you can use Internet Information Services server version 5.0 (which you may have already) rather than the newer version 6.0. In contrast, Windows SharePoint Services only runs on a server that supports the .NET framework, such as Windows Server 2003. To find out more about how to buy Office XP, consult *http:// www.microsoft.com/office/howtobuy/purchasing.asp*.

Understanding How SharePoint Streamlines Production

Each project or document that you want to share with your co-workers can have its own Web site on a Windows SharePoint site. Once you set up the site in FrontPage, you and your co-workers can contribute, using only your Web browsers, or with Office System applications, such as Microsoft Office Word 2003 and Microsoft Office Excel 2003.

When you work with a Web site hosted by an ISP, or that supports the FrontPage Server Extensions, you create or edit pages, then publish them on the remote site. When you create a Windows SharePoint Services site, it is immediately live on the server. You then create and edit pages directly on the server. Those changes become visible immediately—you don't have to publish them, or transfer them from your computer.

Note   One of the advantages of working with SharePoint is the ability to administer the site remotely from any location. You can connect to the site from any computer, as long as you use an account that has administrator rights on the server that is running Windows SharePoint Services.

Installing Windows SharePoint Services

Windows SharePoint Services comes in several varieties. Large organizations that need to connect more than one internal Web site, and provide shared workspaces for teams that are in disparate locations, should install SharePoint Portal Server. Smaller organizations can access SharePoint Services by installing it on a Windows Server 2003 system.

Once you have installed Windows Server 2003, you install SharePoint from the Windows SharePoint Services CD, following the steps presented in the Setup Wizard. When you install Windows SharePoint servers, a SharePoint team Web site is created automatically.

> **Note**   Windows SharePoint Services includes all of the features available with the FrontPage Server Extensions, such as forms processing and discussion groups. In addition, Windows SharePoint Services adds support for document libraries and other collaborative features through a database component, which is described later in this chapter.

Making Sure You Have the Required System Resources

Windows SharePoint Services requires a hardware foundation and system resources to operate. It's worth checking your own system before you begin, to make sure you are installing the software on a server that can operate it correctly. Requirements include:

- A computer with an Intel Pentium III or better processor
- 512 MB of RAM
- 550 MB of free hard disk space
- Windows Server 2003 as the operating system
- A Web application server that runs Microsoft ASP.NET and Internet Information Services 6.0

> **Aha!**   Outsource SharePoint Services
>
> You can also gain access to a SharePoint environment without having to install or configure the software yourself. Just sign up for a monthly account with a service that provides SharePoint to businesses and individuals, such as Apptix (*http://www.apptix.net/sharepoint.htm*).

You also need a database present on the server, in order to proide team members with the ability to create online discussions, lists, and other features. Supported databases are:

- Microsoft SQL Server 2000 with the latest service pack installed
- Microsoft Data Engine (MSDE) 2000

If you don't have SQL Server running on your server, the MSDE is included, and installed by default when you install Windows SharePoint Server.

When you install SharePoint Team Services, the HTML Administration pages are installed on an administration port that enables you to access and configure your site from a remote computer. Typically, you connect to the administative port using Secure HyperText Transport Protocol (HTTPS). Just type the protocol and the port number in your browser's Address box when you connect to the administration pages (for example, *https:// sharepointserver.company.com:443; you obtain the actual URL from your network administrator or your ISP*).

> **Lingo**   A *port* is a virtual opening on a computer that handles services intended to be processed by a particular application. For instance, port 80 is the port used by Web browsers to connect to Web pages, while port 443 is used by browsers to connect to a secure Web server that offers Secure Sockets Layer (SSL) encryption.

Maintaining a SharePoint Services Site

FrontPage makes an ideal front-end tool for creating and editing Windows SharePoint sites. But, in order to take advantage of the Web components that come with SharePoint Services, you need to be a member of the Administrator or Web Designer Site Group. You can then either use FrontPage to access the SharePoint site's administration pages, or connect to them using your Web browser.

> **Lingo**   A *Site Group* functions the same way on a SharePoint site as a Local Group on a Windows network. It gives a user a particular level of access to the pages on the site. Someone in the Reader group has read-only access to SharePoint pages; a Contributor can add content to document libraries and lists; a Web Designer can create or customize document libraries and lists; an Administrator has full control over the site.

You can set up alerts, so that you are notified when someone makes a change to the site. A "page" in a Windows SharePoint Services Web site displays a list of information that enables team members to organize that information any way they want to.

Fostering Collaboration by Administering a SharePoint Site

When you install, and begin to work with a SharePoint site, you gain the ability to establish all aspects of how you and your co-workers can access and use shared information. Windows SharePoint Services is designed to be easy to administer, so that you can focus on creating a site where team members can work together. You administer your site in one of two ways:

- By connecting to the SharePoint site you have created, using your Web browser, and accessing a set of HTML Administration pages that are created when you install Windows SharePoint Services

- By working from the command-line

If you use the HTML Administration pages, you can configure the SharePoint site, either on the server where it has been installed, or from a remote location. Administering the site

See Also   The Web components that come with Windows SharePoint Services—Web Search and Top 10 Lists—are described in Chapter 16, "Making a Site Database-Driven," along with the List View and Document Library View Web Parts.

means that you are able to configure the site's global properties, such as the time zone used to record changes to shared documents. In order to administer a SharePoint site, you need to be either an administrator on the local computer where the site is installed, or a member of the SharePoint Administrators group.

> **Note**   Whenever you need help, or have questions about administering a SharePoint Web site, click Help in the toolbar that appears on any SharePoint Web page. A browser window will open, with a list of topics you can browse.

If you decide to use HTML Administration pages, rather than the command line to administer your site, you fill out a set of Web page forms to do the configuration. These pages fall into two categories:

- Central Administration pages, which control the settings for each SharePoint server, or virtual server

- Site Settings pages, which control the settings for each of the collaborative Web sites you create on the SharePoint server.

Either type of page lets you add or remove users from the Web site, change which group a user belongs to, and create or delete subwebs. The Central Administration and Site Settings pages also let you view any discussion areas that have been created on a site, and view any alert messages that have been set (to tell you that pages have been created or changed, for instance).

Changing Your Site's Visual and Organizational Settings

If you are working locally (on the computer that hosts the SharePoint site), you can access the Site Settings in several ways:

- Click Start, All Programs, Administrative Tools, SharePoint Central Administration.

- Start your Web browser. In the Address box, type *http://servername:port*. The variable *servername* stands for the name of your SharePoint server, while the variable *port* stands for the port where you installed the administrative pages. Make sure *servername* and *port* are separated by a colon. Then click OK.

If you are in the process of editing pages on the site, and you want to access the Site Settings pages from within FrontPage, follow these steps:

1   Make sure you are working within a SharePoint Web site, and have a SharePoint Web page open on screen. Click Tools, Server, Administration Home.

2   Enter your username and password when prompted, and click OK.

3 Your Web browser opens to the Site Settings page for your SharePoint site (see Figure 18-2). This page has the URL *http://sitename/_layouts/IDnumber/ settings.aspx*. (*sitename* is a placeholder for the name of your SharePoint site, and *IDnumber* is a placeholder for the locale ID; for U.S. English Web sites the ID is 1033). The Site Settings pages are located in the _layouts directory on the SharePoint site.

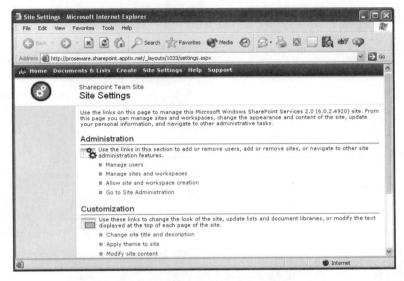

Figure 18-2 Connect to the Site Settings page to change visual and organizational characteristics of your SharePoint site.

> **Note**   You can access the Site Settings pages from the Top Link bar on any SharePoint page: just click Site Settings to open the page.

Adding Users and Changing Access Levels

Once you connect to the Site Settings page, you can switch to the Central Administration pages for your SharePoint site. With the Site Settings page open, just click on the link Go to Site Administration under the heading Administration. The Top-level Site Administration page opens (see Figure 18-3 on the following page).

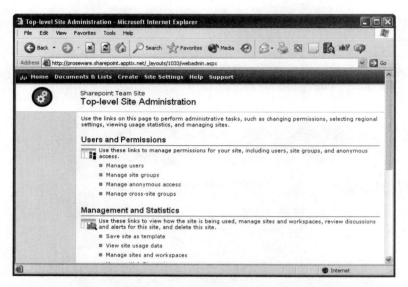

Figure 18-3   Add new users, grant permissions, and view site statistics by accessing this administration page.

One of the things you'll probably be called upon to do most frequently, as your SharePoint site becomes more widely used, is add users and grant permissions levels. To add a new user, follow these steps:

1 From the FrontPage toolbar, click Tools, Server, Administration Home.

2 Enter your username and password when prompted to do so.

3 When the Site Settings page appears, click Go To Site Administration.

4 When the Top-level Site Administration page appears, click Manage Users.

5 On the Manage Users page, click Add Users.

6 When the Add Users page appears (see Figure 18-4), add the user's e-mail address, network username, or group name, in the Users box. Click Address Book, if you want to add a name from your Microsoft Outlook Address Book.

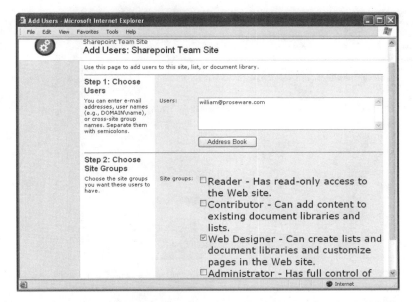

Figure 18-4 You add SharePoint users, and assign access levels, using this page.

7   Assign a permissions level to the user, by checking one of the four Site Groups
listed in the bottom half of the Add Users page: Reader, Contributor, Web
Designer, or Administrator. Then, click Next.

8   On the next Add Users page, verify the e-mail address of the individual you want
to add, and compose an e-mail to the individual, informing them that they have
been added to the list of users for the SharePoint site.

> **Note**   In order to access your Address Book from the Add Users page, or to schedule
> a meeting with a team member, Microsoft Outlook must be configured as your default
> e-mail program.

If you need to change access levels for an individual, return to the Manage Users page, as
described in Steps 1-4 above, then select the check box next to the user's name. Click Edit
Site Groups For Selected Users. When the Add Users page appears, select the new Site
Group for the user. Then complete steps 7 and 8, as described above.

If you want to invite a user to an online meeting, open the Manage Users page, and then
pass your mouse pointer over the user's name. A small box with the letter "i" (presumably,
for "information") appears next to the user's name. Click the down arrow that appears in
the small box, and choose Schedule A Meeting from the menu (see Figure 18-5 on the following page).

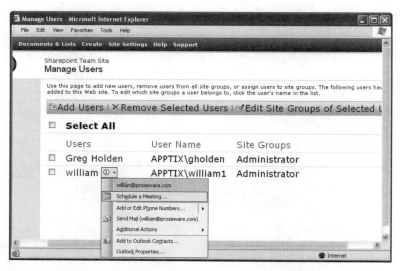

Figure 18-5   It's easy to invite SharePoint team members to participate in online meetings.

It's a good idea to change users' passwords periodically (perhaps once every few weeks) for security purposes, especially if you are working on a SharePoint site that contains mission-critical or sensitive information about your organization. To change a password, open the Site Settings page for the site on which you are working. Then:

1   Under the heading Manage My Information, click View Information About Site Users.

2   Click the name of the user whose password you want to change.

3   When the User Information page appears, click Change Password.

4   Enter the password in the New Password and Confirm New Password Boxes (see Figure 18-6), then click OK.

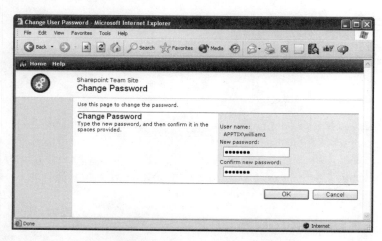

Figure 18-6 It's a good idea to change passwords periodically for added security.

Don't forget to send an e-mail message to the individual whose password you have just changed. Click the user's e-mail address on the User Information page (which appears after you change the password), to open a new message window in your default e-mail program, so that you can send a message easily.

Working with the Collaboration Database

A database is a required part of any Windows SharePoint Services Web site. The information contained in Task Lists, Event Lists, or other lists contained on a SharePoint site, as well as Document Library information, and the threaded comments in Web-based discussions that are contained in a site, are all maintained by a database. You have two choices for setting up such databases when you create a SharePoint site:

■   If Microsoft SQL Server 7.0, or later, is present on your computer, the database will be installed on SQL.

■   If SQL Server 7.0, or later, is not present, the Microsoft Data Engine (MSDE) will be installed when you install Windows SharePoint Services, and MSDE will function as the database.

In each case, the database you use functions as the database for any virtual servers you operate within a Windows SharePoint Services site.

The advantage of using MSDE is that it's free, it doesn't require you to be familiar with SQL Server, and it is installed automatically, if SQL Server is not present. However, MSDE doesn't provide you with management tools so you can administer the database, and it is not as full-featured or flexible as SQL Server. One advantage of using SQL Server is that you can use the SQL Server Enterprise Management tools to manage your database. Another is that using SQL Server for database functions takes the burden off your main Web server when it comes to running your SharePoint site.

Because so much of the critical data on your SharePoint site is contained in the collaboration database, one of the most important administrative functions you can perform on the site is to back up the database periodically. Backing up the data ensures that your site's discussion threads, and other information, won't be lost in case the server crashes. You can back up the files and restore them, if necessary, by using either HTML Administration pages, or command-line instructions.

> **Lingo**   A SharePoint Web site is called a *virtual server*. The virtual server can contain more than one individual Web site. However, each virtual server uses a single database. When you back up the database, you back up the data for each site on the virtual server.

To back up the database using the HTML Administration pages:

1   On the computer that hosts the SharePoint site, click Start, Programs, Administrative Tools, Microsoft SharePoint Administrator.

2   When the Server Administration page opens, under Virtual Servers, click Administration next to the name of the virtual server whose database you want to back up.

3   When the Virtual Server Administration page opens, under Administration, click Backup And Restore Database.

4   When the Backup And Restore Database page opens, under Database Restore, enter the path and filename where you want to store the backed up data (for instance, C:\MSSQL7\BACKUP\Sharepoint.bak) and click Backup.

You can restore the most recent copy of the database from the same Database Backup And Restore page referred to in Step 4, by entering the path and filename leading to the backup file you want to use, then clicking Restore.

Fast Wrap-Up

■   FrontPage enables you to create and administer Windows SharePoint Services Web sites, which foster collaboration among members of a workgroup.

■   Windows SharePoint Services is intended to work with Windows Server 2003, and the Microsoft Office System, enabling team members to post and track information online, all through their Web browsers.

■   Web pages on a Windows SharePoint Services site contain standard navigational elements, including a Quick Launch bar, and Top Link bar, that you can customize using FrontPage.

■   You can administer a Windows SharePoint Services site from the server where it has been installed, or from a remote computer. You configure site settings, using either a Web browser or a command-line interface.

■   You can add new users, remove users, or change user access levels by means of the Site Settings page for the SharePoint site on which you are working.

■   Every SharePoint site makes use of a collaboration database that holds document lists and libraries, and that is installed on either a Microsoft SQL 7.0 server, if it is present, or the Microsoft Data Engine, if it is not.

Administering Web Sites 19

10-Second Summary
- ■ Rename your FrontPage Web and adjust other general settings
- ■ Add comments to Web pages to keep your colleagues informed
- ■ Adjust margins and change other page options to improve readability
- ■ View and clean up your HTML code to keep pages functioning smoothly
- ■ Create and update a Task List, so that workgroup members can be informed
- ■ Make sure your Web pages are accessible to viewers with disabilities

Many essential administrative tasks take place after you've created and proofread the documents that make up your FrontPage-based Web. This is the stage where you make sure your images, links, and forms look and function correctly, and where you specify language, navigation, browser compatibility, and other general settings. The managing of a Web site can be a highly technical undertaking—but Microsoft Office FrontPage 2003 provides the user-friendly tools that make it relatively easy.

In this chapter, you'll learn how to perform some of the basic Web site administration tasks. Some of those tasks require you to make changes to individual pages, such as adding comments to files, and adjusting page margins. Other items in your Webmaster's "to-do list" occur behind the scenes, for your benefit rather than for your visitors'. You can work with a list of tasks you need to complete; you can clean up your site's HTML code so your pages load quickly and display all of their contents; and you can change links that appear on multiple pages at the same time. FrontPage's general Web site administration tools make it possible for you to ensure that your site functions correctly and remains accessible to all of your visitors.

Make Your Site Easier to Find and Update

If you work in a corporate environment, your company might use a proxy server to provide employees with controlled access to the Internet. If that's the case, you'll need to configure FrontPage to connect to the proxy server so that you can connect to your Web server to publish and edit your pages. You can also go to Microsoft's site and make use of online clip art or help files. Not only that, but you can also set up FrontPage to specify how your FrontPage-based Web should be navigated.

Reconfigure Your Site's General Web Settings

If you move your site from one server to another, you may need to rename the files so that they are easier to find for your co-workers. You might need to change a generic name, like site 134, to something clearer, like Customer_Service_Web, for instance. You might also need to change the company name or contact information associated with the site in case your organization undergoes some changes. To change the general settings associated with the currently open Web, follow these steps:

1   Open the Web with the settings you want to change.

2   Choose Choose Tools, Site Settings.

3   Enter a new name for your Web in the Web Name box, shown in Figure 19-1. (This name will be assigned to the folder that holds all of the Web's text files, images, and subfolders.)

4   Click OK.

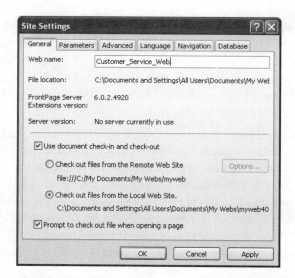

Figure 19-1 Change a Web's name and other general parameters in the Site Settings dialog box.

Checking Pages In and Out

FrontPage is ideally suited for corporate workgroups that create and manage Web sites. In such workgroups, it can be difficult to track who has worked on a file last, and when it was last revised. To prevent members of a workgroup from duplicating one another's edits, FrontPage provides the ability to check out pages when they are edited so that no one else can work on them. When revisions are complete, the file is checked back in.

Enable File Check-In and Check-Out

The General tab of the Site Settings dialog box includes a check box (Use Document Check-In and Check-Out) that you select to turn on this feature.

1 Open the Web you want to edit.

2 Choose Tools, Site Settings.

3 Select Use Document Check-In And Check-Out.

4 Select the option that describes where you plan to edit your files: from the Remote Web Site, or from the Local Web Site, and click OK.

5 When an alert dialog box appears, informing you that the process might take a few minutes, click OK.

The alert dialog box closes; the list of files in the Folder List is refreshed, and the files are ready to check out (or check in).

Note   You must enable document check-in and check-out for each Web you want to work on collaboratively. You can enable this feature for one Web, and choose to not enable it for others.

Check Out a File So That Your Co-workers Know It's Being Edited

Once you enable document check-in and check-out, it's easy to check out a file so that the other members of your development team are aware that you are making changes to it:

1 Right-click the name of the file you want to edit in the Folder List.

2 Choose Check Out from the shortcut menu.

When a file has been checked out, a check mark appears next to its name, either in the Folder List, or in Reports view (see Figure 19-2). To check a file back in when you're done editing, just right-click the file's name and select Check In from the shortcut menu.

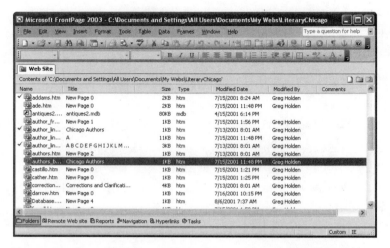

Figure 19-2   Reports view provides workgroup members with a list of files that are currently checked out.

> **Aha!**   Check Out Files to Preserve Your Changes
>
> You don't *have* to check out a file in order to edit it. However, if someone else in your workgroup could potentially open the file and edit it, you should always check out the file to prevent your changes from being overwritten by mistake.

Reports view lets you track which files are checked out (that is, being edited), and which are available for you to edit. Open the Web you want to work on, click Reports in the Views bar. Then click on the down arrow next to Reports (the first button in the Reports toolbar), and choose Checkout Status from the Workflow submenu. A list of files appears, and the Checked Out By column lists who has checked out any documents in the Web.

> **Aha!**   Quickly Undo Your Changes
>
> Choose Undo Check Out from the shortcut menu when you right-click a file, if you want to undo mistakes you made when you edited a file, after checking it out. FrontPage will immediately return to the most recent version of the file before you checked it out.

Adjust Proxy Settings to Make Your Web Available

Many organizations create Web sites that are hosted on their own Web servers, either on an intranet that is available to their own employees, or on an external Web server that is available to anyone on the Internet. Often, their employees access the Internet through a proxy server, which receives connection requests from browsers, and other client programs, and forwards those requests to the destination computer on their behalf. To enable your fellow Web developers to connect to your Web site in order to make changes, you can use FrontPage to enter the proxy server settings:

1 Open the Web you're working on.

2 Select Tools, Options.

3 Click Proxy Settings (see Figure 19-3).

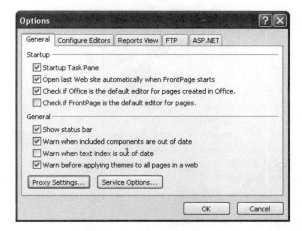

Figure 19-3 Click Proxy Settings to specify proxy server settings for your FrontPage Web.

> **Note** FrontPage 2003 and Microsoft Internet Explorer use the same proxy server settings. If you have already configured Internet Explorer to access the Internet through a proxy server, you may not have to set up your FrontPage Web site to permit access through a proxy. Also keep in mind that any proxy server settings you assign to your FrontPage Web site will affect Internet Explorer as well.

4 When the Internet Properties dialog box appears, Click LAN Settings to change the settings for your Local Area Network (LAN).

5 Check the box next to Use A Proxy Server.

6 Enter the address of your proxy server in the Address box.

7 Enter the Port number you want to use.

8 Click Advanced.

9 Enter the server names, and port numbers you want to use.

> **Note**   The port number you enter depends on the kind of Internet service you want to use. For HyperText Transfer Protocol communications, you would enter port 80. For FTP, Telnet, or other Internet protocols, consult with your network administrator.

10   Deselect the Use The Same Proxy Server For All Protocols button if you want to specify multiple proxy servers—for instance, if you and your co-workers access e-mail, FTP sites, or other services through a proxy.

11   If necessary, enter the beginning of the address for a computer within your company that you can access without a proxy server.

12   Click OK.

> **Caution**   Simply configuring FrontPage to connect to your proxy server might not be enough to get you connected to an internal server, if you want to publish your FrontPage-based Web there. Some companies also restrict access, based on the IP (Internet Protocol) address of the user's computer. Ask your network administrator whether your computer needs to be added to the list of approved IP numbers so that you can edit and publish pages on your internal Web server.

Annotating a Web Site to Keep Co-workers Informed

Sometimes, you need to write notes to yourself, or to your co-workers, about the status of a page you're working on. You can, of course, take a pen, and write the message on a sticky note that you attach to your computer screen. But if your colleagues are in another office, it's just as easy to annotate a Web page, or to add general comments about a file. That way, you can be sure the notes are available when you, or others, begin working on your FrontPage-based Web.

Add Comments

When you need to create a reminder or note to yourself, or to your co-workers, just follow these steps:

1   Position the cursor at the location in the page where you want to add a comment.

2   Choose Insert, Comment.

3   Type your comment in the Comment box (see Figure 19-4).

4   Click OK.

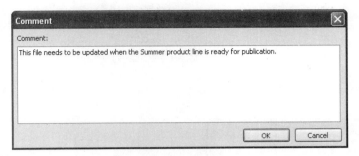

Figure 19-4 Comments about a file can serve as reminders to your colleagues—or to yourself.

After you add your comments, click Save. Then click Preview. The comments that were visible in Normal view won't be visible anymore. Comments are highlighted in a different color than the visible body text on a Web page. They aren't visible when the page is being viewed by outsiders who access your site with a browser—they are seen only by you and your coworkers, when you open the page in FrontPage.

Edit Comments

After you make a comment, you or a co-worker will eventually need to change, or delete it. To edit a comment once you've made it, right-click it, and choose Comment Properties from the shortcut menu. The Comments dialog box opens with your previous comments displayed so that you can change them.

> **Aha!**   Edit Comments Faster
> You can also edit comments by double-clicking on them. The Comments dialog box opens immediately, and you don't have to use the shortcut menu.

Add Comments About a File to Add Factual Information

Comments of the sort described in preceding sections are fine when you need to make a reminder about a page or site. But it's better to add summary comments that you or a colleague can view in Reports View when you need to include simple factual information about a file. To add summary comments, follow thes steps:

1 Right-click the file's name in the Folder List, and choose Properties from the shortcut menu.

2 Click Summary.

3 Enter your comments in the Comments box (see Figure 19-5).

4 Click the Workgroup tab if you want to add more specific details about the content category to which the page belongs, or which workgroup or individuals are working on the file.

5 Click OK.

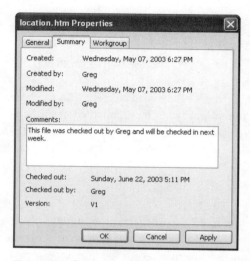

Figure 19-5 Summary comments provide general information about a file, rather than reminders.

File summary comments are visible only in Reports View. You see them when you click Reports in the views bar.

> **Caution**   Make sure you are in any view except Tasks View when you add file summary comments. You can't add comments in Tasks View.

Changing Page Options to Improve Readability

By changing a Web page's general options, you make it more readable for your visitors. FrontPage lets you easily make changes that affect a page's overall design and change content that affects the page as a whole. The Page Properties dialog box contains tools that control a page's title, as well as page margins.

Set a Web Page's General Properties

If you want to change general parameters for a Web site, choose Tools, Site Settings. If you want to change general parameters such as margins, names, and language encodings, only for the currently open Web page, do the following:

1 Right-click the page you want to edit.

2 Choose Page Properties from the shortcut menu. When the Page Properties dialog box opens, in the General tab (see Figure 19-6), check your title, and enter a new one if you want.

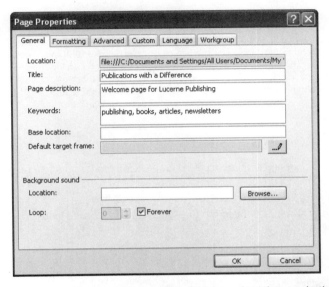

Figure 19-6 Change a Web page's title, base location, and other properties, using this dialog box.

> **Aha!** Keep Your Titles Short
>
> Even if you first created a title for a page, it's a good idea to check the title before you actually publish the page, to make sure it's short and descriptive. Most Web browsers can't display titles of more than 10-12 words, or about 60 characters—but these are maximum lengths; in general it's better to keep titles to three or four words, at most.

3 Enter a URL in Base Location if you want a visitor's Web browser to connect to the pages in your Web in relation to a base location.

4 If you want to add keywords that describe the page's contents, enter them, separated by a comma, in the Keyword box. Keywords are used by some search engines to index a page, based on its contents.

> **Note**   You can't change the location or filename of a page in the General tab of the Page Properties dialog box. You need to choose Save As from the File menu. Then, in the Save As dialog box, you can enter a new filename in the File Name box, or choose a new location from the Save In drop-down list.

Adjust Page Margins to Improve Readability

Web pages can get crowded very quickly. Keeping your content readable ensures that your visitors will return on a regular basis. By increasing the size of the margins around a Web page, you make pages easier to read.

> **Lingo** The *margin* of a Web page is the distance between the contents of the page and the edge of the browser window. Each Web page has default margins (about 21 pixels at the top, and about 12 pixels on the left). Before you begin, though, remember that every Web page created by FrontPage has a margin by default. Before you change the default margins, click Preview In Browser to open the page in your Web browser so that you can see the standard margins. You may decide these margins are OK as is, and don't need to be changed.

To adjust page margins, follow these steps:

1 Open the page you want to adjust.

2 Right-click anywhere in the page, and choose Page Properties from the shortcut menu.

3 Click Advanced.

4 In the Margins section of the Advanced tab (see Figure 19-7), enter a value in Pixels next to one of the margin boxes (Top, Left, Bottom, Right).

5 Click OK.

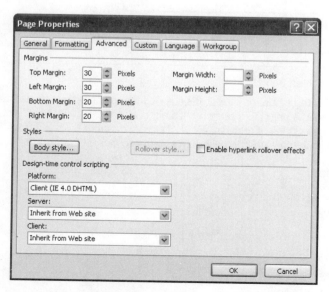

Figure 19-7 Use the Advanced tab to specify margins for your Web page.

> **Aha!** Don't Be Surprised if Margins Decrease
>
> If you enter values in the Specify Top Margin, or Specify Left Margin box that are less than the default margins, you'll actually see the page's margins decrease. If you want to increase the margins, enter values that are more than 21 pixels at the top, and more than 12 pixels at the left.

Select Page Language and HTML Encoding

If you are developing Web sites that have content displayed in more than one language, you need to specify desired language options on the Language tab of the Site Settings dialog box. These options don't actually translate your Web page content into another language for you. (You didn't think it was that easy, did you?) The settings will help you specify the language in which server messages (such as error messages, or form confirmation pages) appear.

> **Note** In order for server messages to be specified in the language you want, you must also have the FrontPage Server Extensions, and the correct Language Pack installed on the server.

If you have the necessary server software installed (as described in the preceding Note), do the following:

1 Choose Tools, Site Settings to open Site Settings, and then click the Language tab (see Figure 19-8).

2 Choose the Language you want from the server message language drop-down list. The list contains only the languages that have been installed on the server; if you haven't installed any, you'll see English (United States) as the only option.

3 Choose an option from the Default Page Encoding drop-down list to change the character set used to encode the Web page. By default, the message appears like this in the HEAD section of your Web page:

```
<META HTTP-EQUIV="Content-Type" content="text/html; charset=windows-1252">
```

This HTML is used for the default English character set. If you want to use non-Western languages on your Web pages, choose an option such as Unicode (UTF-8), which works with many other languages.

4 When you're done, click OK.

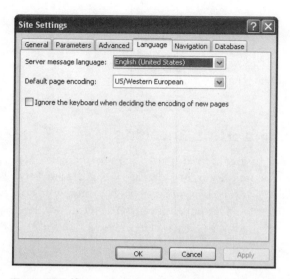

Figure 19-8 If you want your site to be multilingual, setting these options is one essential step.

Check Your Spelling

Another way to make sure your page appears in a way your viewers can understand it is to check your spelling. Spell-checking either individual pages, or all the pages in a site ensures that you look professional as well. Just follow these steps:

1 If you want to spell-check an individual page, either open that page, or select it in the Folder List. If you want to spell-check an entire site, open a page within that site.

2 Select Tools, Spelling.

3 When the Spelling dialog box appears, choose either Selected page(s), or Entire Web site.

4 Click Start.

The spelling dialog box presents you with a list of words that were misspelled. In the status area at the bottom of the dialog box, you'll find a mini-report describing how many misspelled words were actually found, and how many pages were searched (see Figure 19-9).

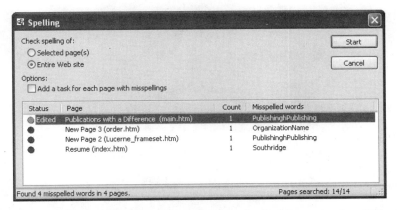

Figure 19-9   FrontPage can quickly spell-check all of the pages in a Web site.

To correct a misspelling, double-click the line where it is listed. A second Spelling dialog box appears that enables you to change the spelling, add the word to FrontPage's dictionary, or suggest an alternate spelling.

Viewing and Cleaning Up HTML to Ensure Consistency

FrontPage is flexible enough to enable both novices and experienced programmers to design Web pages the way they want to. Beginners can use menus, toolbars, and buttons to weave Web pages. Advanced users can work directly with the source HyperText Markup Language (HTML) for a Web page. You can highlight specific HTML commands in different colors, or use search-and-replace to edit multiple occurrences of commands.

View HTML Tags

You can always switch to Code View when you want to view the HTML for a page. But if you're in a hurry, and you like to see the tags in context—that is, wrapped around the Web page contents you create—you can have FrontPage reveal the tags to you in Design View. Just:

1 Open the page you want to work on.

2 Choose View, Reveal Tags.

3 Pass the mouse pointer over a tag to view; the entire text of the tag appears as a screen tip (see Figure 19-10).

See Also See Chapter 10, "Streamlining HTML and XML Markup," for a detailed discussion of FrontPage's Code View, Split View, and other features for viewing and editing Web page HTML and XML code.

Figure 19-10 You can view and edit HTML tags directly in Design view using Reveal Tags.

Once you've revealed the HTML tags for a page you're working on, it's easy to edit them. But you've got to switch from Design to Code View. Just:

1 Position the cursor where you want to insert new HTML.

2 Click Code to switch to Code View. Then, select a word, or entire line of code.

3 Click Cut, Copy, or Paste to make changes to the page's HTML if needed.

Doing an HTML Cleanup

It's up to the editors and writers who provide your Web site's content to make sure the words contained on your Web pages are free of grammatical errors and typos. But it's up to you to make sure your site's behind-the-scenes content—its HTML code—has the correct syntax.

If you create all of your content from scratch using FrontPage, you can be certain that your HTML is correct. But often, Webmasters import text from word processing programs or other Web page editors that sometimes add unnecessary HTML commands to your Web page code. You can tell FrontPage to clean up the code so that your Web pages appear consistently in all browsers, and no unnecessary commands appear online by mistake. Just follow these steps:

1 Open any page in the Web site that has the HTML you want to clean up.

2 Choose Tools, Optimize HTML.

3 In the Optimize HTML dialog box (see Figure 19-11), choose the options you want to optimize. Click Word HTML if you have created some of your Web pages in Microsoft Office Word 2003 and you want to delete the extra commands that Word adds. Click Delete VML content if you have used the Microsoft Office Drawing toolbar to draw images, which use Vector Markup Language (VML) that older browsers cannot display.

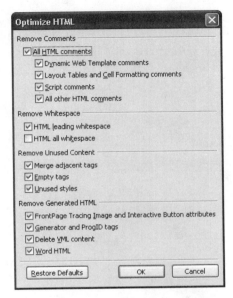

See Also See Chapter 20, "Customizing and Maintaining FrontPage 2003," for more on using the Drawing toolbar to draw images on your Web pages.

Figure 19-11 Cleaning up your HTML ensures that your pages will appear quickly and without commands visible online.

4 When you're done, click OK.

> **Aha!** Optimize HTML When You Publish
>
> You can instruct FrontPage to automatically optimize the HTML of Web pages that you publish—that is, that you move from your local Web site to a remote Web site. In Remote Web Site view, click Remote Web Site Properties. In the Remote Web Site Properties dialog box, on the Web Site tab, click Optimize Published HTML. Select the options that you want FrontPage to optimize, then click OK.

Working with the Task List to Keep Everyone Informed

Task View helps you keep track of the steps involved in completing your FrontPage-based Web. It's useful not only for you, but also for any co-workers or friends who are working on the Web with you. Task View doesn't just give you a "to-do list" of the jobs that remain to be done, however. You can also mark those pages that are finished as Completed, so the members of your team can see where you are, and what needs to be addressed next.

Review the Task List

After a Web site has been created and is online, you might be called upon to perform regular updates. You might receive new files from writers; editors and designers might need to work on pages to change colors or images. When you're part of a larger workgroup of individuals with different responsibilities, you need to keep track of who has worked on a file, and when the work has been completed, to ensure you don't duplicate effort or miss important stages. The need to track workflow becomes more important if more than one team member needs to work on a Web page, and if workers are scattered in different locations. To review the Task List:

1 Open the Web with the tasks you want to review.

2 Select View, Tasks. The Task List opens (see Figure 19-12).

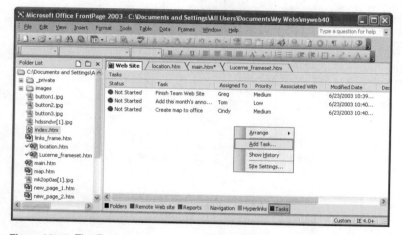

Figure 19-12 The Task List provides a workgroup with a shared set of development jobs or steps to be followed.

> **Note** A filename appears only in the Associated With column in Task View if you create a task while you are editing a page. If that is the case, the name of the page you are editing appears in the Associated With column in Task View.

Add a Task

If you don't yet have any tasks created for the current Web, you need to add one or more tasks by doing the following:

1 Right-click a blank part of Task View area.

2 Choose Add Task from the shortcut menu.

3 Type a name for the new task in the Task Name box.

4 Click one of the three Priority buttons to assign a priority level to the task.

5 Type the name of the individual who is to perform the task in the Assigned To box.

6 Type a description of the task in the Description box.

7 Click OK.

> **Note** If the task you want to add is associated with the editing of a specific page in your Web, it's better to choose Task from the New submenu of the File menu, in order to create a task. When you choose Task, the task becomes associated with the file you're currently editing. You can then start the task by clicking the Start Task button in the Edit Task dialog box. If you right-click the Task View area, and choose Add Task from the shortcut menu, the task is not associated with a particular file.

Mark a Task as Complete

Once you have completed a task on the Task List, you need to mark it as complete, so that no one opens the file unnecessarily or begins to work on it. Just:

1 Right-click the task.

2 Choose Mark Complete from the shortcut menu.

If you need to delete a Task, right-click it, then choose Delete Task from the shortcut menu. Click OK to confirm that you want to delete the task.

> **Aha!** Prioritize Your Tasks
> You can change the order in which tasks are sorted. (By default, FrontPage sorts tasks from highest priority to lowest priority. To change the sort order, click the Priority heading.

Verifying Hyperlinks

Broken hyperlinks can quickly undo the experience you've tried so hard to create for visitors to your FrontPage-based Web. Yet links are alarmingly easy to break, especially on complex sites with dozens, or even hundreds, of pages, and an incrementally larger number of links.

If you change the location or name of a file to which other pages are linked, you might need to make the same link change on many pages. FrontPage functions as both a time and Web saver by automatically verifying links and recalculating those that need to be replaced.

Verify Hyperlinks

After you have completed editing your Web pages, and just before you publish them online, it's a good idea to check the hyperlinks you have already made, to verify that they are properly formatted, and that they lead to the correct destinations within your Web:

1 Open the Web site you want to check.

2 Click View, Reports, Problems, Hyperlinks.

3 When a dialog box appears, asking if you want to verify the hyperlinks in your Web, click OK.

Once you are already in Reports View, you can verify hyperlinks at any time, by clicking Verify Hyperlinks in the Reports toolbar (see Figure 19-13).

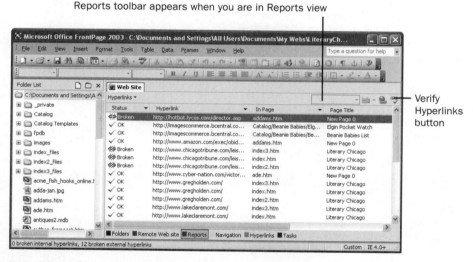

Figure 19-13 You can verify hyperlinks from Reports View as well as other views.

Recalculate Hyperlinks

While verifying hyperlinks make sure they are properly formatted, recalculating checks to see whether the remote Web sites or objects to which the links point actually exist. Web sites move around frequently, and their Webmasters routinely rename files, so it's important to recalculate your hyperlinks to make sure they are up-to-date. Just:

1 Open the Web you want to check.

2 Choose Tools, Recalculate Hyperlinks.

3 Click Yes, in the Recalculate Hyperlinks dialog box, to start recalculating hyperlinks. To view which links, if any, were broken, choose View, Reports, Problems, Hyperlinks.

If you need to fix a link that was reported to be broken after the verification process, right-click the hyperlink in Reports View, and then choose Edit Hyperlink from the shortcut menu. You can then enter the correct destination URL for the link in the Edit Hyperlink box.

> **Note**   You don't have to be in Page View to recalculate hyperlinks for your FrontPage-based Web. The Recalculate Hyperlinks command works in all views.

Making Your Web Pages Accessible to Everyone

While it's a good thing to make sure your Web site contents are accessible to individuals with vision problems, or other disabilities, it can also be a matter of good business. The Federal Rehabilitation Act Amendments that were signed into law in 1998, and administered by the Access Board, require government agencies to create Web content that complies with section 508 of the Act. It also requires resources that are procured by the government to comply with section 508. If you plan to do business with the U.S. government, you need to take advantage of FrontPage's new ability to automatically check Web sites to make sure they are accessible to everyone who wants to see your work. Here's how:

> **Lingo** *Accessibility* is a term used to describe resources that can be used by all people regardless of their physical condition. To make a Web page accessible, text alternatives are added to images, text is presented in a readable font size, and screen colors are easy to read.

1 Open the Web that you want to check for accessibility.

2 Choose Tools, Accessibility, or press F8.

3 When the Accessibility dialog box opens (see Figure 19-14), under Check Where, specify whether you want to check all pages in the Web, only the pages currently open in FrontPage, or the currently displayed page.

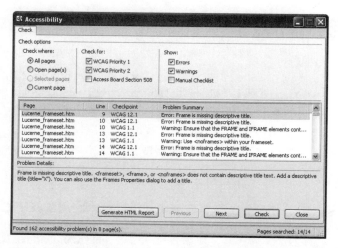

Figure 19-14 This dialog box provides suggestions on how to make your Web pages more accessible to visitors with disabilities.

4   Under Check For, select the set of accessibility guidelines against which you want to check. You can choose the Web Accessibility Initiative's Web Content Accessibility Guidelines (WCAG) or the Access Board's Section 508 guidelines.

5   Under Show, choose the potential accessibility problems you want to display after the check is complete: errors, warnings, or a checklist you develop manually.

6   Click Check. The progress of the check appears in the Accessibility dialog box's status bar.

7   When a dialog box appears, stating that the search is complete, click OK.

8   The first item in the list is highlighted, and details about how to remedy it are presented in the Problem Details section of the Accessibility dialog box. Click Next to move to each item in the list, in turn. When you're done, click Close.

Note   To find out more about the accessibility guidelines used by FrontPage and other programs in the Microsoft Office System, visit *http://www.w3.org/TR/WAI-WEBCONTENT/* (for the Web Content Accessibility Guidelines) or *http://www.access-board.gov/sec508/ 508standards* (for the Access Board's Section 508 guidelines).

Fast Wrap-Up

- Change your Web site's parameters in Site Settings so that you and your co-workers can check pages in or out and connect to your site through a proxy server, if you use one.

- Annotate your Web pages with comments to communicate important instructions to members of your workgroup, or to provide general file information.

- Adjust margins, rewrite titles, add keywords, and change other settings that make pages more readable and visible in the Page Options dialog box.

- Clean up your HTML to make sure your Web pages function correctly, and present a consistent appearance.

- Add tasks to FrontPage's built-in Task List so that you and your co-workers can develop your Web site without duplicating efforts.

- Take advantage of FrontPage's accessibility checker to ensure that your site is accessible to the widest possible number of viewers.

Customizing and Maintaining FrontPage 2003

20

10-Second Summary

- Change the features FrontPage presents at startup, so that you can get to work more efficiently.

- Customize colors, typefaces, and other characteristics of FrontPage's built-in themes.

- Add and remove toolbar buttons to save screen space, and give you the tools you need the most.

- Configure editing programs that launch automatically when you want to edit specified file types.

- Use the Detect and Repair utility to fix common problems you may encounter while running FrontPage.

FrontPage 2003 is all about giving Webmasters like you the tools that match the way you want to work. The View menu gives you more than half a dozen different ways to view your FrontPage-based Web. The Folder List gives you a hierarchical, Windows Explorer-like guide to your site's contents. If you want a more visual layout, you can switch to Navigation view. You can use Design view, if you aren't comfortable with viewing the source HTML, or XML, for a page. On the other hand, if you like to be in control, and understand everything that's going on behind the scenes, you can work in Code view.

But even FrontPage's standard selection of panes, views, toolbars, and menus might not be perfect for your needs. Once you get comfortable with this complex and powerful Web site creation tool, you can assume a higher level of control and customize the program's interface. FrontPage gives users the flexibility to edit and arrange toolbars, menu options, and other parts of its look and feel.

By changing FrontPage's arrangement of tools and options, you can work more quickly and efficiently. You can quickly access those aspects of the program you use most often. In this chapter, you'll discover how to customize the FrontPage window, rearrange—or even create your own—toolbars, and alter the colors or other design aspects of themes. You also examine how to repair FrontPage, if you encounter problems with the software.

Customizing Startup and Interface Options to Match the Way You Work

FrontPage gives you a high degree of control over how its main program window looks. You probably already know that the View menu lets you vary the way you work with a Web page's contents. Besides the different view areas and panes that comprise the FrontPage window, you can also change the appearance and placement of FrontPage's toolbars and status bar. You can even add options to a menu bar, so that you can quickly access the choices you use most often.

Use the Options Dialog Box to Change Startup Features

If you're in a hurry to make a revision to a Web page, you'll save some time by having FrontPage start up while displaying the features that are most valuable to you, such as the Web you worked on most recently. Open the Options dialog box, if you want to change the tools that FrontPage displays when it starts up:

1　Open the Web you want to work on.

2　Choose Tools, Options.

3　When the Options dialog box opens (see Figure 20-1), select Startup Task Pane, if you want the Getting Started version of the Task Pane to be displayed automatically when you first start up FrontPage.

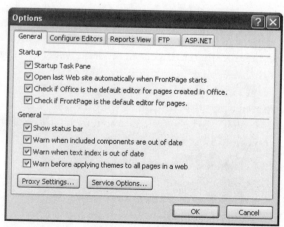

Figure 20-1 Use this dialog box to specify the features displayed when you start FrontPage.

4　Select Open Last Web Site Automatically When FrontPage Starts, if you want FrontPage to automatically open the most recent Web you edited when the program first starts up.

> **Aha!** Update the Same Web More Quickly
>
> If you expect to work on the same FrontPage-based Web consistently from session to session, it makes sense to select Open Last Web Site Automatically When FrontPage Starts. Otherwise, if you think you'll be creating new pages, or new Web sites frequently, select Startup Task Pane.

5 Choose Check If FrontPage Is The Default Editor For Pages, if you want FrontPage to be your default editor for Web pages.

6 Click Show Status Bar, if you want to display the status bar.

7 Click Warn When Text Index Is Out Of Date, if you have created a searchable index for your site, that needs to be updated periodically, as you create new pages, or edit pages. Similarly, select Warn When Included Components Are Out Of Date, if Web Components that have been added to your pages are outdated.

8 Click OK.

> **Caution** If you have more than one FrontPage-based Web open at the same time, the options you apply to one Web won't necessarily apply to other open Webs. For instance, if you make one FrontPage window active, then choose Options from the Tools menu, and then deselect the Show Status Bar box, the status bar disappears for that window. But it remains on other windows you already have open; you'll need to deselect Show Status Bar for each of those windows individually.

Customizing CSS Themes to Match Your Graphic Identity

FrontPage's built-in themes use Cascading Style Sheet (CSS) commands to add graphic interest to a Web site. But the default color, font, and graphics options for the themes may clash with your organization's graphic identity. You might find a theme that uses the right font and general graphic style you need, but the colors don't match the official color scheme that is part of your graphic identity. FrontPage makes it easy to customize many features of themes. Just:

1 Choose Format, Theme.

2 When the Theme Task Pane appears, in the Select A Theme box, pass your mouse arrow over the theme you want to customize. Click the down arrow next to the theme, and choose Customize from the shortcut menu. (Don't click the thumbnail graphic of the theme, or you will apply it to the current page.)

3 When the Customize Theme dialog box appears (see Figure 20-2), click the button for the option you want to customize. If you want to change the theme's font, click Text; if you want to add a custom graphic image (such as your corporate logo) to the background of the theme, click Graphics; to change the theme's colors, click Colors.

Figure 20-2 It's easy to modify a theme's built-in characteristics to match your company's identity.

4 If you click Colors, for instance, a new dialog box appears, that lets you interactively select the colors you want (see Figure 20-3). Click Color Schemes to choose a predetermined set of colors; click Color Wheel to choose your own colors; click Custom to create a color yourself. In each case, the result appears in the Preview area of the dialog box.

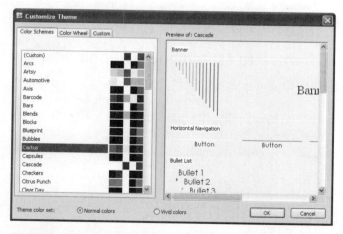

Figure 20-3 FrontPage gives you a great deal of control over colors and other features of a theme.

5 Click Save As to save the theme with a new name. Then click OK to close the Customize Theme dialog box.

Disabling CSS Themes to Return to the Default Page Design

Sometimes, the contents of a Web page are just the way you want them, but the visual appearance is not. If the graphics have been applied from a theme, you can disable the theme for that page. Just:

1 If necessary, click Design at the bottom of the document window.

2 Choose Format, Theme.

3 In the Theme task pane, in the Select A Theme box, pass the mouse arrow over No Theme. Click the down arrow next to No Theme, and choose Apply To Selected Page(s) from the shortcut menu.

If the theme is used on all the pages in a Web, you can also disable it for that Web: just follow steps 1-3 as presented above, but choose Apply As Default Theme from the shortcut menu.

> **Note**   If your Web's pages use different themes, you have to remove each one individually.

Customizing Toolbars to Boost Efficiency

The Web is all about clicking, whether on buttons or hyperlinks, and FrontPage's toolbars give you an immediate and graphical way to perform many basic Web page editing functions, with individual mouse clicks. Sometimes, you need to perform functions that you can (apparently, at least) access only by using FrontPage's menus. Other times, toolbars seem to contain more options than you need, and take up too much valuable screen space. Adding commands to toolbars, and moving—or removing—buttons, can help you work more efficiently.

> **Aha!**   Move Toolbars Where You Need Them
>
> Remember that any of FrontPage's toolbars can be detached from the main program window—just click and drag one of the vertical dividing lines in the toolbar. You can also resize toolbars to fit your monitor's display area—just click and drag on any of the four outer edges of the toolbar after it has been detached.

Adding or Removing Buttons to Maximize Toolbar Space

If a toolbar contains buttons you seldom (or never) use, you can remove the buttons to save some screen real estate. You can also add buttons that aren't available on the toolbar by default (as long as you do it sparingly and realize that your customizations can be lost if you move to a new machine or your system needs to be reinstalled). Here's how:

1 Click the Toolbar Options button at the right edge of the toolbar you want to edit.

2 Click Add Or Remove Buttons to change which toolbar buttons are visible.

3 Choose the name of the toolbar (in this case, we will work with the Formatting toolbar) to view all of its buttons.

4 Deselect a button you don't use often, to remove it from the buttons currently displayed (see Figure 20-4).

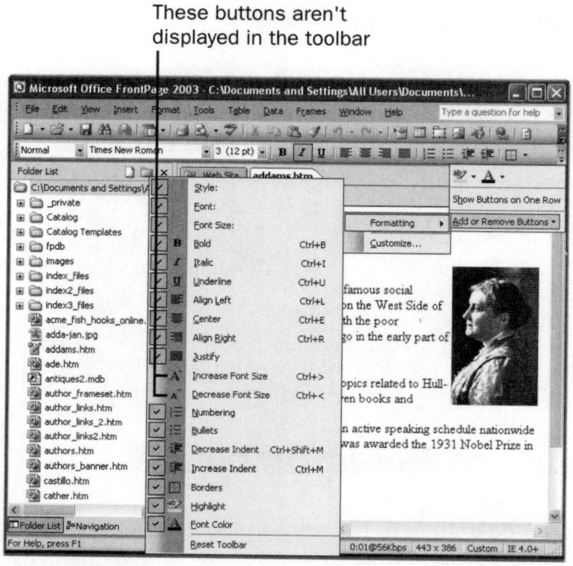

Figure 20-4 You can easily add or remove buttons using the Toolbar Options drop-down list.

5 Click a button that's not currently selected to add it to the buttons currently displayed.

> **Aha!**   Customize How Toolbars and Menus Appear
>
> Another set of options controls how parts of the FrontPage window appear. Choose Customize from the Tools menu, and click the Options tab to access options that control whether full menus always appear, whether the Standard and Formatting toolbars appear on one row or two, and other options.

> **Aha!**   Return to Toolbar Button Defaults
>
> The Reset Toolbar option that appears at the bottom of the list of a toolbar's buttons, enables you to reset the toolbar back to its default selection of buttons.

Changing Graphics Format Settings in the Drawing Toolbar

The Office Drawing Toolbar appears in the set of FrontPage toolbars that is available to you when you choose View, Toolbars. Like any toolbar, the Drawing Toolbar can be customized. You can add or remove buttons by clicking Toolbar Options, and by choosing Add or Remove Buttons from the shortcut menu. However, there's another customization option that applies to the Drawing toolbar alone, which can help visitors to your Web site view the graphics that you draw.

The Drawing toolbar enables you to draw graphics directly on the Web pages on which you are working. However, by default, those graphics are saved in a format called Vector Markup Language (VML), which is complex, and difficult for some browsers to display. You can view the code yourself by following these steps:

1 Click the New button, in the Standard toolbar, to create a new blank page.

2 Select View, Toolbars, Drawing, to display the drawing toolbar.

3 Click the Rectangle button in the drawing tool. Then click anywhere in the blank page, and drag down and to the right to draw a rectangle.

4 Click the down arrow next to the Fill Color button. Choose a color from the shortcut menu, to fill the rectangle you just drew.

5 Select the rectangle you drew. Click the Code button at the bottom of the page display area to switch to Code view. The code used to create the relatively simple rectangle should be highlighted (see Figure 20-5).

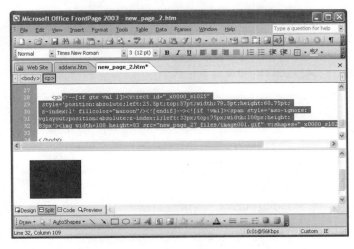

Figure 20-5 Even simple drawing toolbar objects like this rectangle use complicated VML code.

As you can imagine, more complex drawings need longer, more elaborate code to display. If you want to ensure that none of your Web page's graphics contain VML, you can disable this feature in the Page Options dialog box. You'll be disabling your ability to use the Drawing toolbar to add content to your pages. But you, and your fellow Web editors, can use an image editing tool, and save your graphics in GIF or JPEG format to make them visible—and with simpler code. Here's how to disable VML creation:

1 Open the Web site you want to edit.

2 Choose Tools, Page Options.

3 Click the Authoring tab (see Figure 20-6). Then, deselect the VML graphics (Office drawing) box.

4 Click OK.

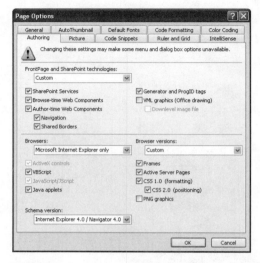

Figure 20-6 Disable VML graphics to ensure that your Web page code remains simple.

See Also By default, many Web browsers can only display *bitmap* graphics— graphics that are made up of little squares called pixels, each of which contains one or more bits of digital informa- tion. In contrast, *vector* images are made up of shapes called paths. Vector Markup Lan- guage allows some browsers to display those paths by inter- preting a com- plex set of instructions that are added to the HTML and XML for your Web pages.

Create Your Own Custom Toolbar

In case FrontPage's selection of toolbars doesn't contain the options you want (or doesn't present the options you want in the right combination), you can create your own custom toolbar as follows:

1 Choose Tools, Customize.

2 Click the Toolbars tab, if necessary, and then click New.

3 Type a name for your new toolbar in the Toolbar Name box.

4 Click OK, and then click Commands.

5 Locate the category that contains the command(s) you want to add to the toolbar.

6 Click the command to select it.

7 Drag the command on top of your new toolbar, which appears above the FrontPage window. When you're done, click Close, to close the Customize dialog box.

> **Note** The Toolbars tab of the Customize dialog box lists some toolbars in addition to those listed in the Toolbars submenu of the View menu—for example, 3-D Shapes, and Shadow Settings. Select these options to view them immediately, and click Close to add them to the Toolbars submenu.

Configuring Editors to Launch Automatically

You work with a variety of files on a Web site, including images, spreadsheets, charts, and style sheets. If you need to edit any of these non-Web-page files, you can tell FrontPage which program you want to identify as the editor for a particular file type. Then, FrontPage will open the file when you specify you want to edit it—for instance, in the General tab of the Picture Properties dialog box, when you click the Edit button, the editor of your choice will automatically launch, and open the file.

Configuring Editors to Enable Detailed Editing

Often, you place an image on a Web page, only to realize that you need to edit it. Maybe you forgot to crop it, you need to adjust the contrast, or you need to make it smaller to fit on the page more easily. Other files, such as spreadsheets, need adjustments as well. To configure an editor to launch when you need it, follow these steps:

1   Choose Tools, Options.

2   Click the Configure Editors tab.

3   Click New Extension (see Figure 20-7) to add a file type that's not listed in the Extensions column.

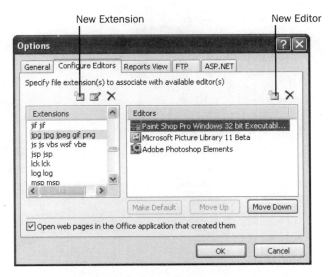

Figure 20-7 Add editors or new file types using this dialog box.

4 When the Open With dialog box appears, type the three-letter filename extension for the type of file you want to add (see Figure 20-8).

Figure 20-8 Specify an available editor and the file extension you want to associate with it.

> **Note**   You don't need to include the dot before the three-letter filename extension when you type it in the File Type box in the Add Editor Association dialog box—just type **gif** instead of **.gif**, for instance.

5 Scroll down the list of available programs and select the editor you want to use, or click Browse for more to locate a program that's not on the list.

6 Click OK.

> **Aha!**   Right-Click to Open a File with a New Application
>
> Even if you associate a particular type of file with an application, you can still open that file with another application. Right-click the file's name in the Folder List, and then choose Open With from the shortcut menu. Choose the application from the Open With dialog box, which lists available editors on your computer.

Modify a File Type to Work with New Software

See Also You can customize many of the options that control how HTML, XML, and other Web page code appears in Code View. See Chapter 10, "Editing HTML and XML Markup," for more on changing the colors in which code is displayed, as well as font size, font type, and word wrap.

Sometimes, you obtain upgraded software, or new programs that enable you to edit text files, images, or other Web content more efficiently than you could before. If you want FrontPage to open the new, or updated, software automatically upon encountering a specified file extension, you have to modify the editor that is currently set to open that extension. Follow these steps:

1 Choose Tools, Options.

2 Click Configure Editors.

3 In the Extensions list, select the type of file you want to modify.

4 Click New Editor.

5 Select the new editor in the Open With box.

6 Click OK to close the Open With dialog box and return to Options. Click Make Default, if you want to make the new program the default editor for the specified file type.

7 Click OK.

Using Detect and Repair to Get Out of Trouble

Occasionally, software programs encounter problems that don't result from obvious causes. Some information about the program stored in the Windows Registry might become corrupted, for instance. Or some of the files the software needs to operate is accidentally discarded. If you encounter problems running FrontPage, the quick and easy solution is to call on the built-in repair application that's common to all Microsoft Office System programs.

Aha!   Save Your Custom Changes

Before running Detect and Repair, write down any customization changes you've made to the program, so that you can recreate them later on.

Just do the following:

1 Close and save any open files, or open Webs.

2 Choose Help, Detect And Repair to display the Detect And Repair dialog box (see Figure 20-9).

Figure 20-9 The Microsoft Office System Detect and Repair utility can fix many problems with FrontPage.

3 Leave Restore My Shortcuts While Repairing selected so that you keep a shortcut to FrontPage on the Windows Start menu. Choose Discard My Customized Settings And Restore Default Settings if you want to undo any customization you have done and return to FrontPage's default settings.

4 Click Start. You might have to wait a few minutes for FrontPage to be configured. When a dialog box appears, stating that the configuration process is finished, click OK.

> **Note**   If you have customized FrontPage's toolbars, menus, or other aspects of the program, much of your work will be undone when you run Detect and Repair. You'll also need to re-enter your username and initials when you restart FrontPage, after running the repair program.

Fast Wrap-Up

■ The controls in the Options dialog box let you control how FrontPage starts up, and what features are available, to match the way you work.

■ FrontPage's built-in themes can be customized to fit your organization's graphic identity. You can also disable themes, when you don't want to apply them.

■ The default buttons included on FrontPage's toolbars can be removed, or supplemented, to present you with the options you use most often.

■ FrontPage enables you to configure editing programs that launch automatically when you want to edit specific types of files, such as images.

■ The built-in Detect and Repair utility can be used, if you encounter problems running FrontPage.

HTML/XML Reference   A

Microsoft Office FrontPage 2003's core function is to translate your design input into clean HTML code that Web browsers can interpret quickly. At the same time, many of the features that are new to FrontPage, which enable groups of Web developers to work collaboratively, take advantage of the power and flexibility of XML. Hopefully, you won't need to spend time manually altering your Web page code and can focus on designing pages the way you want to. But if you ever need to manually edit the HTML or XML that FrontPage generates, the new Code view tools will streamline the process considerably.

Code view, Split view, Code IntelliSense, and Code Snippets all help you work directly with your Web page code when you need to. Sometimes, making slight changes to the code and then seeing the effect in Preview mode can help you learn how the individual commands work. Occasionally, working directly with HTML or XML code can be quicker than using FrontPage's toolbars, menus, or dialog boxes. To help you edit more effectively, the following sections present you with some of the basic commands found in virtually all HTML pages. If you can become familiar with them, you'll better understand what you're viewing and editing in Code or Split view. Table A-1 describes the most common commands used to define HTML or XML documents, and to format text, images, and other elements.

Table A-1   Common HTML Structural and Formatting Elements

Element	What It Does
\<HTML\> \</HTML\>	Identifies an HTML document
\<HEAD\> \</HEAD\>	Encloses the HEAD section of an HTML document
\<TITLE\> \</TITLE\>	Defines the title of an HTML document
\<META\> \</META\>	Contains information about the HTML document as a whole
\<!DOCTYPE\>	Identifies what type of document this is, usually by giving the version of HTML or XML being used
\<BASE\> \</BASE\>	Specifies the location of external files, or objects needed by a browser
\<BODY\> \</BODY\>	Encloses the BODY section of an HTML document
\<!-- --\>	Encloses comments made by the author of the Web page
\<P\> \</P\>	Defines a new paragraph
\<A\> \</A\>	Creates an anchor for a hyperlink to another location
\<IMG\>	Inserts an image file into the Web page being created
\<BR\>	Creates a line break
\<HR\>	Creates a horizontal line

The most basic kind of content on a Web page is text, and HTML provides a variety of commonly-used elements for formatting that text. Some examples are shown in Table A-2.

Table A-2 HTML Elements for Formatting Text

Element	What It Does
`<I> </I>`	Encloses text to be displayed in italic type
`<B> </B>`	Encloses text to be displayed in bold type
`<U> </U>`	Encloses text to be underlined; this is seldom used, as it can be confused with hyperlinks
`<BLOCKQUOTE> </BLOCKQUOTE>`	Encloses text to be formatted with narrower margins than the surrounding text
`<Hx> </Hx>`	Defines a Web page heading; x is a variable from 1-6. An H1 heading is displayed in the largest type; an H6 heading is the smallest
`<EM> </EM>`	Adds emphasis to text; exact formatting depends on browser
`<STRONG> </STRONG>`	Adds stronger emphasis to text; exact formatting depends on browser
`<CITE> </CITE>`	Designates a citation or reference; formatting is browser dependent
`<DFN> </DFN>`	Designates a definition; formatting is browser dependent
`<SMALL> </SMALL>`	Displays text in smaller type than surrounding text
`<BIG> </BIG>`	Displays text in larger type than surrounding text
`<SUP> </SUP>`	Displays text in superscript
`<SUB> </SUB>`	Displays text in subscript
`<INS> </INS>`	Displays text as an insertion; exact formatting depends on browser
`<ABBR> </ABBR>`	Displays text as an abbreviation; exact formatting depends on browser
`<ADDRESS> </ADDRESS>`	Displays text as an address; exact formatting depends on browser

A number of HTML tags are used to define content so that Web page authors can tailor HTML to their own needs. Often, these commands are used with Cascading Style Sheets. Some of these commands (see Table A-3) are usually employed together, such as `<DIV ID>` or `<SPAN CLASS>`.

Table A-3 **Elements that Add Structure to Documents**

Element	What It Does
`<DIV> </DIV>`	Used to enclose a block of code
`ID`	An attribute used with DIV, SPAN, or other commands to identify a type of content, such as a name or message. ID is also used as a target anchor for hypertext links
`CLASS`	An attribute used with DIV, SPAN, or other commands to identify a type of content
`<SPAN> </SPAN>`	A container that identifies an inline object, rather than a block of code

In Chapter 11, "Advanced Layout with Tables and Layers," you learned how to design pages using tables. If you ever need to edit the HTML code for a page that uses tables, you'll need to recognize the common table-related elements shown in Table A-4.

Table A-4 **HTML Table Elements**

Element	What It Does
`<TABLE> </TABLE>`	Encloses a Web page table
`<CAPTION> </CAPTION>`	Defines a caption for a table
`<TH> </TH>`	Creates a table header for a column
`<TR> </TR>`	Creates a row within a table
`<TD> </TD>`	Creates a cell within a row

In Chapter 14, "Working with Forms," you learned about creating Web page forms that add interactivity to a Web site. In case you want to edit the HTML for a form that you create, the form-related elements shown in Table A-5 should provide you with a starting point.

Table A-5 HTML Form Elements

Element	What It Does
`<FORM> </FORM>`	Encloses a Web page form
`ACTION`	An attribute used with the FORM command to specify a URL or other location to which data should be submitted
`METHOD`	An attribute used with the FORM command to specify the method used to process form data; the two common methods are GET and POST
`<INPUT> </INPUT>`	A command that can be used with TEXT to create a single-line text box, PASSWORD to create a password box, CHECKBOX to create a check box, RADIO to create a radio button, and so on
`<LABEL> </LABEL>`	Used to designate an input variable
`<BUTTON> </BUTTON>`	Creates a push-down button
`<SELECT> </SELECT>`	Designates a drop-down menu list
`<TEXTAREA> </TEXTAREA>`	Creates a multi-line text input box

Keep in mind that, if you use one of FrontPage's Web components to process your form data, you will see commands such as `<!--webbot bot="SaveResults" -->` in your HTML. Such commands are specific to FrontPage (not to HTML or XML) and designate the Web component to be used to process the data.

Index

Symbols and Numbers

<!– –> element, HTML, 329
3-D Shapes and Shadow Settings toolbar, 324

A

<ABBR> element, HTML, 330
Absbottom, picture alignment, 104
Absmiddle, picture alignment, 104
access control, SharePoint Services, 289, 291
accessibility, 313–14
Acrobat Reader plug-ins, 212
ACTION attribute, HTML, 332
Action option, custom scripts, 247
Active Hyperlink color indicator, 70
ActiveMovieControl, 212
Active Server Pages (ASPs), 246
ActiveX Control, 212
Additional Links option, 87
Add Link option, 87
<ADDRESS> element, HTML, 330
Administrator, SharePoint Site Groups, 287
advanced buttons, forms, 229
advanced features, Web browsers, 17–20
<A> element, HTML, 329
AIFF audio format, 118
AIFF-C audio format, 118
alerts, SharePoint Services, 287
Align Center, text alignment, 63
alignment
    horizontal lines, 64
    pictures, 104
    table cells, 133–34
    tables, 128
    text, 62–63
    WordArt, 107
Align Right, text alignment, 63
All Available Themes, 74
anchor tags, bookmarks, 40
animation, Flash, 212
answers, FAQs, 42
Archive page, project Web site, 53
articles, discussion Web sites, 49
ASCII file, 230
aspect ratio
    Keep Aspect Ratio option, 105
    maintaining, 115
ASPs (Active Server Pages), 246
attributes, hidden fields, 249
AU audio format, 118
Authoring tab, browser support, 15, 18
AutoFormat tables, 131

automatic updates, TOC, 44
AutoShapes, adding to Web pages, 108
autostretching tables, 167
AVI video format, 120

B

background colors
    adding to table cells, 135
    adding to tables, 132
    frames and, 189
    shared borders and, 83
    themes and, 70
background pictures
    setting, 110
    shared borders and, 83
    themes and, 78
Backspace, line editing, 62
back ups, Web sites, 277
banners
    creating, 88
    themes and, 78
    updating, 52, 54
<BASE> element, HTML, 329
Baseline, picture alignment, 104
bCentral, 236
<B> element, HTML, 330
bibliography page template, 40
<BIG> element, HTML, 330
bitmap graphics, 324
Blank Page template, 36
<BLOCKQUOTE> element, HTML, 330
<BODY> element, HTML, 329
Bookmark dialog box, 68, 69
bookmarks
    bibliography entries and, 40
    editing, 68
    indicating with dashed underlining, 42
    linking pages, 67
    removing, 69
borders. See also shared borders
    settings, 94
    showing/hiding frame, 188
    table cells, 135
    tables, 130–32
    thickness, 104
    visibility in browsers, 160
    width settings, 128
Bottom, picture alignment, 104

 element, HTML, 329
Browser Compatibility tool, 19
browsers. See Web browsers
bulleted lists
    style of, 66
    when to use, 65
Bullets, page element styles, 94

William R. Stanek

William R. Stanek has 20 years of hands-on experience with advanced programming and development. He is a leading technology expert and an award-winning author. Over the years, his practical advice has helped millions of programmers, developers, and network engineers all over the world. He has written over two dozen computer books. Current or forthcoming books include *Microsoft Windows XP Professional Administrator's Pocket Consultant*, *Microsoft Windows 2000 Administrator's Pocket Consultant 2nd Edition*, *Microsoft Windows Server 2003 Administrator's Pocket Consultant* and *IIS 6.0 Administrator's Pocket Consultant*.

Mr. Stanek has been involved in the commercial Internet community since 1991. His core business and technology experience comes from over 11 years of military service. He has substantial experience in developing server technology, encryption, and Internet solutions. He has written many technical white papers and training courses on a wide variety of topics. He is widely sought after as a subject matter expert.

Mr. Stanek has an MS degree with distinction in Information Systems and a BS Computer Science degree magna cum laude. He is proud to have served in the Persian Gulf War as a combat crew member on an electronic warfare aircraft. He flew on numerous combat missions into Iraq and was awarded nine medals for his wartime service, including one of the United States of America's highest flying honors, the Air Force Distinguished Flying Cross. Currently, he resides in the Pacific Northwest with his wife and children.

Greg Holden

The writings of Greg Holden take many forms. He prepares documentation for companies and creates online courses. He writes columns and articles for both print and electronic publications. His previous books include *E-Commerce Essentials with Microsoft FrontPage* (Microsoft Press), *Guide to Network Defense and Countermeasures* (Course Technology), and *Starting an Online Business for Dummies* (Wiley). He took a short break from computer-related material to write *Literary Chicago: A Book Lover's Guide to the Windy City,* which was published in 2000 by Lake Claremont Press. He also has published a number of his short stories and poems. Among the publications he produces are the prodigious output of his bright, funny, and very creative daughters, Zosia and Lucy Holden. They are currently collaborating on a play based on Queen Elizabeth. To find out more, visit his personal and business Web sites at *www.gregholden.com*, or send e-mail to greg@gregholden.com.